IN THE SERVICE OF OUR COUNTRY

USS ZELLARS DD 777
THE SHIP AND HER MEN

COMPILED BY
ARTHUR H. BARNES and SHIPMATES

Fideli
Publishing

IN THE SERVICE OF
OUR COUNTRY
USS ZELLARS DD 777
THE SHIP AND HER MEN

ISBN: 978-1-60414-517-5

First printing, June 1998

Second printing, 2012

Published by
Fideli Publishing, Inc.
www.FideliPublishing.com

There is no named dedication of this book on the history of the U.S.S. ZELLARS. I know that every destroyer that went to sea had a similar crew whose family members were equally proud of their support of our country during World War II. Therefore, I take the liberty of saying that the following story of our ship is meant to HONOR all destroyer sailors who went to sea and met our enemy.

**If there were a dedication,
it would be to honor the memory of the 44 shipmates
who never came home.**

Their names are listed in a special part of the text.

GOD BLESS THEM ALL.

*Nov 1 2016,
JACK HEVLY,
THIS BOOK IS REAL HISTORY
EMby, THANK You
Arthur H. Basner*

TABLE OF CONTENTS

Regardless of service, these were special shipmates from beginning to end.

Personal Stories from those who served on the ZELLARS

USS ZELLARS (DD777)

December 1997

As the writer of all the information contained herein, I do not wish to make any kind of dedication of the ZELLARS history. It is, and was, a part of the finest crew that ever served on any destroyer. I prefer to say that all that is contained between the covers of this book is in memory of the 44 shipmates killed on April 12, 1945 off Okinawa.

To acknowledge any person or persons for their assistance would take many pages. Therefore, I chose to say to all who bothered to compile their personal histories, review the past and make suggestions, if you approve, your shipmates thank you.

I do wish to thank those of you who sent photographs and documentation:

Beth Walsh   "Howie" Walters
Daughter of John Walsh   Red Peterson
Naval Historical Center   Bath Iron Works, Bath Maine
Harold Buck   Leonard Bell

Further I would like to note, a majority of the photos taken on the ship during 1944–1945 were the work of Chief Electrician Cushing.

Arthur H. Barnes, Plank Owner, U.S.S. ZELLARS DD 777

Definition of PLANK OWNER: During the time of wooden ships, if a commissioning crew member was logged on board, that DAY. He was referred to as PLANK OWNER and proudly carried the title throughout his Naval carrier.

IN THE SERVICE OF
OUR COUNTRY

Our Brothers' Keepers

Young sailors gathered to place a new "Man of War" into commission, they came from many different parts of our great free country: New York, Texas, Nebraska, Washington State, Oregon, California, Mississippi, and you name it. They have attended boot camp and some have served from the beginning of the war. Petty Officers, Chief Petty Officers, Seamen and Officers of varying ranks.

As the crew stood in the slight mist on the docks of the Seattle shipyard, they listened to high ranking officers state that the ship was a fine ship and ready to begin the crew's training. They also made reference to the total objective of our time: "To go in harms way, search out our enemy, and destroy them."

On October 25, 1944, the ZELLARS stood at dockside and listened to those words, not really knowing that in just a few months, ship and crew would be tested to the ultimate in a faraway place that none of them had ever heard of — OKINAWA.

Not withstanding, every sailor had in his heart the part he must play in order for the ship to achieve that task. The training was very specific to the task: ship handling, watches at many different stations, gunnery, engine room services demanded in order for the ship to steam at all speeds, and the routine of basic housekeeping for all 345 officers and men.

There were never ending General Quarter drills at all times of the day and night. There was seldom a moment that every man was not involved in some effort that lent itself to the final objective.

The more senior Petty officers paid close attention to the seamen as the training intensified, until each man was a master at his duty.

As days passed the bond between shipmates grew, with one shipmate always ready to help another. Lesser tasks usually had many more hands to help than was required, the extra hands just wanting to be an active part of whatever was going on. The "taking on" of fuel at sea was always a great spectacle as heavy fuel lines were passed from a larger ship such as an aircraft carrier, battlewagon or fleet oiler. Stores and ammunition, not a pleasant task, was accomplished with a few groans.

It seemed that each shipmate was determined to hold his fellow shipmate's hand if ever needed. As the ship drew closer to the enemies' islands, the bond grew even closer. Each shipmate knew that he would depend on the others for assurance and security in the days to come.

Without it being said, *you hold my hand and I will hold yours.*

Thus, the ZELLARS entered the war and stood out in the pursuit of duty, honor and country.

The following pages represent just a part of the events of this great ship. The personal histories contained herein are just as sent to the author except for modest editing and a few spelling adjustments. It is their story.

I was very proud to have served with everyone of the men that I spent some two years with during the ship's most trying time and more proud to have been in a country where freedom is our foundation and to have served our country when she was in great need.

Arthur H. Barnes FC3c, plank owner.

USS ZELLARS, DD 777 FACTS

Thomas E. Zellars

Namesake:	**THOMAS E. ZELLARS USN.**
Destroyer class:	Allen M. Sumner
Keel Laid:	December, 24, 1943
Launched:	July, 19 1944
Commissioned:	October, 25 1944
Displacement:	2200 tons
Length:	376.6 Ft.
Width, Beam:	40.10 Ft.
Draft:	15.8 Ft.
Speed:	35.2 knots.
Complement:	345, Officers and Enlisted Men
Battle Stars:	WWII 1, Okinawa; 4 Korea

ARMAMENT

6	5" 38-CAL MAIN BATTERY
12	40MM CANNON
11	20MM MACHINE GUNS
10	21-INCH TORPEDOES
6	K DEPTH CHARGE GUNS
2	DEPTH CHARGE ROLLING RACKS

USS ZELLARS (DD777)

DECEMBER 1943

A great struggle of war was raging across the whole of the Pacific Ocean, from Pearl Harbor out to the many far flung Islands that few had ever heard of. Island groups and Atolls scattered in far away places like Midway, the Gilbert Islands with Tarawa and Makin Islands that our Marines paid heavy prices to capture. The Marshalls and Solomans that few will ever forget, again because of the price our country paid at Guadalcanal and Bougainville. And now the Islands of Guam, Tinian and Siapan.

The United States had been struck a very cowardly blow on December 7th of 1941 and was fighting in many different places with her resources stretched to the limit. The Airplane factories were turning out new and faster aircraft. Fighter planes and bigger bombers that were mandatory for the march to victory over Japan.

Our Navy had to have much needed ships of all kinds and sizes. Aircraft Carriers, Battleships, Cruisers, Troop Transports and Cargos ships, but most of all, the fast new GRAYHOUNDS of the fleet, the DESTROYERS, the smaller of the Navy's men of war

In Seattle Washington, a shipyard situated inside of the Pudget Sound great waterways, was a first class ship building company that had the responsibility to turn out as many of the new destroyers as they could. As one hull was completed and sent down the ways, the shipbuilding way was cleaned checked and a new beginning for another ship was already being lifted into place.

Heavy overhead cranes lifted single keel plates onto the center keel footing and carefully aligned it making sure the most important part was as perfect as possible.

As each keel plating was placed in position from the stern to the place where the bow would be, additional plates about six-feet by ten-feet were welded alongside to form the outer ship's hull. The plate that formed the very bottom of the keel had been cupped and was four-feet wide. As each keel hull plate was completed, an "H" keel brace was lowered into the ways, giving a rigid backbone that would support the whole of the outer hull. As the "H " spine was set in place, welders ascended like flies and secured the "H" spine to the hull plating. This completed, additional hull plates were welded into place until some three plates to a side

had been secured and final welding done. As each plate was placed into position, heavy timbers were placed along on the outer hull to support the additional structure. On and on this construction went night and day. It was urgent to build as many ships as the shipyard could, in the shortest period of time, but they had to be made with utmost quality. At every point of construction, quality control specialists observed and tested every weld and section as it was laid down.

From bow to stern, the shipyard workers made sure that the "keel" was straight as an arrow. It took several weeks for the final pieces to be set in place. The "keel" was the back bone of the ship and it had to be perfect. The first major bulkhead to be set in place was the forward boiler room bulkhead. This part had been put together in another area of the shipyard and set in place by heavy cranes. 'It had all the different levels measured for their additions and went from the bilge to the main deck. In the engineering spaces, of which there were four, two boiler rooms and two engine rooms. These compartments were set in place first. From the stern, to the bow, the main hull grew as each compartment bulkhead was completed and made ready for the different deck levels that had to be added before any upper structure could be set in place. The very large and heavy machinery had to be installed before a next

level deck plate could be added. Again, as the hull grew, heavy timbers were set in place to brace the outer hull. It looked like a lumber yard had gone crazy from the floor of the ways up the side of the hull as it grew.

As each section of the hull was complete, and smaller spaces completed, the swarm of electricians and plumbers would take over. The mass of wiring and pipes that went into these spaces and joints was inspected for quality and proper placement. The foundation plates for the large steam boilers had to be very precise in their placement and as soon as this was done and approved, the boilers were lifted down into the cavity and fixed firmly to the foundation plates. Again, as in some of the other spaces, a different group of workers descended and began to complete the final installation of accessory parts, pipes, some small and others very large. Due to the crowded spaces that all parts had to fit into, many of the pipes were preformed in the shipyard assembly area next to the ways. They were bent in many different directions so as to fit just right for the need that they would perform. Each was checked and quality measured for correctness before it was mated to the number 1 boiler room. As each module was approved, welders swarmed over the two sections and began the final coupling, making them into one.

Ladders and stanchions, walkways and lesser bulkheads would fill the requirement for passage from one level to another. As the different spaces were "outfitted," the next deck level would be put into place, closing off that compartment except for the entry hatch or other critical unfinished need. Except for the engineering spaces, as the compartments were basically finished, the main deck plates were added and for the first time parts of the construction began to look like a ship.

In the two boiler spaces, each level began to fill up with many complex and important parts Here would be the source of the many different functions required for a destroyer: normal steam from the boiler rooms', super heated steam for maximum flank speeds, fresh water for the boilers and crew requirements, and fueling demands. Piping seemed to run all over the compartments. Valves that controlled the steam, water, and fuel were set in their proper space. Electrical wiring by the mile to carry orders and all communications were strung about the inner hull, all going to a station where needed.

With the main parts of the hull in place for power to run the ship and provide services for the crew, and most important, fulfill the purpose of the ship, other modules began to be put in place. The main fuel tank, one of many crew compartments, frozen food storage compartment and, finally, the bow section.

Toward the aft section just behind the number 2 engine room there was another crew compartment, a machine shop and a dry storage space. This compartment would be home for some 60 young seamen, bunks for rest and personal lockers for storage. Of course, there was bilge space just below these compartments.

Aft of the second crew's compartment was another different space, because in the center of the space was the barbet for one of the main battery 5" 38 guns (gun number 3). The barbet was a circular configuration that would hold a ready supply of both powder and projectiles. Around the peripheral of the barbet was space for other crew members. The last large compartment was another crew space, the damage control workshop. Another very important space was aft steering in the center. And on the port side there were several very small storage spaces for whatever might be needed. Each of these modules were outfitted with all the needed plumbing, wiring, stanchions and other support structures.

In the bow section, the same "outfitting" of each space was underway. In the very bottom of the hull under the number one and two main battery guns, two very strategic spaces for both the powder and projectile storage were fitted with emergency sprinkler systems. Should the emergency demand, because of fire, or damage to the ship require it, a valve above decks could be turned on and these spaces would be flooded immediately. Above them was a crew compartment and aft, another crew space, plus a "head," toilet-shower facility for the forward part of the crew.

In the "head," the showers were nothing but open stalls. The wash basins were attached to the bulkhead with a very narrow shelf just above them. The more interesting item was the "toilet." A trough-like bench where three-to-five persons at a time could sit cheek to cheek and do their task. To support the behind, two well-polished boards that resembled a toilet seat were set across the trough, with not too-much space between each set of seats. There was nothing personal but it was not the best of situations when one had to "go."

AND THIS IS HOW I BEGAN ...

At first I had no idea how I would be built and in what order of construction. Now that my basic form was in place, shipyard workmen began to swarm all over my hull. The smell of burning welding torches, the pounding of the ship fitter's heavy hammers readying the next module, and cables and lines being dragged all over the place.

Sub-assemblies began to be set in place. Some from the bow, and others from the stern. Each compartment had its purpose and each was labeled by deck and frame so that any crew member would be able to find any space that he would need.

In this early stage, the boiler and engine room spaces were the center of attention. They were the source of my power to drive the ship at all speeds, churning the seas so that I could show off my highest speeds.

So far I had only part of what was called the main deck in place. The area of my boilers and engine rooms were open so that heavy large parts of the boilers and engines could be lifted into place. In the cold Seattle weather, I felt just a little bit naked but at the pace that the workers were moving, this would not last too long. I am not sure but I think that I am becoming excited.

After several months, I could see and understand how I would look when finished, at least the hull part of me. My outer hull was taking shape up to the main deck. The ship's propeller shafts, one for the starboard screw and another for the port screw had been set in their bearing mounts and tested for alignment. The propellers would be attached to the shafts much later.

Forward near the bow, the first of the super structure began to take shape. A large hole in the main deck was made ready for the number 1 main battery 5" 38 gun and just aft of this open space was the first structure for entry to the forward officers' quarters. Also the ladder leading down to the forward crew's quarters, the upper handling room for mount 1, frozen food storage and aft to another crew's quarters and the crew's mess deck.

Just aft of the crew's mess on the port side was the food service space where food would be served steaming hot from steam-furnished tables. On the starboard side, going aft was the scullery and the main battery fire control plotting room. Just below the scullery was the forward power generating room.

The space for the officers' ward room, on the main deck was a forward port to starboard passageway, and then a real important space, the ship's galley and then on back to the area just forward of the midship's passageway "the sick bay, the ship's laundry and across the passageway, the ship's office, aft officers' quarters and along the passageway, the ship's store. Cigarettes, soap, "pogy bait" candy, shaving supplies and a number of other personal items would be purchased. It would be an important place. Next, just above the main deck was the aft crew's head, and except for being a little larger, it was configured the same as the forward head. The next "BIG" item would be the space for the number-three 5" gun. On the very stern was a triangular gun tub for three 20MM machine guns, the smoke generator, and a port and starboard roll rack of depth charges.

Things were looking great and I could feel added strength in myself. I still had a number of holes in my structure where other needed space would be fitted out as required. This level was referred to as the "0-1" deck. Most funny were the two stacks. The forward stack was behind the forward torpedo tubes and the aft stack was set just aft of the forward torpedo tubes.

There was enough of me somewhat finished that I could see onto the dock area just forward of the ways that held me in place. For the first time I learned what my hull number was. Three big "7s" had been painted on a large back board and stood out to let everyone know who I was, "DD 777." Boy what a number! That should be lucky for all who would sail aboard.

Every day new pieces were welded in their places on both the port side and starboard side, some 20 to 30 feet aft of the number 2 stack. I learned that they were for two quad 40MM cannon guns that would have a ready ammunition storage space built inside the ring. On the port side of the number 2 stack above the 01 deck, the workers also fitted a space for 2 20MM Guns to be set in place later. Anyone with duty in that space would have one heck of a view.

Security cables or lines around the edge of the main deck had been installed sometime when I was not paying attention. The lines were to protect shipmates from falling overboard and I guess also to lean on as they admired the passing seas or felt a little sea sick.

I began to feel that something special was about to happen to me. I think that it was July 18 1944. I had not been able to keep track of time and dates. The shipyard workers began to string many colorful banners and flags, draping a great red, white and blue banner across my bow. I had been carefully painted from my keel to my main deck and all the superstructure that was exposed topside. The color was a nice light gray with the keel to what would be my water line, a black, black.

All the unnecessary planking, the gangway, welding machines, cables, and numerous other types of equipment were removed. A stand for people to sit had been erected just in front of the ways. The only thing holding me in place on the ways was a number of heavy timbers that had been installed when they began my keel and hull.

About 1:00 the next day, July 19th, a small stand was placed just in front of my bow and more colorful banners draped around it. The stand was so close that I could almost touch it, I now knew that something very big was about to happen.

Within an hour, Naval Officers, several nicely-dressed ladies and a number of guests began to walk toward my bow. A large number of the shipyard workmen and women gathered in the stands and others just stood nearby.

A Navy Officer unfolded some papers from his coat pocket and made a statement about my being. I learned that I had been named after an outstanding Naval Officer who had given his life during an on-board gun mount explosion and this (LT.(jg) THOMAS E. ZELLARS, USN.

Several other visiting members made some very warm and complimentary statements about why I had been built and what the objectives for me would be. If I'd had buttons on my chest, they would have exploded off, I felt so proud, and I was only about half finished.

Then a marvelous thing happened. A rather graceful gray-haired lady who was in, called champagne. It had several colorful ribbons attached to the small part of the bottle. As she stepped very close to my bow, she commented:

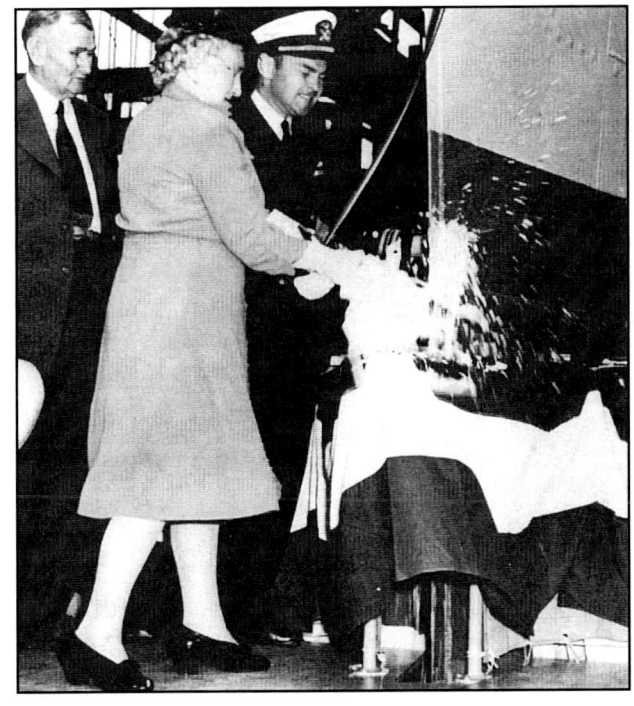

"In the name of my son, Thomas E. Zellars, LT.(JG) USN, I christen thee, the U.S.S. ZELLARS, to go forth and serve our country with great honor and distinction.

I know that you will serve our country well."

Mrs. ZELLARS then crashed the bottle across my sharp bow and the bubbly stuff ran down into the way. I did not even get to taste the stuff.

There followed a lot of hand clapping, and to my surprise, loud horns began to honk, whistles sounded throughout the shipyard and the few workmen who stood under the ways, swinging sledge hammers, released the blocks that held my hull and I began to slide down the ways, tasting salt water for the first time. The water of Pudget Sound felt cool and gentle. I knew that a new and final building phase was about to begin as I slid farther out into the sound.

The noise continued from the docks and many of the yard workmen stood proud at their achievement as I moved farther away.

Some 40 to 50 shipyard workmen rode down the ways on my deck. They also shouted and made proud comments about their efforts to make me the best they had ever achieved.

Shortly after moving away from the way, a small tug came alongside and gently began to move me toward a dock called an outfitting dock.

Somewhere I had heard about the "Little Tug that would." I knew that the little tug that was now moving me to my new birth "would" be very careful and not mar my new paint job. The

tug crew moved very slowly. As they neared my new temporary home dock, workers stood at the ready with heavy lines, ready to secure my hull to the docks. Men on my deck threw a small line to the dock workmen who then tied the smaller line to the larger line. The men on deck then pulled the larger line to my main deck ballards and slowly pulled me to the dock, making me fast. I was at my new home for awhile as the shipyard began to finish the construction.

I had barely been tied to the dock when more and more workers began to come on board. The welding machines began to arrive and all sorts of cables and hoses were being dragged across the deck and down into compartments and to upper deck spaces. Soon followed prefabricated modules for the superstructure, gun mounts, bridge and mast.

Beginning at the stern, was the aft steering space. The hydraulic rams that moved the rudders were installed and the associated electrical wiring attached to the terminal boxes. After each installation, the workmen charged the system with special hydraulic fluid and began the necessary testing. The system made growling sounds at first but as the workmen adjusted the system, the noise changed to a soft murmur. Now when the time came, I could be guided any direction that the crew wanted me to go.

Installing air flow ducts for ventilation throughout the whole of the ship was a real struggle

for the workmen. It seemed that everyone wanted to work in the same space and there was just not that much room. Some loud voices could be heard at times as tempers got a little out of hand. Then a boss-type person would step in and make the decision as to who should have the space at that time.

On and on it went for days and some nights. In the crew spaces, lockers and bunk frames begin to appear. Lighting had been strung out as the light was needed, but permanent lights were installed and tested.

I was amused with the outfitting of the crews "head" space. Open shower stalls were no great concern but the human waste disposal was. A stainless steel trough about six persons long had been set along the bulkhead of the starboard side. Across the trough was placed two boards that took the place of a regular toilet seat. Salt water constantly flowed from one end of the trough to the scuppers on the outside of the hull. Absolutely no privacy.

There were a series of wash basins somewhat separated from the shower and "can" part of the "head." I don't know who first called the rest room "the head." It just doesn't fit.

On each side of the bridge, the plan was for a twin mount 40MM cannon just aft of the signal part of the bridge. They sat high and offered a great view of all that anyone might want to survey. Just below each mount was a 40MM ammunition ready room. The trunnion ring for the guns was being carefully set in place. I thought that it would not be to long before I would be called, "bristling" with guns.

In the mess deck, the steam tables were being set in place and the plumbing for the steam connected. Tables for the crew to eat at also were being welded to the deck and the scullery outfitted for washing the trays. A strange piece of equipment was being manhandled into the plotting room. The Philco/Ford Company built the main battery firecontrol computer. It would be a most valuable instrument needed for firing the main battery weapons. The aft bulkhead of plot was a maze of switches that allowed the main battery guns to be switched on for automatic control and many other functions that were part of the weapons systems.

Early one morning, I as I took inventory of the changes that had happened in the last few days, a crane was lifting a twin mount 5" 38-gun system into place on the bow. It looked awesome even hanging in the sky. The workmen put it into place as gentle as one would hold a woman. (I have not had that experience.) As it was set in the final position, flange bolts secured it into place. Within a few minutes, the 5" 38 mount for the number 2 gun was also slung into it's position. Each gun had all the power drive system attached under the main part of the gun so that all that was required for final installation was the power connections and final adjustments.

I thought that the space between the two stacks might be for an exercise space but to my amazement, came the five tube torpedo system. It was massive and took up all the space on the 01 deck from port to starboard. Gosh, what would be next?

Next were the two 40MM gun systems on the aft part of the 01 deck. The starboard unit would be numbered Mount 43 and the port one, number 44. It seemed that the Navy always numbered everything this way. Everything on the port side was numbered in even numbers and the starboard side with odd numbers.

My bridge area still needed a lot of work. First there were the radio and sonar spaces, at least that's what the blue prints said. Just in front of this space was one of the most important areas, the C.I.C., "Combat Information Center." This would be the heart of the battle command for information regarding the proposed target. It would also serve as a constant source of

radar data as to the ship's position. In fact, it would be on constant alert for everything going on about the ship at all times when at sea. We get a little fancy with the next forward space. Should there be a "Commodore," one who commands a squadron of ships, a special "state room" is provided. It is more spacious than the Captain's state room. Pretty darned first class.

The deck above this level is the bridge. The Captain's main world. On the stern of this deck is the flag bridge. On the starboard side of the ship is a cavernous "bag" for the ready storage of all the signal flags. From several rails, many lanyards hang high to the yardarm at the top of the mast. Just a few feet below and outboard of the signal bridge are two 40MM twin gun positions. The fire control directors, one port and one starboard, are respectfully located forward of the signal area. Forward of the control directors are another two directors. Each side has a torpedo director for firing either to port or starboard. As I become more complete, these items are installed and all controls connected. I am beginning to "shape up."

As all the gun systems, radar, sonar, radio and such are installed they are tested for operation and in some cases, calibrated.

I am not sure when, but all of a sudden strange faces begin to wander about my decks and compartments. As I listened, they were the first of some of the crew to be assigned to take care of me. There were some 40 "pre-commissioning crew," officers, chiefs and enlisted men. They would begin to check things out, preparing for the full permanent crew. Boy oh boy was I looking forward to them. It was great to have some "Navy" men on my decks.

I could tell that my construction was nearing an end. Waist-high stanchions were placed around the entire length of the main deck and, where needed, on the 0-1 deck. Skid proof sheets installed on all the deck surfaces and painting was going on all over the ship. Bulkheads and decks from the water line to the main mast; I was looking real NAVY.

A number of the commissioning crew would become plank owners and permanent crew.

I learned that it was sometime in October. It was like a swarm of bees. Sailors in work dungarees, officers and chiefs in work khaki came from every direction. My crew had arrived. It would not be too long before I would be going to sea.

The 24th of October was "sweepers man your brooms," clean sweep down fore and aft. All tools that were used in the final days to finish me off were removed and I was made "spick and span" from bridge to keel. Stem to stern. I was ready for whatever and the order for tomorrow was passed out.

USS ZELLARS (DD777)

BOOT CAMPS

While ships are manufactured, sailors are being trained in basic seamanship in many different "recruit training centers" around the country. It is important to understand that a sailor does not just hold up his right hand and swear to defend his country and go to sea. He must endure the weeks of being subject to some hazing, being "helled" at and maybe given some unpleasant extra duty. The objective is to have the recruit learn and understand harsh discipline that is mandatory in any military service, For the Navy, that is "BOOT CAMP."

There were some boot camps that lasted only three weeks at the beginning of our war with Japan. The U.S. had a long and empty pipeline to fill and the urgency placed on new sailors was extreme. Most boot camp durations were in the eight to thirteen week schedule and were crammed with many different serious activities.

Upon arrival at a boot camp, there was always another physical. The one that was given at the recruit center was just to see if you were alive and war material. The physical at the training center was to see if you could stand up straight, march in an orderly fashion and do physical exercises.

Then came a hair cut, clothing issue and strong words on how to store clothes, make up a bunk and the many routine requirements for doing laundry, self hygiene shots and keeping the barracks spotless.

The "spotless field day" would be a very important duty that would follow each sailor all thru his Navy career. It was on Friday so that EVERYTHING would sparkle on Saturday morning's inspection and it had better "sparkle. "Saturday morning breakfast was also the first introduction to "NAVY" beans, a tradition that goes back a long way.

In the following week's marching seemed the most important. Each different place a group would go, it was by marching format — to chow, the gym and, of course, to all the functions that were part of routine training. At Farragut, Idaho, the longest march was to the heavy rifle range and the next was to lake Pend Oreille. The lake was a beautiful deep lake with high cliffs almost all around it's edge. Sand Point was the only town that the sailors saw but was the dock area for the oar pulled boats that were used for boat pulling exercise. The crews would row the boats out from the dock with the training petty officer giving the command of "stroke, stroke," and always one or more had trouble keeping up the rhythm.

The rifle range came later in the training. It was about three miles from the "boots" camp and was a nice outing. In small groups, they would fire a small number of rounds just to get the feel of a 30:06 rifle. As one group fired, another group would go to the pits and man the targets. They would pull them and show the hole if the recruit happened to hit it, so that the firing line could see if a hit had been made, then lower the target and patch the hole for another round.

Other training efforts that seemed important were Swimming, to practice life saving of one's self and maybe a shipmate, basic first aid, seamanship, knot tying, chemical warfare, standing watches, (this also would follow everyone throughout his Navy career), also ship and aircraft identification.

Toward the end of boot training, everyone was given a battery of tests to determine his knowledge and attitude. It was supposed to allow the personnel staff to place each recruit in the most adaptable duty after his boot training. Each recruit was given three choices as to the kind of duty that he would like to be sent to and the kind of ship he would prefer. This was to make sure that almost every person was sent in the opposite direction. When the "boot camp" experience was complete, a short leave was issued, at the conclusion of which each man had to be back to the center for assignment. Some went to what was called "A" school, others directly to a base for more training in some specialty, while the balance went to a disbursing center for assignment to a ship or new construction and more training. But the main purpose was to give some semblance of what to expect when a young man became a "sailor" and joined the fleet.

USS ZELLARS (DD777)

BLINN VAN MATER

BLINN VAN MATER was appointed to the Naval Academy in 1923 and graduated with the class of 1927. On graduation, he served successively in the battleship Colorado, the destroyers Paul Hamilton, Stottert and the Tatnall: the cruiser Indianapolis and sea plane tender Gannett (conducting survey of the Aleutian Islands in 1934).

Later assignments included U.S.S, Argonne: Hydrographic Office, Washington DC: destroyer Barker in the Asiatic Fleet. He received a letter of commendation from the CinC Asiatic Fleet for performance of duty in hazardous rescue operations for SS President Hoover which had run aground in Japanese waters. Subsequent duties were in destroyer, Farragut and NROTC Northwestern University.

WWII assignments include command of destroyers Anthony and the **ZELLARS DD777**, ComDesRon 6- participating in campaigns at Guadalcanal, the Solomans, Saipan, Guam, the first battle of the Philippine seas, the Okinawa invasion and occupation of Tori Shima.

He was awarded the Bronze Star Medal, and 3 Gold Stars in lieu of awards of the 2nd, 3rd, and 4th, Bronze Star Medals all with combat "V" and Commendation Ribbon with combat "V."

BLIN VAN MATER
U.S. NAVAL ACADEMY, CLASS OF 1927
COMMISSIONING COMMANDER OF
U.S.S. ZELLARS DD 777,
OCTOBER 25, 1944

Post war duties included, OpNav, Oni, Naval Attache to Turkey, staff of NATO command (CinC Med) at Malta; Hdq. of 6th. NavDist; Commanding Officer of cruiser Columbus and a return tour in OpNav.

In addition to his personal decorations, cited above, he earned the following medals: China Service, American Defense, American Campaign; Asiatic Pacific with 7 engagement stars: World War II Victory and National Defense Service.

Upon retirement in 1957, RAdm Van Mater joined the staff of the National Academy of Science as Administrative Officer.

RAdm Van Mater passed away June 1, 1991.

USS ZELLARS (DD777)

COMMISSIONING CEREMONY
25 OCTOBER 1944

1. The commissioning ceremonies will take place at 1430, 25 October 1944

2. The uniform for commissioning will be:

   Officers   Service Dress Blue Baker
   Enlisted Men   Dress Blue Baker

   NOTE: If weather is inclement, raincoats will be prescribed for officers and chief petty officers and peacoats for enlisted men.

3. Parade: Officers, chief petty officers, and watch squad on forecastle. Crew in tight ranks on deck.

4. Preliminary procedure:

   1345 — Meet guests, escort them to assigned spaces.

   1400 — Pass word, "All guest are kindly requested to leave the ship."

   1405 — Crew to quarters at commissioning parades. Muster and report to P.X.O.

   1420 — P.X.O. reports to Captain Van Mater, " Ready to proceed with ceremonies, sir."

   1425 — Captain Van Mater will greet Captain Wallin at brow. As Captain Wallin approaches forecastle, bugler sound "Attention". P.X.O. will call officers and men to attention.

   1430 — Captain Van Mater to Captain Wallins, "We are ready to proceed with the ceremony, sir."

5. CEREMONY:

   Mr. Packard introduces Miss Jules Wagner to Captain Van Mater. Miss Wagner presents colors to Captain Van Mater. Captain Van Mater delivers colors to quartermaster.

   Quartermasters and signalmen take stations at jackstaff, flagstaff and mast (pigstick).

P.X.O. to officers and crew: "Uncover - two. Spectators will please rise for the Chaplain's invocation.

Prayer by Chaplain.

P.X.O. to officers and crew: "Cover - two". Captain Wallin reads commissioning directive.

P.X.O. orders "Face aft". Officers will left face; chief petty officers will right face; watch squad will about face; men on dock will right face.

P.X.O. " Hand Salute" (Men in ranks do not salute). Band plays National Anthem. Two-block colors, jack and commission pennant smartly.

P.X.O. " Ready — two. Face forward — face." Officers and men will face to original position.

Captain Wallin will make a few remarks, declare the ship in commission, and deliver the ship to Captain Van Mater ("Publish your orders").

Captain Van Mater reads his orders and accepts the ship.

The Commanding Officers reads the letter from the Secretary of the Navy.

The Commanding officer addresses the crew.

Commanding Officer to Executive Officer, "Set the watch."

Executive Officer to CBM Ambrose, "Pass the word — set the watch — first section."

CBM Ambrose pipes the watch. Watch squad breaks ranks, proceeds to stations on the double.

CBM Ambrose to Executive Officer: Sir, the watch has been set."

CBM Ambrose takes his place at the brow to pipe Captain Wallin ashore.

Executive Officer to Commanding Officer, "Sir, the watch has been set."

Commanding Officer to Captain Wallin, "The ceremony is complete sir."

Commanding Officer escorts Captain Wallin aft.

Captain Wallin is piped over the side.

Executive Officer " Leave your quarters". Officers and men salute and fall out.

Buffet lunch in wardroom for officers and their guests.

Civilian guests are not allowed in plot, gun mounts, radar room radio rooms, or space below the main deck.

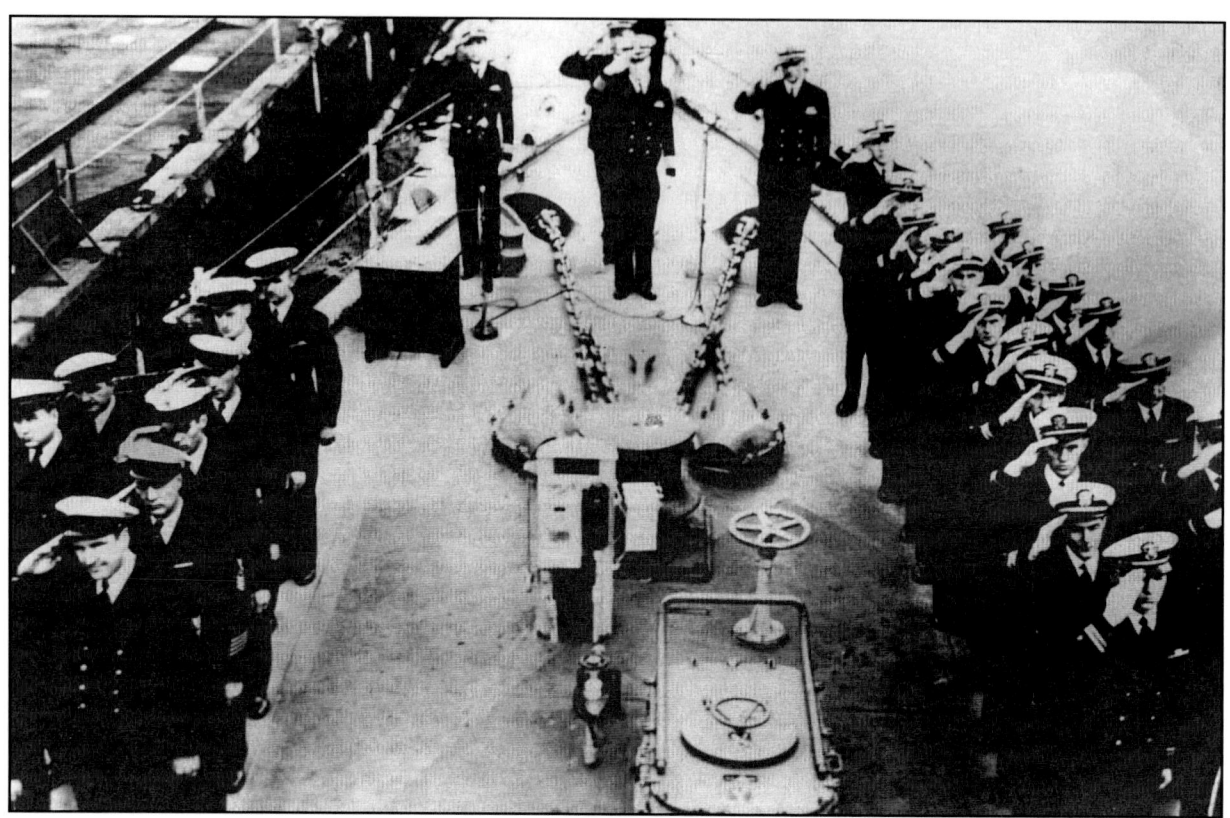

Just after noon, with all the officers and chiefs standing at attention and all the enlisted men on the dock also at attention, Captain Wallin addressed all the assembled crew and special guests. He stated that the ZELLARS was a fine new ship and would serve our country well. The crew had been carefully selected and were some of the best the NAVY had. They would go in "harms way" and do well.

With all hands piped to colors, the order was given to hoist our great American flag. The Stars and Stripes caught the breeze and unfurled for the first time. Each step allowed me to become more proud of all the young men who would be taking care of me.

He then turned over to Commander Van Mater the ship's first orders, placing me in Commission and part of the best Navy in the world.

A chaplain then stepped forward, hats were ordered removed and he gave a strong request for the ship's safety and deliverance of the crew from harm.

The ZELLARS DD 777 would go with God as she began her service to our country.

MAYFORM - 136 (REV. 1-44)

DECK LOG—LIST OF OFFICERS

CONFIDENTIA

LIST OF OFFICERS
ATTACHED TO AND ON BOARD THE U. S. S. ZELLARS (DD-777) , COMMAND

BY Lt. S. KINTBERGER, Commander, U. S. N. , DURING THE PERIOD COVERED BY THIS LOG BOOK, WITH DATE (

REPORTING FOR DUTY, DETACHMENT, OR DEATH, FROM 1 April , 19 45 , TO 30 April , 19 45

NAME AND FILE NUMBER (Show File No. below name)	RANK	DATE OF REPORTING ON BOARD DATE OF DETACHMENT (Show detachment date below reporting date)	PRIMARY DUTIES
KINTBERGER, L. S. 71416	Comdr.	2/8/45	Commanding
DUPZYK, R. R. 85208	Lt. Cdr.	10/25/44	Executive Off.
SMYLIE, C. A. 123316	Lieut.	10/25/44	Gunnery Off.
JONES, B. W. 139239	Lieut.	1/18/45	Engineer Off.
CLEVELAND, D. D. 185345	Lt. (jg)	10/25/44	1st Lieutenant
LINDH, A. L. 179192	Lieut.	10/25/44	Communications
ROBBINS, S. E. 165724	Lieut.	10/25/44 4/12/45	Automatic Weapons Officer
SMITH, N. E. 215098	Lt. (jg)	10/25/44	Navigator
RITTER, A. J. 92402	Lt. (jg)	10/25/44	Ass't Engineer Officer
BIRD, K. W. 324008	Lt. (jg)	10/25/44	Recognition Officer
GUNTHER, W. M. 328619	Lt. (jg)	10/25/44 4/12/45	Ass't First Lieutenant
BERNSTEIN, S. E. 87065	Ensign	10/25/44	CIC Officer
MARLOW, M. L. 311614	Lt. (jg)	10/25/44	Ass't. Engineer Officer
ROBINSON, J. P. 355943	Ensign	10/25/44	Ass't Communications Off.
BROCKMAN, E. E. 355494	Ensign	10/25/44 4/12/45	Ass't Gunnery Officer
FREEMAN, R. D. 335614	Ensign	10/25/44	Torpedo Off.
SCHAEFFER, H., Jr. 355961	Ensign	10/25/44	Radar Officer
HRUSHESKY, W. M. 332824	Ensign	10/25/44	Intercept. Off.
SOUTHALL, D. L. 333351	Ensign	10/25/44	Sound Officer
KINCAID, I. F. 140233	Lieut.	10/25/44 4/12/45	Medical Officer
KOCH, J. W. 271964	Lt. (jg)	10/25/44	Supply Officer
BARNES, O. C. 269384	Lt. (jg)	2/ 4/	...icer 132

Nelson E. SMITH, Lt. (jg). U. S. N. R. NAVIGATOR

20

USS ZELLARS (DD777)

COMMISSIONING

MUSTER ROLL OF THE CREW
FOR THE QUARTER ENDING OCTOBER 25,1944

ACUFF, William R.	629-92-87	S1c
ALGOOD, James H.	864-77-60	S1c
AMBROSE, Joseph S.	404-88-41	CBM
ANDERSON, George L.	303-35-30	RM2c
ANDERSON, Richard (n)	893-40-63	S2c
ANDERSON, Robert T.	877-83-23	SoM3c
ARDEN, Peter (n)	945-49-43	S2c
ARONSON, Chester C.	632-38-33	M1c
ASHBY, Oran L.	965-88-46	S2c
ASSELIN, Ernest, (n)	666-19-70	MM2c
AVERTT, Willard M.	359-87-35	FC1c
BAILEY, Broadus, (n)	576-69-95	Cox
BAKER, Harold E.	671-73-55	S1c
BARKLEY, Calvin J.	767-86-99	S1c (SK)
BARNES, Arthur H.	378-78-82	S2c
BEAVERS, Gorden E.	640-00-74	WT2c
BECKNER, Roy (n)	356-81-59	GM2c
BELL, Leonard A.	313-41-27	S2c
BELL, Russell F.	941-36-16	F2c
BENAVIDES, Manuel (n)	864-86-53	S2c
BENNETT, Floyd D.	965-90-83	S2c
BERTELSON, William K.	960-90-09	S2c
BIEBER William J.	961-16-03	S2c
BILYEU, Jimmie M.	274-43-19	GM3c

BISCONTI, Nick (n)	949-47-94	F2c
BLACKFORD, David H.	280-10-86	F2c
BLANKENSHIP, Ernest E.	849-13-02	S2c
BLANKENSHIP, D. Jr.	866-35-70	RT2c
BONNY, Denny. G.	387-07-47	S2c
BONOS, Eugene L.	250-46-14	CQM (AA)
BOREN, Glenn R.	393-43-44	SK1c
BRADLEY, Andrew (n)	296-05-72	StM1c
BRADY, John W.	871-74-75	S1c
BRANSOM, Thuopholus	562-58-62	MoMM1c
BRIGGS, John C.	886-98-23	F1c (BE)
BRIM, LeRoy R.	849-66-08	S1c
BROKOP, Henry F.	943-16-22	F1c (BE)
BROWN, Vir1 V.	975-04-74	S2c
BUCK, Harold C.	654-60-63	TM1c
BURDETTE, Charles R.	393-25-99	CCS (AA)
BUSSE, Emmett A.	849-84-92	F2c
CADWELL, Harry N.	317-13-60	S2c
CALL, Helaman P.	964-28-15	S1c RdM
CAMPBELL, Loyd E.	755-99-36	S2c
CARD, Richard D.	368-81-75	S2c
CARLSON, Richard K.	638-50-99	S1c
CARNATHAN, David A.	356-42-99	SM1c
CASSIDY, Weslay M.	871-11-60	S2c
CEBULSKI, Matthew R.	711-36-92	S1c
CHERRY, Homer W.	628-01-46	BM2c
CHILTON, Clyde A.	663-66-87	MM1c
CHOVAN, Daniel (n)	410-64-61	WT1c
CLARK, Miren D.	566-02-74	SoM3c
CLEVENGER, FLOYD T.	648-48-80	GM2C
CONKLIN, Dale E.	952-37-44	F2c
CONNOR, Joseph E.	208-64-82	TM3c
CORBIT, Richard L.	758-16-77	S2c
CORP, Bobbie J.	618-97-95	FC2c
CRAFT, Charles B.	660-87-95	S2c
CRAIG, David S.	891-03-84	S2c
CREIGHTON, John C.	612-16-22	GM2c

CROSBY, Carl E.	317-13-26	S2c
CUNNINGHAM, Jerome E.	951-58-83	S2c
CUSHING, Frank H.	363-64-88	CEM (PA)
CUSTER, Dallas H.	317-13-34	S2c
DALY, John H.	202-69-51	MM2c
DANIELS, Joseph R.	859-17-28	S1c
DANIEL, Norman R.	342-96-55	S1c
DANKERT, Fred J.	961-03-92	S2c
DAVIS, Mack E.	605-27-40	FC2c
DAY, Ted Jr.	755-98-22	S1c (FCR)
DE BOER, William (n)	961-63-59	SC3c
DEDIC, Joseph (n),	321-59-29	MM1c
DERBY, Leo L.	973-08-36	S2c
DINIUS, Peter J.	877-87-36	TM3c
DOIRING, Robert E.	202-83-94	Bkr3c
DUDLEY, Robert O.	376-44-45	MM2c
DURAN, Cypriano (n)	619-33-60	S2c
EATON, Robert L.	654-70-69	SM2c
ENSLEY John R.	619-24-45	PhM3c
ERICHSON, Lester O.	638-03-25	BM2c
ESGUERRA, Jaun B. (?)	663-22-96	StM3c
JESSE, Lyman J.	973-03-52	S2c
EVANS, Donald D.	316-61-76	CMM (AA)
FANIEL, Robert A.	322-14-30	S2c
FEHL, OrrieL.	923-41-12	Flc(WT)
FERRELL, James W.	677-20-69	Flc(EM)
FLEMMING, Cyril J.	341-96-30	WT1c
FLETCHER, Arthur L.	668-15-91	EM1c
FLOREY, Arnold R.	730-84-72	QM3c
FOLK, Andrew R.	262-34-76	MM1c
FORD, Russell D.	783-51-05	S2c
FRAHM, Gilbert G.	317-06-86	S2c
FRAZIER, William F.	967-69-66	RdM3c
FURGHMER, Donald N (?)	660-87-96	S2c
FURMAN, Calvin L.	961-70-99	S2c
GEDMAN, Stanley (n)	212-23-48	CTM

GEORGE, Richard W.	617-04-24	S1c
GIBBS, Ernest F.	888-18-38	F1c(MM)
CIERER, Robert W.	873-31-38	S1c
GIONFRIDDO, Paul J.	400-23-73	WT3c
GOGAN, William L Jr.	648-81-63	PhM2c
GOLDBERG, Herman J.	624-87-69	StM1c
GOLDBERG, Joseph (n).	642-18-32	MM2c
GOLDATE, Bernard T.	645-38-89	S1c
GOREE, William A.	381-74-76	S1c
GOWEN, Paul H.	842-91-22	S1c
GRABOWSKI, Frank C.	821-81-32	Cox
GRAY, Robert A.	945-35-74	S2c
GREGORY, Marvin L.	872-04-16	S1c
GRIGGS, Dewitt (n).	272-40-61	MM2c
GROTHOUSE, Leonard P.	864-43-99	S1c
GROULX, Roger (n).	951-62-34	S2c
HAINLINE, Clyde H.	765-29-82	S2c
HAJICEK, Henry G.	961-20-24	S2c
HAMILTON, Maurice L.	662-55-24	S2c
HARRIS, Charles F.	669-34-84	EM2c(GY)
HARRIS, George E.	342-99-91	F2c
HARTIGAN, Mathew D. Jr.	853-23-87	S2c(GM)
HARVEY, Charles F.	600-18-54	QM2c
HAWES, Donald M.	924-06-59	SoM3c
HAYES, Rodger B.	890-63-21	QM3c
HEISEL, Oscar H.	975-03-59	F2c
HHENLEY, Alfred J.	844-14-49	F1c
HEREFORD, Stanley G.	654-59-98	S1c
HESLEY, Quency T.	355-25-43	CMM (PA)
HILL, Cicil L.	393-23-79	MM1c
HIRST, Carl J.	283-29-18	CPhM
HIXON, Charles	880-71-94	S2c
HODGE, Robert E.	357-96-87	S1c
HOLBOROW, Frank M.	382-45-54	Cox
HOLLY, LaValle.	848-61-65	F1c
HOMICK, Michael (n)	244-45-25	TM3c

HOPSON, Wayne W.	888-03-07	SoM3c
HORIST, Joseph A.	853-48-42	FC3c
HORNER, Willis W.	883-64-86	F2c
HUGHES, Charles E.	849-38-08	F2c
HUMRICHOUSE, Roy L.	662-30-72	S2c
HUSAK, Otto (n)	317-01-31	S2c
HUTCHINS, EIdon T.	368-34-88	WT1c
INGRAM, Cicil C	938-90-74	S2c
INGRAM, Clyde W.	885-46-65	S1c
JACOBSON, Robert A.	951-41-53	F2c
JANIGA, Joseph J	865-38-59	S1C
JIMENEZ, Rudolph M.	879-60-10	S2c
JIRRELS, Floyd E. Jr.	342-25-54	S1c
JOHNSON, Carl D.	612-69-55	EM1c
JONES, William F.	650-46-54	TM2c
JORGENSEN, Darold J.	317-07-33	S2c
KAWULA, Julius F.	622-17-40	S1c
KEANE, Clair V.	973-08-91	S2c
KENNEDY, Kenneth A.	610-98-00	MMlc
KENNEDY, Theeodore (n).	606-23-41	TMlc
KIEFERLE, Frank M.	945-38-32	S2c
KING, Alfred Q.	756-05-33	S1c
KLEMME, Edgar A.	874-42-63	S2c
KLIENDL, Darwin L.	757-91-20	S2c
KOTSCHWAR, Vernon L.	317-13-53	S2c
KRAJCA, Frank J., Jr.	617-05-89	S1c
KRAMER, John A.	368-47-07	BMlc
KREIENSIECK, Arthur J.	553-03-98	S1c
KROMBAR, Emmet.	810-40-58	S1c
KUHNS, Jack M.	413-54-42	RM3c
KUZMICH, Joseph (n)	207-32-59	GMlc
LAMY, John D.	948-40-84	S2c
LANFORD, Francis E.	605-15-34	S1c
LAWSON, Kenneth K.	973-08-57	S2c
LEE, William L.	964-47-87	S2c
LEVERTON, Dwight, J.	386-72-72	S1c

LEVITZ, Eugene J.	563-64-89	SF1c
LIGHTBODY, Thomas H.	952-02-11	S2c
LINDSEY, James L.	843-78-20	S1c
LISK, Eddie L.	957-20-02	S2c
LISTON, John W., Jr.	393-76-66	S1c
LIVINGSTON, James H.	973-08-32	S2c
LOEBER, John (n).	377-90-45	S1c
LONG, George H.	869-65-65	S1c
LUTA, Stanley (n)	852-59-03	S1c
LYNAS, Stanley (n).	626-79-82	S1c
MAC KAY, Warner P.	886-94-90	S1c
MAPIE, Stanley C.	957-02-21	S1c
MAREK, Walter J.	853-27-32	S2c
MARMON, Chester G.	961-14-31	S2c
MATTHEWS, William L.	891-03-08	F2c
MAXWELL, Chalmer O.	865-36-12	F1c
MC ALLISTER, Robert M.	956-27-35	F1c
MC BRIDE, Donald B	888-39-89	F2c
MC CRACKEN, Howard W.	875-40-93	F1c
MC CURDY, Harvey M.	963-14-96	S1c
MC FARLAND, Richard D.	875-90-71	S2c
MC GEE, George W.	285-57-68	F1c
MC GEE, Joseph J.	860-39-27	S2c
MC GREGOR, Cecil K.	652-26-90	MM1c
McLEOD, Richard E.	250-57-71	GM3c
MC MATH, Laney M.	839-78-17	FCR3c
MC VIE, William J.	404-47-10	GM2c
MEDINA, Raul C	317-13-25	S2c
MELCHER, Ernest H, Jr.	860-50-21	S2c
MELING, Richard E.	943-29-72	F1c
MERRIMAN, Jack L.	888-30-56	S2c
MIER, Raymond H.	312-58-06	S1c
MILTENBERGER, Robert B.	321-79-45	MM3c
MINSON, Lawrence A.	957-22-96	F2c
MIRACLE, Ralph D.	650-37-25	S1c
MOHR, John R.	815-24-96	S1c (FC)

MOORE, Howard J.	860-76-67	S1c
MORGAN, Charles R.	615-80-35	S1c
MORGAN, Steve R.	356-17-57	GM1c
MORSE, Otis A.	654-13-69	S1c
MORTON, Ralph O.	375-57-88	CRM (PM)
MUHL, Robert L.	860-10-40	S2c
MUNOZ, Richard D.	565-75-59	S1c
MURO, Vincent P.	876-46-75	S1c
MURPHY, Charles E, Jr.	641-65-15	S1c
MURPHY, Raymond J.	961-19-26	S2c
MYERS, Cecil M.	632-46-02	FC2c
NAVA, Jaun L.	624-17-20	SC1c
NEAL, Herley C.	895-35-27	S1c
NEFF, Jacob H.	956-81-66	F2c
O'BRIEN, Thomas J.	755-04-86	S1c
PADGETT, Leonard J.	386-59-53	S1c
PALMIERI, Antonio.	878-79-17	F2c
PAPIERNIK, Poleslaus A.	857-72-37	F1c
PARKER, James B.	550-06-02	Y1c
PASCHAL, Raymond E.	660-88-34	S2c
PASSIELY, Burl H.	885-35-58	S2c
PATTERSON, Kimble C.	640-90-74	F1c
PEDEGANA, William J.	890-15-05	RM3c
PEEL, Elmer (n)	943-61-69	S2c
PELLETIER, Joseph R.	202-04-01	GM2c
PETTERSON, Verlyn H.	306-69-94	F1c
PHILLIPS, Milton S.	873-82-61	S2c (SM)
PITTS, Elmer E.	658-09-60	Cox
POOL, Kay (n)	346-38-03	CWT (PA)
PORTER, Glen A.	874-27-48	S2c
PORTER, Paul W Jr.	975-62-80	S2c
POTTER, Clifford L.	883-88-04	S2c
POTTER, Paul L.	973-08-31	S2c
PROVITOLA, Armando J.	802-06-29	S1c
PUCKET, Wilbum E.	888-36-29	S2c
QUARTOROLI, Joseph Jr	327-13-71	S2c

RALSTON, Charles F.	245-02-82	GM3c
REA, Earl F.	942-41-95	S1c(FRC)
REED, Sterling D.	279-90-17	EM3c
REED, Oscar H.	360-49-14	MM2c
RHONE, John E.	563-07-79	MM2c
RICHARDSON, Donald W.	385-90-47	MoMM3c
RISLING, George W.	962-01-29	S2c
ROACH, Billy Joe.	356-75-70	FCM2c
POBERTSON, Jack P.	829-78-55	TM3c
ROBINSON, James G.	651-11-01	WT3c
ROCHEFORD, Harold J.	869-68-00	F1c
ROGERS, Henderson C.	933-64-05	StM2c
ROHLFER, Kermit G.	613-17-84	FC2c
RUSH, William B.	258-42-97	MM2c
RUTKOWSKY, George A.	820-98-43	Cox
SALDANA, Cenero (n).	619-42-61	S2c
SAUNDERS, Basil B.	848-52-84	S1c
SAYE, William T.	967-97-16	S2c (RdM)
SCHUH, Bernard J.	869-05-03	S1c (FC)
SCHULTHEIS, Joseph E.	955-72-21	S2c
SCHULTZ, John J.	285-23-54	S2c
SCOTT, John P.	885-27-69	S2c
SCRUGGS, Jimmy G.	721-95-98	GM3c
SEALS, Fred (n)	887-37-35	StM2c
SEIGEL, Marvin M.	815-26-13	F1c
SEXTON, Lester (n).	291-63-24	GM2c
SEXTON, Owen (n)	659-61-18	Y2c
SHEAHAN, William T.	554-78-17	S1c
* SHIPLEY, Lawrence T.	871-59-87	F2c
SHULMAN, Lester M.	814-90-18	F1c
SIMS, Harry E.	620-36-11	WT3c
SIMS, John B.	633-31-45	SoM2c
SIROIS, William R.	224-99-07	S1c
SLUGOCKI, Thaddeus C.	821-34-80	EM2c
SMITH, Roy L.	393-58-63	S1c (RM)
SMITH, William E.	840-12-45	S1c (GM)

SOMMERFIELD, Raymond J.	611-81-79	B2c
SPAN, Norman E.	317-13-52	S2c
SPOSATO, Paul (n)	810-71-90	S2c
STADELHOFER, Richard.	411-29-55	QMlc
STEHLIN, Herman A.	342-85-70	S2c
STERLING, James A.	815-26-18	F1c
STETSON, Richard, (n).	827-14-70	RT3c
STEVENS, Harold W.	883-82-29	S1c (RdM)
STEWART, Herman (n)	967-61-10	F2c
STEWARD, Lawrence E.	885-01-69	F1c (EM)
STONE, Clarence R.	864-09-21	EM3c
XSTRICKLER, Raymond V.	819-56-05	F1c
SURRATT, Bob R.	617-28-62	Bkr2c
SYRES, Charles A.	888-23-02	S2c (RdM)
TACKETT, Isaac H Jr.	295-08-43	BM2c
TASHJIAN, Mural R.	382-72-43	F1c (MM)
TEMPLIN, Richard F.	854-08-92	SM3c
THOMAS, George M.	888-20-44	S1c (RdM)
THOMAS, Ralph W.	640-07-95	MM2c
THOMPSON, David (n)	755-03-57	S2c
THOMPSON, Ernest R.	861-92-13	S2c
THOMPSON, Wilfred C.	961-77-68	S2c
THORNTON, Thomas M.	570-27-22	S2c
TOLLESON, Oras E.	938-89-07	F2c
TRACY, Lawrence (n)	641-17-09	S1c
TRAEGER, Casper W Jr.	842-83-11	SoM3c
PROVATO, Ignatius J.	810-70-48	S1c
TURNER, James M.	847-82-61	S1c (Y)
ULKU, Stanley J.	758-22-31	S2c
UPTON, Ray (n)	838-23-08	S1c (GM)
VAITKUS, Albert F.	299-99-70	FC(R)lc
VAUGHN, Joe A.	356-57-00	CMlc
VOLPEL, Richard H.	883-09-15	F1c (MM)
VON HINKEN, Fred H.	710-63-90	FC3c
WADE, Clarence W.	372-21-79	SC2c
WADKINS, Gerald M.	357-67-71	S2c (RM)

WALKER, Ross R.	765-28-25	S2c
WALLING, Julios B.	261-37-43	CMM (T)
WALSH, John F.	854-44-71	S2c
WALTERS, Howard B.	891-03-79	S2c
WATSON, Preston K.	510-02-99	GM1c
WELO, Earling A.	871-23-42	S2c (RdM)
WELT, Lewis W.	321-05-40	CGM (PA)
WESTNEDGE, Leonard A.	891-03-69	S2c
WHARFIELD, Miles C.	853-70-46	S2c
WHITE, Roy C.	840-80-29	GM3c
WHITLOW, Glen E.	293-02-28	S2c
WILBER, Howard E Jr.	382-99-33	MM2c
WILCOX, Deward (n)	958-70-53	S2c
WILLIAMS, Douglas V.	565-75-27	S1c (QM)
WILLIAMS, George A.	295-96-75	Ck2c
WILLIAMS, Kenneth E.	207-31-50	TM2c
WILLIG, Glenn E.	620-17-11	WT2c
WILLISON, Richard C.	620-09-85	WT2c
WOLF, Paul J.	961-04-04	S2c
WOODS, David R.	212-84-54	S1c
WOOTEN, Fred Jr.	680-49-21	S1c
WYATT, Chester L.	883-89-40	S2c
WYCKOFF, Harold R.	382-32-61	SoM3c
YOCUM, Robert L.	632-37-91	MM2c
YOUNG, Glen R.	317-07-05	S2c
YOUNG, John W.	251-03-09	S2c
YOUNG, William L.	893-40-06	S1c
ZELK, Wilber H.	622-14-56	MM2c
ZICMA, Fred (n)	401-98-50	F2c
ZUNT, Raymond E.	880-18-18	S2c

The commissioning pennant was ordered to the top of the yardarm and crews set the first watch. I now had sailors to care for me, to give life to the purpose for which I was built. I had become alive! The American flag was two-blocked to the flag stay on the stern. I knew everything was now complete.

The Captain briefly spoke to the niece of Lt(jg) ZELLARS and she presented the Captain with a photo of the ship's namesake officer.

There were a total of 20 officers from Ensigns, Lieutenant Jgs, Lieutenants and to the Captain, a full Commander.

Eleven Chiefs, usually one for each division. Their job was to keep everything on the ship running smoothly, both in their specialty and the men serving under them. The rate "chief" was looked upon as a goal for the lower ratings and retirement after a full career.

Most of the crew were very young and just out of Boot Camp with a stopover for special sea duty and training. From the Captain on down, the seamen and other ratings that had never been at sea before would be well trained by the more experienced crew members. Most of the training would be the responsibility of the senior Petty Officers. Gunnery, fire control, radar, sonar, and all the other specialties would be pounded into a well functioning proud crew.

Now the shakedown part for approval began. Food, fuel and general stores were placed on board. I kinda smiled as all hands turned to in bringing the stores onboard. Senior petty officers supervised the lesser ratings in the art of carrying the goods to the correct storage spaces. It was also interesting how some of the more ready-to-eat supplies found their way to different gang work areas. Apples, oranges, canned Vienna sausages and many other goodies made a few moments special.

For several days, with some of the shipyard workers on board, the crew charged me up and down the Sound. They checked my engines and spun my main battery and gun director to make sure of their correct operations.

When the Navy was satisfied with the basic performance of the ship, orders were passed that I was to get my first taste of deep blue water.

All of us were going to San Diego for more extensive training and sea trials I was going to be tested to my limits and I was real nervous, I did not want any problems or deficiency, I just wanted to be perfect.

There were few moments of rest. An example was late one night, about November 3rd or 4th, a noise on top of the bridge gave me concern. The main battery gun director was moving about and mount #1 was moving with it. Upon self inquiry, I learned that both were pointing at the moon and the pointer in the director was talking into his head phones saying "mark, mark" as the director and the gun mount was being "bore sighted" on the left side of the moon. Boy, were the ZELLARS big guns going to shoot accurately; minute adjustments in the gun mounts were made so that each 5" mount was aligned exactly the same as the gun director. It was after midnight before the gunners' mates and the firecontrolmen were satisfied with the drill and quietness about the ship was resumed.

Early on a very wet November morning, a Bos'n pipe sounded and the voice that went with it commanded "all hands to your special sea details, make preparations for going to sea." As each division reported, the Captain ordered "single up all lines, let go all forward lines, let go aft, all slow astern" and the ZELLARS got underway headed for deep salt water.

We headed out thru the Strait of Juan de Fuca and the Pacific blue ocean. Some miles out, the Captain ordered to come left to a course that would drive us South and make turns for 20 knots. Everyone on the ship could feel the change in our speed. The decks began to rumble and the stern sorta tucked down to bite deeper into the sea. The Bos'n piped call to lunch and soon after, change of the watch to the second section.

Later in the afternoon, a plane towing a sleeve target came across the horizon, and our first general quarters was sounded. A comedy began. Some of the new crew forgot which side was up on the starboard and down on the port side. Some strong words were expressed as sailors ran into other sailors going the wrong way. Each would soon learn.

The target sleeve plane could have cancelled the flight. Our 5 inch blasted away; the 40MM, all twelve barrels, cut loose and the range for the 20MM was too great. Round after round screamed in the general direction but not one hole was put in the sleeve.

Typical sailor's words came from the bridge as the Captain expressed his dissatisfaction. He left a firm impression that we would be doing a lot of gunnery practice in the near future.

The ship was some 40 miles out to sea nearing the channel Island group and, as guessed, another plane surprised us and away went the guns again. The gunners did a little better this time. After some strong words from the mount captains, big black puffs of exploding flack crept nearer and nearer to the target until the bursts were right on top and the sleeve parted from the tow cable and drifted down into the sea. The gunners felt a little better but knew that they had a long way to go before the Captain would render praise. The crew was learning that the Captain would not accept anything other than perfect and on time.

The ZELLARS entered the port of San Diego late in the evening after being at sea for five days. It was a relief for everyone to just see land again and anticipate liberty and a cold beer. Our first anchorage was near the destroyer base which was at the end of the bay, south. Many other ships of varying types were at the repair service docks being serviced and cared for the ship had it's turn for some minor tune-up and resupply of general food stuff. For several days nothing happened. The Captain was spending a lot of time at the base commander's headquarters. We learned that he was setting up our next several weeks of intense training. A ship just didn't charge out of the harbor and rush around making a lot of noise. Each day was carefully planned with a lot of support from the base. When we did slowly move out to the blue sea, we had a schedule that was to be followed, and carefully monitored by the training command at the base. Each part of training was "eyeballed" by a referee who made notes for correction during the next session. They were very exacting in their task.

Days passed into several weeks ...

We had a lot of anti-aircraft gunnery and believe us, we got a lot better as we became used to the drills. The one drill that caused some new excitement was the ASW, (anti submarine warfare). A sub from the sub base would meet us at a designated location, radio words spoken and then it would submerge with its periscope high in the air. As we cruised close to the sub, grenades were thrown from the stern of the ZELLARS noting the accuracy and closeness of the charge. It was supposed to simulate the depth charges against an enemy undersea sub. Once the ship dropped a real depth charge just to show the sub crew what it was like to have such an explosion nearby.

The training cycle was almost routine, out to sea in the early morning to rendezvous with another ship, submarine or a sleeve towing target plane. All hands would go thru their assigned responsibility and be observed by one of the training team. As the whole ship became efficient in the close by training, another challenge was added.

Not too far from San Diego was an island called San Clemente. It was the official shore bombardment range. It also harbored a large herd of goats and a trillion sea birds. The southern end of the island was the target range. Large circles and squares had been set in some of the more strategic places and they were what the ships were supposed to hit. For several days the gun crews blasted away at the various white shapes and did very well. I am not sure if they killed any of the wildlife on the island but it sure scared hell out of the goats. Shooting at a stationary target was easier than a moving sleeve. I was really becoming proud of the crew and their great attitude in taking care of me.

As the training team became more friendly and smiled as each task was completed, we knew our stay in sunny California was coming to an end. On a perfect day in late December, with fresh supplies on board and the fuel tanks topped off, the ship slipped out of the harbor and turned North just out of Point Loma and added a good measure of turns to the engines.

As I, the ship, and they, the crew, steamed North, I began to take stock of all that had happened to me from the first day that I began to realize that I was to be a ship. Each day there seemed to be less for me to be concerned about. I was in the very best of hands and knew that it was about time to let the crew take full charge. I had a lot of thinking to do and decided to hold on until our return to Seattle.

Something kinda crazy, at least to me, had slipped by. It had been going on from the very first day the crew reported on board. It was the Fridays. Each Friday just after the crew had breakfast, every man on the ship "turned to." Scrub brushes, buckets, mops and lots of clean rags with a sailor attached went from one end of my hull to the other, from bilge to the bridge cleaning every nook and cranny. It was an all-day affair.

The living spaces were scrubbed and mopped. The light fixtures were cleaned behind each reflector and every hidden place where a grain of dirt might be found was searched out and scrubbed clean.

The gun mounts were given the same attention, and if needed, the bore of each 5" 38 was polished and oiled. It seemed funny to me to see several sailors aligned on a long pole, with special scrubbing brushes attached, going back and forth as they made sure the bore would meet the Captain's inspection. In the Plotting room, where it was always neat as a pin, the shiny aluminum deck plates were even polished to a bright reflection. The Galley got a very special scrubbing for food service was one of the Captains pet "better be clean "areas. By the end of Fridays, the crew was pretty spent. On most occasions, when field day had been completed, the division officer for each space would hold his own walk-thru inspection to make sure that nothing had been missed for it could be his neck if a space did not meet and pass inspection. The funny part was on Saturday morning. After all the hard work preparing for inspection, the crew was given a breakfast of "NAVY beans and corn bread." I learned that this unusual meal was a long standing NAVY tradition. The whole purpose was not to mess up any part of the ship before the Captain had a chance to do his Saturday morning thing.

The other item was each morning. At 6AM the Bos'n pipe wailed it's command and a gruff voice would order," now hear this, sweepers man your brooms, clean sweep down fore and aft." It was often repeated in order to make sure it was heard throughout the ship. Sailors, still half asleep, would struggle out to cleaning lockers, retrieve the necessary brooms and sometimes mops, go to the part of the ship that they were responsible for, and without a great deal of enthusiasm, begin the before breakfast general sweeping. I always felt that they could have waited until after breakfast and let the crew have a couple more "Zs." Routine is routine, especially in the NAVY.

The intense training continued all the way up the coast. Even as we were about to enter the Straits leading into Bremerton Navy Shipyard, a sub met us and again repeated the ASW drills.

The ship was assigned docking space next to the great aircraft carrier, FRANKLIN. She was being re-outfitted after a long cruise in the war zone and was about to return. The ZELLARS was dwarfed, tied alongside her massive hull. The ZELLARS spent Christmas in Seattle but the readiness pace increased. Shipyard workers moved all over the ship adjusting and making final corrections of any deficiencies that had been noted during the shakedown cruise. Some of my crew was given a short leave and others were let loose to have a few days of liberty in Seattle.

The period of Christmas allowed me to come to a point of final terms about myself. The quiet with most of the crew on the beach and the rattle of the shipyard let me count my blessings. The crew now had everything that was needed to meet our country's enemy and I need not be further concerned. They were in command.

USS ZELLARS (DD777)

MAXIMUM READINESS TO GO IN HARM'S WAY

As each crew member returned from either leave or liberty, they settled into making final preparations for departing for Pearl Harbor, and on to an assigned task force.

On January 25, 1945, with full fuel and stores on board, the now familiar order, "single up all lines, make ready for going to sea." Our orders simply read, "proceed to Pearl Harbor for further training and assignment to the active fleet." The trip to Pearl Harbor was more training but we were now headed in the right direction, to do what we had been training to do from day one.

Upon entering Pearl Harbor, some of the dastardly deeds done by the Japanese on December 7th was still in evidence. A small amount of the upper superstructure of the Arizona was on our port side as we passed and stood at attention, paying honor and in memory "of the shipmates still sailing below her rusting decks. On the ZELLARS there were tears of sadness, even though we did not know the Arizona's men personally, they as all sailors, were our shipmates. Their loss was our loss and they died in the defense of our country. It sounded as though the ZELLARS growled in anger as we passed and the words were "rest easy, I am going deep in pursuit of the bastards who did this and I will rain vengeance on them to my fullest ability."

After the ship had anchored in the destroyer anchorage, the Executive Officer gave a brief summary of liberty and some details of how we should act while on liberty, the first section was piped to liberty beginning at 13:00. There was a rush for the first section to change to Navy whites and obtain their liberty cards. The harbor was full of ships and one could imagine the number of service men who would fill the streets in Honolulu.

The crew had several days to go over the ship and make ready for Admiral's inspection. Every effort was made to polish all the brass and scour the bulkheads and decks. Inspection day came and selected men were standing by to welcome the Admiral. As his barge made it's way alongside the ship's ladder, the Bos'n piped attention and as he stepped on board, the "side boys" saluted smartly as Captain Van Mater welcomed him on board. The Admiral had a staff with him and the inspection was a real doozy. Ensigns, Lt.(jgs), Lt's, Chiefs and several other higher ranking staff went thru the ship like a tornado. Every little space was opened for evaluation by the inspecting staff. In the end the ZELLARS was heartbroken. She had not passed. In fact we gained a new and very unwelcome name, "The dirty Z." Every one on board felt that this was the Admiral's way of welcoming "new" destroyers to the fleet, just to take any edge off of some cockiness that the ship may have acquired. Not the "Z!" We were just proud, not boastful. Like heck we weren't.

After the inspection team departed the ship, guess what happened? Every item that the inspection team had noted as deficient received special attention. Paint scrapers, wire brushes and paint were issued. Everyone "turned to." The Captain was really pissed and so informed the crew, "This will never happen again as long as I am the Captain of this ship." Very final words.

A fuel barge came alongside with stores. It was time to meet the challenge of the Pearl Harbor training command. Again it was out in the early AM and back late at night. At first it was seamanship, with other destroyers undergoing the same routine as the ZELLARS. Then an old friend arrived. The FRANKLIN that we had shared dock space with in Seattle came steaming over the horizon with a great white foam of salt water running up her prow. We, along with the U.S.S. FOX, our sister ship, met the Franklin miles from Pearl and were assigned plane guard detail. The Fox stood off the FRANKLIN's bow and the ZELLARS was assigned to tag along at her stern. Our responsibility was to rescue any of the carrier's pilots that happened to miss her flight deck. From time to time, the carrier would fly an SBD (a dive bomber) over our station and we would have anti-aircraft gunnery. We had become very good at "killing" that darned sleeve but began to wish that it was a Jap Zero. An air of anticipation for real combat was beginning to form among the crew. Eager, yes but very wary for we had seen some of the ships at Seattle that had met the enemy and they had suffered some very devastating damage, with many of the crew killed. The ZELLARS was not without concern.

Every day, and some nights, were busy. Replenishing of fuel, ammunition and food stores went on like routine. The ship was constantly being cared for with the ever present paint scraping and repainting where any rust dared to show. Guns being cleaned and the bores swabbed and oiled. The main battery was bore sighted often and used the moon, when it was available, to align all the guns and gun director. Every inch of the ship from bow to stern, bridge to bilge, received full attention. Each division was always on the alert for any unsatisfactory event or space. The crew tended themselves just as well.

As the days melted into one another, the training became more intense

During a weekend ship cleaning, Chief Cushing, electrical gang, arranged for each division to muster on the fantail for a photo session. Cushing was our official and unofficial photographer. As one division stood before his camera and was recorded, another division was called to standby. It took most of the afternoon to complete the picture taking.

Many of the names have gone from memory and even the faces, but the lasting bond that developed will never fade from those crew members who really care about each other.

From the following, a few names will be noted with special comments where they have a meaning.

(Editors note:) Every effort was made to find a photo of each division that was taken at Pearl Harbor. Several are missing.

Each deck division had a Bos'nsmate as leader and one senior Bos'n as boss. It is difficult to explain how an iron ship can get so dirty when at sea with the closest dirt some hundreds of feet below the keel, but it does happen. Burning bunker oil spreads black dirt all about the ship. The three deck divisions are constantly scrubbing both above deck and in all the living spaces. Each day the division Bos'n inspects his area to make sure that when the leading Bos'n comes along, all is well and shipshape.

From left to right, BMlc KRAMER leading Bos'n; BM2c ERICKSON, third division; Ensign HRUSH-ESKY, deck officer; First division Bos'n TACKETT BM2c; BM2c CEBULSKI, second division Bos'n.

BMlc Kramer had a strong, forceful way of handling the deck crew but did a great job of managing responsibility.

The writer was unable to find a photo of the FIRST DIVISION as well as some others. (*Sorry shipmates.*)

There are three deck divisions and they are mostly responsible for the routine maintenance of housekeeping of the ship. When the Bos'n blows, "sweepers man your brooms," it is the seamen that jump to the call.

The ship is divided into three sections from bow to stern. The first division begins at the bow and does their thing up to the weather break or about 1/3 of the forward part of the ship. This includes cleaning the crew's compartment, seeing that the crew's laundry is taken to the laundry service per the schedule. Even policing the "air bedding" when it's called, (each man is responsible for carrying his mattress topside for about 1/2 day to freshen the pad.)

The first division took care of all topside decks and some bulkhead maintenance, scrubbing the bulwarks and if any rust stains should dare show, the paint scrapers could be heard all over the ship as they chipped away the offending site. The chromate, Navy gray, or deck gray was applied, after which the division Bos'n inspected the completed work. It had better meet his satisfaction, per NAVY regulations.

SECOND DIVISION

The second division takes over where the first division leaves off. (Naturally)

On a Sumner class destroyer, they have more topside area to care for. All of the 01 deck, some of the outer bulkhead around the 40MM gun tubs, boat davits for the motorwhale boats and of course the basic decks and bulkheads. Per square foot area, they have the greater space to care for.

The Coxswain for the moterwhale boat was assigned from the second division and fell to DAROLD JORGENSEN, S1/c as one of his regular duties. This position also held the distinction of "leading seaman," an important responsibility leading to Petty Officer 3c (Coxswain.) "Jorgie" is in the back row far left. Barnes, S1/c is second from right, same row.

For special sea details, each sailor had an assigned duty; each stood a watch in some part of the ship. As the ship prepared to "get underway" depending on whether from anchored or docked position, the Bos'n in charge of the particular division assigned each sailor to a function; line handler, line gun thrower, gun shooter, etc. Everyone turned to until the ship was underway and the "tools" of the situation were properly stored and secured. If the motorwhale boat was used, it had to be brought in and set in its place with boat davits turned in. The midship passageway held the ship's winch, the only means for lifting the whaleboat from the water, holding it in place while the davits were shifted to the secured position. Heavy lines had to be laid out on the deck from the whaleboat along to the midship passageway, turned by means of heavy pulleys then to the drums or capstan heads. Due to the tension on the lines as the lifting was taking place, it was a dangerous place to be. One could easily get a leg or foot caught in the line and be hurt. It was everyone's job to be very careful.

For General Quarters' assignment, seamen from all three divisions were assigned based upon their early training. They would be selected to GQ positions on any one of the guns, depth charge racks, damage control, lookout, phone talkers, etc.

The crew compartment for the second division was also where most of the gunnery division "bunked." Gunnersmates, torpedomen and firecontrolmen all shared the space. Their compartment was the first compartment on the aft part of the ship, forward of the number 3 5" gun. It was a very friendly place as were all the crew compartments. They had to be, with 345 men on the ship that was 376 feet in length, a little more than a foot per man in length,

When liberty sounded, the cramped quarters became one traffic jam as those going on liberty made ready for the shore. It was a good idea for the shipmates with the duty to be topside or somewhere else at that time.

THIRD DIVISION

PEARL HARBOR, JANUARY 1945
Front Row: Lynas, Wharfield, Kreiensiek, Hrushesky, Thompson, Slalin, Leverton, Goree, and Custer. Second Row: Quatralo, Young, Cubowski, Benavides, Ashby, Tackett -(?), Lightbody, Gray, Lawson, Bertelson, Hartigan. Back Row: Groulx, Allgood, Crosby, Sposato, Brim, Provttola, Erickson, Grabowski, Lober, Lee, Bailey, And Acuff.

The third division was housed in the stern part of the ship, just above the noisy screws. There were several service or "shop" compartments in the very aft part of the ship. On the starboard side was the damage control or carpenter shop. In the center compartment was the secondary "helm" emergency steering system. Should the bridge lose steering control, it was shifted to aft steering where the sailor on watch took control with the command coming from the bridge. On the port side was a very small compartment that was used for the barber shop and a training device for firecontrol. (Rangefinder simulator).

Third division officer was Ens Hrushesky, one of the shortest men on the ship, but a really good officer. Third division's primary housekeeping duty was their compartment, and as stated with the second division, they shared with cleaning and painting the aft head. From the very end of the 01 deck to the very stern of the main deck was also their area.

There was a 20MM gun tub on the stern between the port and starboard depth charge roll racks. It was a favorite place to watch the wake of the ship, especially at high speeds, and share great "sea stories."

Mount number 3, 5" 38 , the third main battery gun on the ship, was the most prominent structure on the stern main deck. When the gunnersmates scrubbed the bore of the gun, it was show time as a number of the crew watched the event. With a long pole, one of the rated gunnersmates, along with several GM strikers and maybe a few brave deck hands, would gang up on the pole, jockey back and forth thru the barrel, cleaning and then oiling the bore.

They made it into fun by splashing the soapy water and cleaning stuff on each other and if the onlookers made too many comment, they also got a dousing.

GUNNERY GANG

Front row, (as remembered) second from left, JIMMIE BILEU, Third from right, (in whites) PAUL GOWEN. Second row, left to right. SCRUGGS, fourth from left DANIAL, fifth from left, WHITE, sixth, P.K. WATSON, and Lt ROBBINS (asst. gun boss) back row, left to right. Lt. SMILYE (gun boss), third from left, MACKAY, sixth, BAKER, seventh, KUZMICH, then BROWN. *It is hoped that as shipmates view the photo, they will be able to name some of the others.*

What a motley crew. The gunnery gang aboard any man-of-war is the heart of the ships main purpose, to keep the ship's weapons in the finest order. Each gun mount is assigned a leading gunnersmate along with the required number of assistants. The lead gunnersmate in the main battery is a GMlc and knows the mount inside and out and every detail of his gun.

This requires constant training for the lower ratings and strikers. A 5" 38 gun is a complex electro/mechanical monster and on the ZELLARS each mount held two systems with train and elevation driven hydraulic power. Besides keeping the basic "rifle" super clean, they also maintained the breech mechanism, the ammunition hoist to the magazines and the fuse setting systems, etc.

The only item that the gunners did not do was bore sight each mount. This was the responsibility of the firecontrolmen, a part of the ordnance division. The gunnersmates were always on hand to give assistance when the guns needed to be aligned with the main battery gun director.

The 40MM guns (four of them) had a gunnersmate for gun captain and was responsible for all aspects of the gun. Training, cleaning and operation. He also over saw the ammunition for the gun. Each gun had it's own magazine. A ready supply was stored in the inner circle of the gun barbet with a much larger supply housed in a magazine near the gun, usually below the gun on the next deck. A master magazine held the major supply that was at the very bottom of the ship.

Paul GOWEN was the gun captain of mount 44, on the port side aft and Warner MACKAY was captain of mount43 on the starboard side. Each gun was a quad, four barrel weapon and could fire a stream of deadly rounds per minute. The Navy has a numbering system for everything. All port side numbers are even and starboard side are odd.

20MM machine guns had a round magazine that held some 60 rounds and was controlled by one highly trained sharp shooter. Two other shipmates assisted in the operation. The ZELLARS had two 20MM guns on each side of the bridge, two more on the port side of number two stack and one just aft of mount 43. Three more guns were on the stern in a triangle type gun tub. For a destroyer, this was considered a well-armed ship that could do a lot of serious damage.

TORPEDO GANG

Torpedo Officer, Ensign B.D. FREEMAN (assistant gunnery officer), Stanley GEDMAN, CTM, Theodore KENNEDY, TM1/c, Harold BUCK, TMl/c, Joseph E. CONNOR, TM2/c, William F. JONES, TM2/c, K.E. WILLIAMS, TM2/c, J.P. ROBERTSON TM3/c, M. HOMICK, TM3/c, Otto HUSAK, S1/c, striker, Pete DINNIS, S1/c, striker, Charles MORGAN, S1/c, striker.

The torpedo gang had their workshop on the starboard side just aft of the weather break. It looked out to sea without any obstructions and at sunset, it was the best place on the ship to be. They served the very best coffee and as the sunset closed the day, it was special to hold one of the big white mugs of fresh hot coffee and dwell upon what a great experience it was to be at sea with some of the very best friends one could ever have.

The coffee cups were always sitting in a bucket of not so fresh cold water and if invited which most everyone was, you reached down in the coffee colored water, retrieved a cup and poured your own with cream and sugar if required, stepped out into the evening and enjoyed some of the best sea stories ever told. Gosh, what a time to be young and in the service of our country!

The torpedomen had two sets of torpedo tubes to care for and all the depth charges. Besides the two roll racks, there were two "K" gun throwing systems on each side of the ship toward the stern. The "K" guns threw a depth charge some 50-60 yards to either side out to sea. A shell charge was inserted in the barrel of the gun and lifted the depth charge to it's target. The charge gave one heck of a bang when fired.

It seemed that the torpedomen were fussing over the "fish" almost constantly. They would pull the black tipped fish out as far as they dared, clean the protective coating off and then redo it over again. If required, a routine test of the firing circuit would be made and sometimes the guidance system would also be checked.

There have been many "sea stories" about the torpedomen and their "torpedo juice." The ZELLARS torpedo gang were such a straight bunch of sailors that no juice was ever reported missing, (ha)

On the bridge, both port and starboard, toward the aft portion of the area, were two torpedo firecontrol directors. This was their main station when at General Quarters. Target information was fed into the directors manually with sightings thru a special scope to the target. When all was ready and the Captain gave the order to fire, "launch torpedoes" meant something special was about to happen. The ZELLARS fired her torpedoes only one time and that was on a training exercise. Had there been a need to fire at a real target, it was a sure thing that they would have gone straight to their intended target.

One more time, "A very special bunch of shipmates."

FIRECONTROL GANG

Firecontrol Officer, Ensign E.E. BROCKMAN, Avertt HILLARD FC1c, M.E. DAVIS FC2c, John MOHR, FC3c, Ted DAY, S1c (striker), Bernard SCHUH S1c (striker), Harry CADWELL S2c (striker), Fred VON HINKEN, FC3c

The heart of the ordinance division. The ordinance division is made up of "Gunnersmates, Torpedomen and firecontrolmen. They were very closely related in the defense and attack requirements of the ZELLARS.

The ship has a main battery firecontrol gun director mounted above the pilot house which is part of the bridge. The main battery gun director houses the firecontrol radar that is needed to seek out and target an enemy ship or plane. In conjunction with the radar is an optical range finder, trainer, and a pointer along with the radar operator and the "gun boss." The pointer and trainer manually move the director from hand controls when they see a target. If one is visible then the range finder operator gets in the act and computes the correct range with the range finder. The director could be set in "automatic" using the radar to control pointing, elevation and range. A real handy system for good shooting.

Full control for all 5" 38 main battery guns could be made with one mount or all three. The torpedo system could also be operated from the director.

Again, all of the firecontrolmen's names cannot be remembered but those who are, are listed below the photo.

Besides the gun director, they were also responsible for the plotting room where all firecontrol computing was done and the bulk of electrical switches for guns, and the gun director stable element were located. The computer was a Ford/Philco model that could receive data from the gun director for firing at planes or surface targets. For shore bombardment, data had to be manually fed into the computer by the firecontrolmen in plot. The stable element controlled the ship's motion and kept the gun director and the guns on target regardless of the ship's motion. The plotting room was one of the few spaces where a sign on the Hatch read, "restricted, authorized personnel only."

Members of the firecontrol gang had several other duties to keep track of. The 40MM guns had a Mk 14 lead-computing sight which gave the operator a reasonably accurate ship-to-target aiming point.

CIC GANG, (combat information center)

Members of the CIC gang, front row, left to right: LAMY, CLARKSPAN, STEVENS, TREAGER and CALL. Center row: PASSLEY, SYERS, WYKOFF, Ens. HURSHESKY, Ens. BERNSTEIN, Ens SOUTHALL, Ens. SCHEAFFER, ANDERSON, BROWN, HOPSON, and MELCHER. Third row, MAPLES, HOWES, SOMMS, and THOMAS. Back row, WELO, WALKER, SAYER and FRAZDER. "C" DIVISION (communications) Record keeping, Yeomen, Quartermaster, Radiomen and several other specialties made up the "C" division. Front row left to right: second man, MUNOZ, S1c , fourth from left, PEDEGANA, RM 3C, fifth man, T. THOMPSON, S2C, seventh, C. DURAN S2c. Second row: far right MORTON, CRM, fourth R. FORD S2c, eighth, G. ANDERSON, RM2C, ninth, BONNY, S2c. Back row: fourth, R. HODGE S1c , ninth, H. WALTERS S2c. *Some of the names might be identified in the wrong position, again, after so many years it is impossible to properly and accurately record each name.*

The most important defensive and underway area of the ship. As the word "single up all lines" is given, the watch in CIC has been standing by for several minutes, ready for work. Their radar and ship's position plotting has already begun.

Every movement of the ship is very important to the bridge and Captain. In the darkened CIC room with only the glow from the radar scopes to see by, the CIC officer and his watch meticulously plot every movement on a large plastic screen. Glowing radar screens, with swirling sweep traces of the radar, show all that is going on within miles of the ship. The bridge has to know just where and what is in the neighborhood of the ZELLARS. This measure of control goes on at all times when the ship is underway.

During a training or real enemy situation, CIC passes several different pieces of target information down to plot. Regardless, the bridge is kept informed about everything at all times. The firecontrol plotting center, several decks below, receives target information which is fed into the main firecontrol computer and sets all required data for firing the main battery guns.

The CIC gang is very close to the sonar and radio gangs' space which is also manned at underway stations. Radio has a trained radioman on watch at all times to receive any radio messages that can come at any time.

"C" DIVISION (communications)

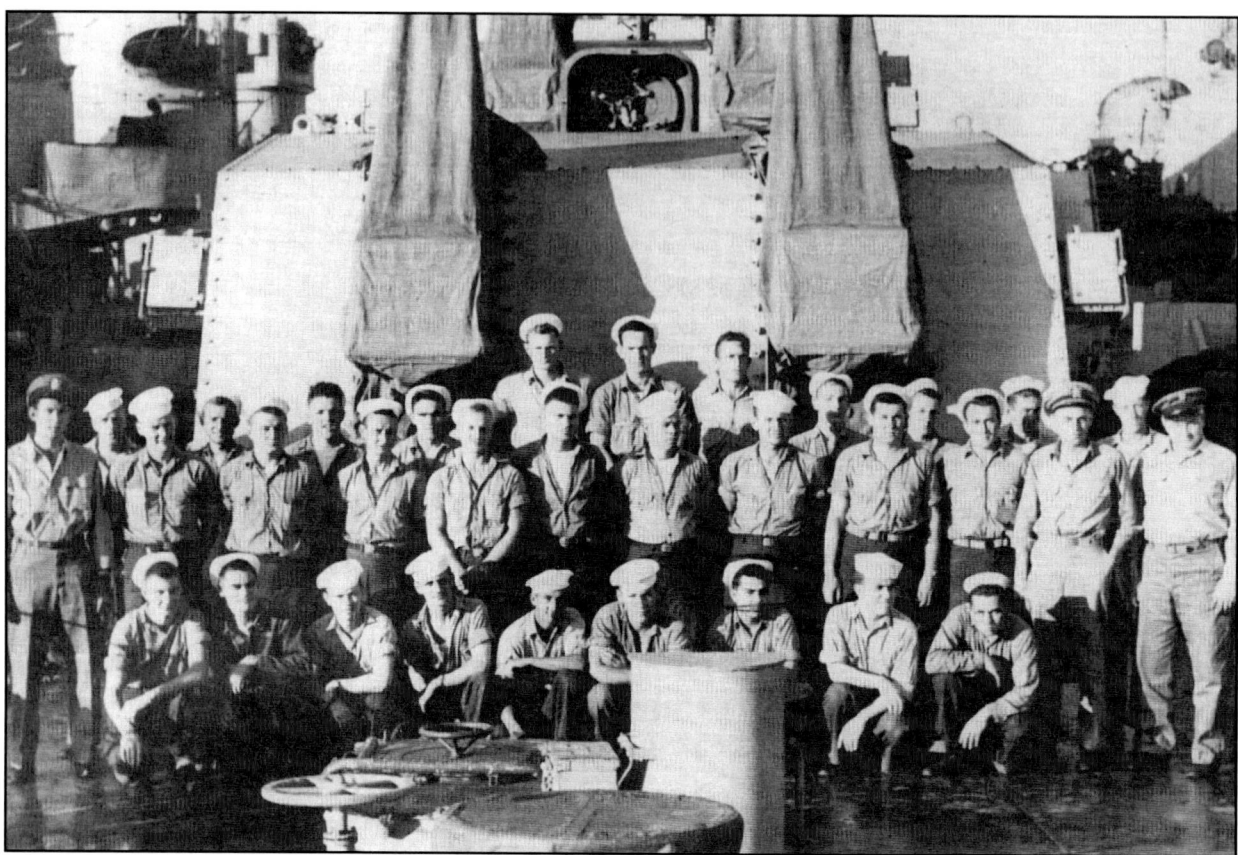

Record keeping, Yeomen, Quartermaster, Radiomen and several other specialties made up the "C" division. Front row, left to right: second man, MUNOZ, S1c, fourth from left, PEDEGANA, RM 3C, fifth man, T. THOMPSON, S2C, seventh, C. DURAN S2c. Second row: far right MORTON, CRM, fourth R. FORD S2c, eighth, G. ANDERSON, RM2C, ninth, BONNY, S2c. Back row: fourth, R. HODGE S1c, ninth, H. WALTERS S2c. Some of the names might be identified in the wrong position, again, after so many years it is impossible to properly and accurately record each name.

WATER TENDER GANG, (Some of shipmates names may be incorrect.)

Front row left to right: BLANKENSHIP S2C, MCALLISTER, F1c, unknown, ROBINSON, WT3c, BROKOP, F1c, unknown, CHOEAN, WTlc, FHEL, F1c. Second row: HERMAN,. NEFF, F2c, HEISEL, F2c, MINSON,. F2c, WALTERS, LIVINGSTON, S2c, MAXWELL, F1c. Back row. LT.(jg) RITTER, SHIPLEY, F2c, LT. (jg). MARLOW, OTOOL, SHULMAN, F1c, PETTERSON, F1c, BELL, F2c, REED, MM2c, J. ROBINSON, WT3c, WILCOX, F2c, ZICMA, F2c, WILLIG, WT2c, HAMILTON, F2c.

The Water Tender gang was responsible for all fresh water for the boilers, laundry, personal hygiene food service and such. Fresh water was always critical for steaming. The crew had to suffer at times, like missing a shower or having to delay the laundry due to the demands made by the engines. No steam, no go.

February 8, 1945, Commander VAN MATER was relieved and our new Captain was one with great experience. He had been the captain of the U.S.S. HOEL, DD 533 and had the Hoel shot from under him by a fast moving Japanese major battle group. It had three Battlewagons and a number of Cruisers and Destroyers. One of the Battlewagons was the largest ship of it's kind in the world, the mighty YAMATO with 18 inch main battery. The new Captain was Leon S. KINTBERGER and he wore the Navy's highest honor, the Navy cross, earned for his part in the Battle of Leyte Gulf off the Straights of Samar, October 25, 1944. It was the same day the ZELLARS was placed in commission. When the ship went into harms way, she would go with a very experienced Captain

Commander KINTBERGER was somewhat of an easier going "skipper." He allowed liberty in Honolulu to begin at 10.00 for one section and then another section at 13.00. All hands had to be back on board by 20.00 and no excuses. VAN MATER allowed liberty to begin at 13.00.

USS ZELLARS (DD777)

COMMANDER KINTENBERGER ASSUMES COMMAND

From the date of commissioning, the ZELLARS was not as happy as she should have been. The day that Commander KINTBERGER took command, it seemed to change. There was a different spring to the steps of all the crew.

The ZELLARS was in an intense training period with usual long days and nights, practicing the many routines of war. KINTBERGER was a seasoned destroyer skipper having experienced one of the most heroic battles of the war, the battle of Leyte Gulf. He lost the destroyer HOEL DD533 at Samar by attacking a major part of the Japanese fleet.

The ZELLARS had no elusions of what lay ahead. Knowing that the ZELLARS was going into battle with a very experienced Captain, made the crew feel assured that all hands would stand fast and do an outstanding job. It was not unusual to have the Captain just show up at different stations to share a cup of coffee asking about the welfare -of the members of the crew.

BIOGRAPHY OF CAPTAIN LEON S. KINTBERGER
UNITED STATES NAVY CLASS OF 1932

Captain Leon S. Kintberger, USN was born on April 4, 1910 in Zanesville, Ohio. Prior to entering the Naval Academy, his education included four years at Baltimore Polytechnic Institute and two years in Johns Hopkins University, before being appointed to the U.S. Naval Academy, graduating with

LEON S. KINTBERGER, U.S.S. Naval Academy Class of 1932. Assumed command of U.S.S. ZELLARS February 8, 1945, relieving Commander Blinn Van Mater.

the class of 1932. He served his apprenticeship on the Battleship New York and Cruiser Minneapolis. In June 1935 he was ordered to his first destroyer, USS Evans. This was to be a colorful and exciting thirteen years in Destroyer types which has thus far included the command of six ships and two Destroyer divisions.

Within 18 months after reporting aboard Captain Kintberger served in every department of the USS Evans (DD-78) and in November 1936 he assumed command, thereby earning the distinction of being the first of his Naval Academy class to have command of a destroyer.

He continued to serve in the destroyer Gridley, USS Argonne and recommissioned the USS Bernadou in 1939 for neutrality patrol duties. Two years as instructor in thermodynamics at the Naval Academy was followed by duties at the Subchaser Training Center at Miami Florida. His first wartime command was at the helm of the USS Charles Lawrence (DD-53). Next Atlantic duty was as Skipper of USS Coolbaugh (DD-217). With this background of convoy and anti-submarine operations, Captain Kintberger was ordered to command escort division 65.

In August of 1944 he took command of USS Hoel, (DD533) in the Pacific, engaging the enemy in the battle off Samar, Philippines. This critical action saw three other destroyers and two destroyer-escorts in company with the USS Hoel fighting a Japanese battleline consisting of battleships, cruisers and destroyers. The Japanese battle force was thwarted in its attempt to sink our carrier force by what historians have described as " ONE OF THE MOST GALLANT AND HEROIC ACTS OF THE WAR." Although the torpedo attack by the U.S. ships succeeded, the U.S. Hoel was sunk due to enemy gunfire. Captain Kintberger was among the survivors and was in the water for 52 hours before being rescued. For this action, Captain Kintberger was awarded the Navy Cross, it's highest honor. His unit was also awarded the Presidential Unit citation for his successful engagement with the enemy.

February 8, 1945 he became the commanding officer of the USS Zellars (DD-777) in Pearl Harbor. During the battle of Okinawa, his ship destroyed seven Japanese suicide planes before being badly damaged in a Kamikaze attack (April 12,1945). For this action, he was awarded the silver star.

In 1947 destroyer division 22 came under his command, then successive tours of duty under the Commandant Potomac River Naval Commands and Chief of Naval Operations in the Naval reserve program.

He graduated from the Industrial College of the armed forces in 1951 and has had an additional tour in Chief of Naval Operations Office. The most recent being head of Navy overseas bases.

The troop transport USS Noble (APA-218) became his eighth command in August 1955. Next he was ordered to Tokyo, as Chief of Logistics Plans branch of Commander-in-Chief, far east, and served in that capacity until assigned as Commanding Officer of the USS Norfolk (DL-1).

In 1959, now Rear Admiral KINTBERGER, retired and settled in Annapolis Maryland. For the next 15 years, he was an official of the Electromagnetic Analysis Center, a private company under government contracts.

Retired Rear Admiral LEON S. KINTBERGER, at age 73, passed away September 4, 1983.

More Training

The training took on another dimension. Maybe it was due to our Captain, fresh from a recent battle that was considered the greatest sea battle of modern warfare, or maybe he had a greater feeling of what we were in for. Anyway everyone on the ship worked harder, if that was possible.

On one occasion we had another exercise with a submarine and at the conclusion of the drill, a target ship steamed out to meet us. It was a torpedo drill with a live firing. On the bridge, both port side and starboard, are special torpedo firing directors. They are manned by well-trained torpedomen, usually a First class at the director. The "torpedo officer" stands by to give assistance in making sure that the correct data is made available to the director.

The torpedo that had been selected to be fired had the "warhead," which normally has a very high explosive war head attached, removed and a dummy head filled with water. As the torpedo completes it's run, an air tank in the center of the weapon blows the water out of the dummy warhead and the device hopefully floats to the surface for recovery. The Captain began the run on the target ship and without a great deal of emotion, let the torpedo fly. It made a very successful run and was recovered. This event required all hands topside to observe. Few of the crew had ever seen the live firing of a torpedo and it created a lot of new excitement

More plane guard detail with the carrier FRANKLIN and back into Pearl. On March 21, the ZELLARS, under a full head of steam, departed Hawaii, passed Diamond Head and the compass

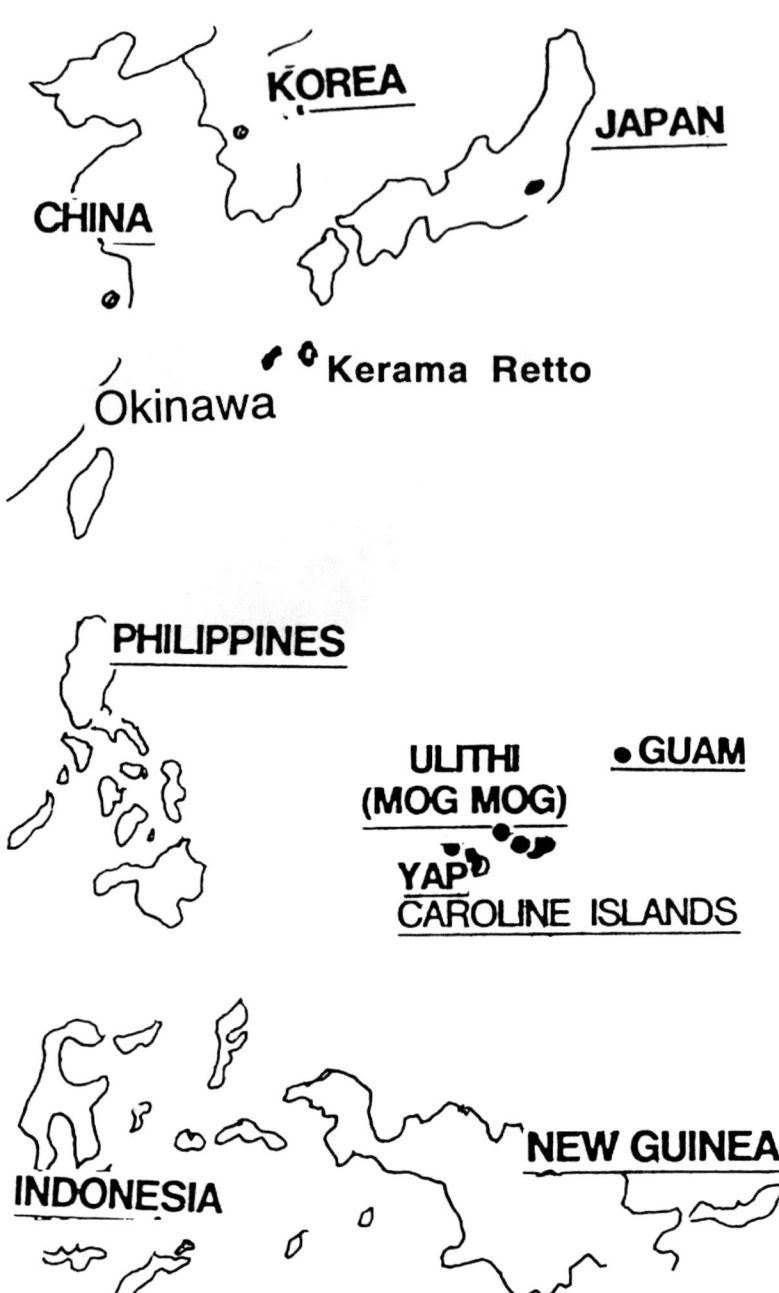

ULITHI was made up of several Islands and the one heard most often was MOG MOG. The other Islands are

PIG ISLAND

PUGELUG ISLAND

FURAYA ISLAND

reading was due west. She joined up with a number of major units and headed for the Carolina Island group and a place called Ulithi, arriving on March 24. Other than the routine of plane guard detail and active ASW, the journey was uneventful.

Ulithi was located some fifty miles from the Jap-held Island of YAP. Usually at night the Jap planes would fly out and cause a great deal of anxiety among the hundreds of Navy ships anchored in the Ulithi anchorage. One aircraft carrier had a suicide plane crash onto her deck doing a great deal of damage.

Ulithi was a time of island liberty of sorts. The islands of MOG MOG, PIG ISLAND, PUGELUG, and FURAYA ISLAND. Pig Island was the destroyer base anchorage. On the eastern side of the island the sea was very deep and on the western side one could walk out for hundreds of feet and still be only knee deep in the coral-bedded ocean. The shallow waters offered inspection of many different and colorful fish. The coral was very sharp and would render tennis shoes soleless in a few yards. To many it was too much to pass up. Each had to stand yards away from shore and enjoy the scene at their feet.

Several different destroyers shared the warm beer and cokes, usually for an afternoon. Exploring the island did not take long. Something resembling football and baseball was the only energy-spending exercise that the many sailors could find. Some were poorly informed about the hundreds of cocoanut trees which covered the island and shimmied up to capture a fresh cocoanut. It was fine going up, but coming down shaved a fair amount of chest hair and skin. When the islands were the only escape from the ships, it was a real great time.

Each night several destroyers were ordered out away from the anchorage for night security patrol. YAP was a Japanese-held island about fifty miles from Ulithi and unwelcome visitors did sneak into the area. The ZELLARS had such orders and according to the ship's navigator, there were several times that the ZELLARS was within fifteen miles of the Jap stronghold

On Saturday, March 17, the ZELLARS had such a night security patrol. At 0118 the radar lit up a target at about 25,000 yards. The bridge challenged the target twice with no response. The Captain gave the order, "Fire a star shell over their heads and see what happens." In a second the surface of the surrounding area was alight with blinker lights from the target.

Per the ship's log, "0259, target identified as one merchantman escorted by PC 1375. Proper minor warship recognition signals exchanged. Set course 000 degrees, T standard speed 15 knots (140 RPM) ammunition expanded, two star shells.

An example of how fragile a situation can become if the target ship had not responded in a short time, the next sound that they would have heard was one big bang and a disaster would have happened.

On the same early morning patrol as the ship returned to the Ulithi anchorage, per the ship's log, "at 0712 sighted 26' motor whaleboat adrift; set course to pick up the boat, secured the boat aboard, set course 110 T speed 20 knots" and so it went on the edge of the enemy's front door.

The weather at Ulithi was a very pleasant warm. During the day working hours many of the crew working topside went without shirts to add to their tan and just plain comfort. It was a tension time, but looking forward to the next order — going deeper into harms way.

Ulithi and Some Warm Beer

First it needs to be noted that the beer was made in America. OLYMPIA from Tacoma, Washington, warm, it was still great.

As noted earlier, Ulithi was a group of low islands and covered with a variety of shrubs and cocoanut palm trees. With respect to their place on the globe, they were tropical somewhat pretty islands. The sandy beaches were clean white sand with one side a beautiful coral bottom that let a sailor wade out for many hundreds of feet. The ocean was full of very colorful tropical fish in many different sizes and shapes.

In lieu of a beer, cokes were available, only two bottles of either beer or coke per person. Some traded their beer for the warm coke. It was a great stopover for a short break from being at sea.

Left front, our ship's doctor, Lt. J. F. KINKAID, MD, and in back row, third from left, JOHN MOHR FC3c. Both shipmates were killed April 12, 1945. *Other shipmates' names have slipped the mind, but their faces will be part of all shipmates' memories forever.*

A few more happy faces! At least all smiles

The beer parties were always a mix from the different divisions.

The wrinkled dungaree shirts are not poor personal keeping, the ship laundry did do a very good job of washing, but they did not do ironing. At some times, a shipmate would wash out his own dungarees because it might be several days before his division laundry was due to be sent to the laundry or once in a while, shortage of fresh water cause clothes to be hanging from several places out of sight of the bridge. It was not to smart to allow drying clothes to be seen by the Captain from the bridge.

Front row, left to right: First person, P.K. WATSON, GM1c, fourth from left, HAROLD BUCK, TM1c Back row, second from left, LEONARD BELL F1c. *Many of the faces are remembered, just the names have slipped from memory.*

Ulithi and More Warm Beer

The island looked like real jungle but friendly. This bunch of beach dwellers look like they have gone native.

The island was about 1/2 mile long and at low tide had a reef that allowed for the more adventurous souls to walk out on the reef for over a mile. The tide change was so rapid that if one ventured out to the end, they would have to run like hell to beat the tide change. The western side of the island was very shallow and allowed sailors to walk out very far enjoying the beautiful clean clear water. The shallow reef was full of tropical fish and was a great delight to those who took the opportunity for a lesson in tropical fish culture. About all the island offered was a little recreation and was void of native islanders. It did offer a change in ship routine of which the crew took full advantage.

Front row left, first person, DURAN S1c; second person, Owen SEXTON Y2c; far right front, ERICKSON, BMlc. Back row, left, PITT, Cox; fourth from left, CUSTER, S2c

The Ulithi R&R was for all who dared to go. The officers joined in the sand games with the crew and some paid the price when tackled. It should be noted by their dress, which was always very regulation and neat, also joined the frivolity of the crew. The ZELLARS was lucky in having so many very fine officers and a great bunch of sailors who carried out their duty as one would expect.

Left to right, ARTHUR LINDH, Lt, DL. SOUTHALL, Ens, W. HRUSHESKY, Ens. H. SCHAEFFER, Ens. S. BERNSTEIN, Ens. Just how Ens. Bernstein managed to get his pants so wet is anyone's guess. It had to be fun!

It's amazing what a sandy beach and a couple of bottles of almost-cold beer can do to a bunch of sailors who have been at sea for several weeks. They let it all hang out! The normal ship's dress code didn't exist. Baseball hats appeared and shipmates running around without shirts cause not a ripple of concern to anyone.

In the shelter of cocoanut trees, standing so close that one had to walk around them, a sun blistering those who disregarded the intensity of the heat and would show serious sunburns. Others did things that they had never done before, like climbing a cocoanut tree that shaved their skin when they slid down the trunk. Such craziness added to the close relationship that was bound to become closer as they delved deeper into harms way.

Front row right, with a startled look on his face, V. MURO, Sic, back row left to right, P.K. WATSON GM1c. *Faces are still sharp in memory, but names faded with the passing of time.*

All Smiles

All were so young and feeling very infallible about their reason for being at a place very much in harm's way, and nothing to really smile about except for faces that were all smiles for the camera.

There are always several in every crowd! As can be seen, the beach was littered with all forms of dress and undress even down to those who had no dress at all.

With no females to worry about (if it would have made a difference), there had to be those who went native, There were so many sailors using the beach that it was all but impossible to find enough sand for a simulated ballgame of any kind. The beach was the anchorage side of the island and had the best beach. If one walked away from the group, the end of the island had a long reef that at low tides allowed for a long walk out onto the reef. When the tide began to change, it was a race to get back to sand before the tide made it into a swimming challenge. The reef was made up of very sharp coral and could cut the soles out of shoes in a matter of steps. All the reefs were full of small beautiful fish of many

A few names, front to back left to right; third man, L. ERICKSON, BM2c, Lt.(jg) K. BIRD; sixth, BARNES ,S1c. Half hidden in back of BARNES is CORBIT S2c. Next to Corbitt is CEBULSKY BM2c. Third from left, second row, C. HIRST ChPM. Third row, third from left, WALTERS, S2c; fifth from left is PITTS, Cox; and LEVERTON is to the right of PITTS. Other names remembered, BRIMM S1c , MORTON, CRM, HAJICEK, S2c, WESTNEDGE, S2c. *It is wished that all names were available and could be matched with the faces for such great sailors (sorry).*

From either the front or back, not one sailor can be identified.

Our ship stands ready in this island retreat,
Sailors, sure of the task they'll meet,
Fuel, food and ammunition stored as planned,
Orders known, course plotted, enemy be damned.

At evening sky, the colors not shy,
Gentle seas, as storms passed by,
For the morrow we sail,
From this safe anchorage to a place full of hell.

The Captain has checked, and made his rounds,
Officers, Chiefs and each sailor mustered, ready to go,
All systems calibrated, not a fault to be found,
The ZELLARS tense, for not far away lays our foe.

Each shipmate has recounted his bond with friends,
Worked, trained and cared; shipmates to the end,
Darkness covered the stillness of the night,
There's a feeling of assurance by dawn's early light.

For the morrow, the anchor will rise,
Engines will sound, the helm ready to respond,
Sailors at stations, signal flags will fly,
The ZELLARS will glide quietly into the early dawn.

Over the horizon, not too far away,
A silent enemy lies defiant, angry at bay,
Our ship knows the deadly task that lies ahead,
Each man aboard, not frightened of war's dread.

For all, as they look and take account,
A great feeling of pride the ZELLARS has found, '
Cause, she's everything: hope, prayers to survive,
Our country, God, and shipmates bound.

Regardless of what tomorrow might bring,
Our ship will go forth, her position to stay,
She will account, do more than asked,
A great ship of the fleet, **going in harm's way.**

Several different destroyers shared the warm beer and cokes, usually for an afternoon. Exploring the island did not take long. Something resembling football and baseball was the only energy spending exercise that the many sailors could find. Some were poorly informed about the hundreds of cocoanut trees which covered the island and shimmied up to capture a fresh cocoanut. It was fine going up, but coming down shaved a fair amount of chest hair and skin. When the islands were the only escape from the ships, it was a real great time.

Each night several destroyers were ordered out away from the anchorage for night security patrol. YAP was a Japanese held island about fifty miles from Ulithi and unwelcome visitors did sneak into the area. The ZELLARS had such orders and according to the ship navigator, there were several times that the ZELLARS was within fifteen miles of the Jap stronghold.

On Saturday, March 17, the ZELLARS had such a night security patrol. At 0118 the radar lit up a target at about 25,000 yards. The bridge challenged the target twice with no response. The Captain gave the order, "Fire a star shell over their heads and see what happens." In a second the surface of the surrounding area was alight with blinker lights from the target.

Per the ships log, "0259, Target identified as one merchantman escorted by PC 1375. Proper minor warship recognition signals exchanged, set course 000 degrees T standard speed 15 knots (140 RPM) ammunition expanded, 2 star shells."

An example of how fragile a situation can become if the target ship had not responded in a short time, the next sound that they would have heard was one big bang and a disaster would have happened.

On the same early morning patrol as the ship returned to the Ulithi anchorage, per the ship's log, "at 0712 sighted 26' motor whaleboat adrift; set course to pick up the boat, secured the boat aboard, set course 110 T speed 20 knots" and so it went on the edge of the enemy's front door.

The weather at Ulithi was a very pleasant warm. During the day working hours many of the crew working topside went without shirts to add to their tan and just plain comfort. It was a tension time but looking forward to the next order going deeper into harms way.

On Wednesday, March 17, 1945 at 0621, the ZELLARS ship's log again reads:

> "Underway from birth #336 Ulithi, Caroline Islands enroute Okinawa Gunto, Nansei Shoto, Captain at the com. Passed entrance buoys; entered international waters. Commenced patrolling according to sortie plan, Task force 54. Proceeding to point Oboe for formation of disposition."

The ship was now headed where it was intended to be from the very beginning, into the jaws of the enemy.

As the ship found its place in the Task force, as far as one could see were ships of all sizes and purpose. From one horizon to the other, from bow to the furthermost stern, hundreds of men of war, all flying the American flag, steamed as one, course set for Okinawa.

NAVPERS-134 (REV. 1-44)   DECK LOG—REMARKS SHEET

UNITED STATES SHIP _____ ZELLARS _____   Saturday 17 March , '45
                                              (Day)   (Date) (Month)

0-4

0000: Steaming independently on radar picket station #4, west of Ulithi, Caroline Islands on course 180°T and PGC, 179°PSC. Speed 15 knots (140 R.P.M.) Under boilers #1 and #4 split plant operation Ship is darkened, material condition Baker, condition of readiness II. 0015: Changed course to 000°T and PGC, 359°PSC. 0045: Changed course to 180°T and PGC, 179°PSC. 0115: Changed course to 000°T and PGC, 359°PSC. 0118: Unidentified radar surface targets bearing 080°T, 25,000 yards. 0125: Exercised crew at General Quarters. 0134: Changed speed to 25 knots (246 R.P.M.), maneuvering on various courses closing unidentified targets. 0148: Challenged unidentified targets; no reply. 0150: Maneuvering on various courses at various speeds maintaining position on starboard bow of target. 0258: Fired starshells to illuminate unidentified targets. 0259: Targets identified as one merchantman escorted by PC-1375. Proper minor warship recognition signals exchanged. 0243: Set course 000°T and PGC, 359°PSC, standard speed 15 knots (140 R.P.M) Resumed radar picket patrol. Secured from General Quarters, set condition II. Ammunition expended: 2 rds. starshells and flashless powder. 0351: Changed course to 180°T and PGC, 179°PSC.

Arthur LINDH, Lieut., USNR

4-8

0400: Steaming as before. 0415: Changed course to 000°T and PGC, 005°PSC. 0500: Changed course to 090°T and PGC, 088°PSC, changed speed to 20 knots (190 R.P.M.) 0515: Changed course to 082°T and PGC, 083°PSC. 0651: Changed course to 090°T and PGC, 088°PSC enroute Ulithi, Caroline Islands. 0709: Changed course to 095°T and PGC, 092°PSC. 0712: Sighted 26' motor whale boat adrift; maneuvering on various courses at various speeds to pick up boat. 0727: Boat secured aboard, set course 110°T and PGC, 115°PSC, speed 20 knots (190 R.P.M.) 0749: Changed course to 035°T and PGC, 033°PSC.

D. D. CLEVELAND, Lt.(jg), USNR

8-12

0800: Steaming as before. 0806: Changed course to 000°T and PGC, 005°PSC. 0812: Changed course to 345°T and PGC, 347°PSC. 0834: Changed course to 298°T and PGC, 300°PSC. 0835: Passed through anti-submarine net gates. Stationed all special sea details. 0838: Changed course to 290°T and PGC, 292°PSC. 0841: Secured all condition watches. Maneuvering on various courses at various speeds to conform with channel. 0900: Made daily inspection of magazines and smokeless powder samples; conditions normal. Maneuvering to go alongside U.S.S. PRARIE STATE (IX-15) to fuel ship. 0925: First line over to PRARIE STATE. 0929: Moored port side to U.S.S. PRARIE STATE (IX-15) in berth 295, Northern Anchorage, Ulithi, Caroline Islands with six (6) five inch manilla lines and one (1) three-fourths inch (3/4") wire cable. 0947: Commenced receiving fuel; draft forward 13'0", aft 14'2". 1030: Completed fueling having received on board 27,900 gallons of Navy Special fuel oil. Draft forward 13'4", aft 14'6". 1036: Underway from alongside U.S.S. PRARIE STATE proceeding on various courses at various speeds to assigned berth. 1105: Let go the port anchor. 1107: Anchored in southwest corner of berth 336, Southern Anchorage, Ulithi, Caroline Islands in seventeen fathoms of water with seventy-five fathoms of chain to the port anchor on the following bearings: Feitabul Island Beacon 039°T, Pugalug Island Beacon 137°T, and Pig Island Beacon 185°T. 1115: Secured the special sea details, set the port watch. 1120: Let fires die under boiler #1. Boiler #4 in use for auxiliary purposes.

C. A. SMYLIE, Lieut., USN

1120: Anchored as before.

Owen C. BARNES, Lt.(jg), USNR

12-16

1200: Anchored as before. 1215: MALFATTI, Melvin LeRoy, Slc, USN, 378 37 97 transferred with baggage, records, and accounts to the U.S.S. YOSEMITE (AD-19) for treatment by authority of BuMed form "G".

D. L. SOUTHALL, Ens., USNR

16-20

1600: Anchored as before.

Nelson E. SMITH, Lt.(jg), USNR

20-24

2000: Anchored as before.

Herman SCHAEFER, Jr., Ens., USN

APPROVED:

L. S. KINTBERGER, Comdr., U.S.N COMMANDING.

Nelson E. SMITH, Lt.(jg), U.S.N.R. NAVIGATOR

CONFIDENTIAL

NAVPERS-134 (REV. 1-44)

DECK LOG—REMARKS SHEET

PAGE _____

UNITED STATES SHIP _____ ZELLARS _____ Wednesday 21 March , 19 45

(Day) (Date) (Month)

0-4

0000: Anchored at Berth 336, Ulithi, Caroline Islands in 17 fathoms of water with 60 fathoms of chain on the port anchor; #2 boiler in use for auxiliary purposes. #1 generator in operation for light and power. Ship is darkened.

A. J. RITTER, Lt.(jg), USNR

4-8

0400: Anchored as before. 0500: Lit off #4 boiler. Made all preparations for getting underway. 0600: Set all special sea details. 0621: Anchor aweigh. Underway from berth #336, Ulithi, Caroline Islands enroute Okinawa Gunto, Nansei Shoto Captain at the conn, Navigator on the bridge. Steaming on various courses at various speeds conforming with channel and traffic. 0711: Passed entranbe buoys; entered International waters. Commenced patrolling according to Sortie Plan, Task Force 54. 0755: Proceeding to point "Oboe" for formation of disposition.

Arthur LINDH, Lieut., USNR

8-12

0800: Steaming as before. Set base course 070°T and PGC, 067°PSC at 15 knots (140 R.P.M.) conducting sortie with Task Force 54. 0835: Arrived at point "Oboe", changed course to 000°T and PGC, 005°PSC. 0840: Maneuvering on various courses at various speeds to form and maintain screen ahead of capital ships during sortie. 1002: Forming a straight line screen 6000 yards ahead of U.S.S. ESTES (AGC-12) 2000yards between destroyers. Order from left to right: BOWER, WILLMARTH, DORSEY, MILES, LONGSHAW, WESSON, ABELE, ZELLARS, BRYANT, BARTON, O'BRIEN, PRESTON, PORTERFIELD, GALLAGHAN, IRWIN, ENGLAND, WITTER, and FOREMAN. 1010: Made daily inspections of magazines and smokeless powder samples; conditions normal. 1015: On station, set course 325°T and PGC, 320°PSC at 15 knots (140 R.P.M.)

C. A. SMYLIE, Lieut., USN

12-16

1200: Steaming as before. 1225: Commenced zig-zagging in accordance with plan #6, USF 10A. Changed speed to 15½ knots (145 R.P.M.) 1323: Manned General Quarters stations of main battery, plot and combat. 1330: Ceased zig-zagging, returned to base course. 1346: Commenced firing main battery at towed sleeve target. 1400: Manned General Quarters stations of 20 MM and 40 MM batteries. 1402: Broken fire main reported in C.P.O. Quarters forward. Repair party #1 called away. 1415: Commenced firing 40 MM and 20 MM batteries at towed sleeve target. 1417: Fire main reported repaired; loose union; no damage caused. 1542: Completed firing exercises. Ammunition expended: 73 rds. 5"38 AA common, 39 rds. 5"38 flashless powder, 34 rds 5"38 smokeless powder. 1545: Secured main and secondary battery, plot and combat from General Quarters, set condition of readiness II.

Arthur LINDH, Lieut., USNR

16-20

1600: Steaming as before. 1700: Steaming on various courses at various speeds to take picket station 30° on port bow of U.S.S. ESTES (AGC-12) distance 12 miles. Guide's speed 12 knots (111 R.P.M.) 1737: On picket station, changed speed to 12 knots (111 R.P.M.) 1859: Sunset, darkened ship. 1900: Set clocks back one hour to zone -9 time. 1805: Changed speed to 15 knots (140 R.P.M.)

D. D. CLEVELAND, Lt.(jg), USNR

20-24

2000: Steaming as before. 2028: Changed course to 335°T and PGC, 340°PSC.

for S. E. ROBBINS, Lieut., USN

APPROVED:

L. S. KINTBERGER, Comdr., U S N COMMANDING.

ED:

Nelson E. SMITH, Lt.(jg) U.S.N.R. NAVIGATOR

<u>S U N D A Y</u>

25 March 1945

<u>PLAN OF THE DAY</u>   <u>CONT</u>:

1730   (About) Form retirement unit #2 consisting of 10 OBB, 7CA, 3CL, 14DD (including ZELLARS) 2DE, 2AVD and 6APD.

SUNSET   DARKEN SHIP

1930   Eight o'clock reports
2000   Dump trash and garbage.

<u>N O T E S</u>

1.   All hands are urged to do their share to keep the ship shooting, livable, and covered against surprise close in attacks by suicide planes, PT boats, swimmers etc.
To this end, do all jobs assigned you promptly and with a will whether it be to carry ammunition, mess cook, sweep compartments, act as lookout, or be a messenger. Be alert to detect jobs that should be done; do them without being told. Lend a hand every chance you get. <u>BE A SHIPMATE</u>

2.   Stay as close to your battle **station as conditions permit**, even when the ship is not at general quarters. If possible, sleep near your GENERAL QUARTERS STATION.

3.   Keep your life jacket and helmet near at all times.

4.   If you see anything that the bridge should know about, get the word to the bridge immediately.

5.   Expect long hours at GENERAL QUARTERS, irregular meals and meal hrs.

6.   Keep yourself as rested and as mentally fit as possible.

7.   <u>K I L L   J A P S</u>   <u>K I L L   J A P S   K I L L   M O R E   J A P S</u>

R. R. DUPZYK

NAVPERS-134 (REV. 1-44)

DECK LOG—REMARKS SHEET

PAGE _____

UNITED STATES SHIP _____**ZELLARS**_____ Tuesday 27 March , 19 45
(Day) (Date) (Month)

0-4
0000: Steaming with Task Force 54.3.2 in retirement formation 5RD from objective area on course 215°T and PGC, 221°PSC at standard speed of 13.5 knots (125 R.P.M.) Fleet axis 345°T, U.S.S. TENNESSEE (OTC, CTG 54.3.2 and Guide) in station 2130. Screen consisting of 20 vessels on circle 8.5, Station #1 000°T from guide. ZELLARS on station #9, guide bears 241°T distant 7500 yards. Radar guard "Dog". Sound search beam to beam. Radar search 360°. Steaming on boilers #2 and #4 in split plant operation. Ship darkened, material condition Baker set, in condition of readiness II. 0010: Resumed zig-zagging in accordance with plan #6, USF 10A. 0053: Ceased zig-zagging, resumed base course. 0100: Changed course to 131°T and PGC, 137°PSC. Changed speed to 15 knots (140 R.P.M.) 0108: Commenced zig-zagging in accordance with plan #6, USF 10A. 0350: Ceased zig-zagging, returned to base course. 0400: Changed course to 162°T and PGC, 168°PSC.

Arthur LINDH, Lieut., USNR

4-8
0400: Steaming as before. 0410: Commenced zig-zagging according to plan #6, USF 10A. 0430: Ceased zig-zagging resumed base course, changed speed to 14 knots (129 R.P.M.) 0453: Enemy aircraft in area, went to General Quarters. 0536: Changed course by turn movement to 135°T and PGC, 137°PSC. 0555: Changed course by turn movement to 345°T and PGC, 348°PSC. 0630: Maneuvering radically on various courses at various speeds, enemy aircraft attacking formation. 0640: Took aircraft on starboard bow under fire. 0641: Ceased firing. 0645: Took enemy aircraft on starboard bow under fire. 0649: Ceased firing. 0720: Secured from General Quarters having expended 66 rds. 5"38 AA common projectiles, 57 rds. 5"38 AA special projectiles, 123 rds. mixed smokeless and flashless powder. Set course 180°T and PGC, 182°PSC, took station #4 screen 54 USF 10A, U.S.S. BIRMINGHAM guide, formation speed 10 knots (92 R.P.M.) 0745: Changed course to 225°T and PGC, 228°PSC.

D. D. CLEVELAND., Lt.(jg), USNR

8-12
0800: Steaming as before. Changed course to 090°T and PGC, 093°PSC. Changed speed to 10 knots (92 R.P.M.) 0825: Changed base course to 070°T and PGC, 072°PSC; changed base speed to 15 knots (140 RPM.) 0838: U.S.S. BARTON left screen to investigate possible mine. Commenced reorienting screen to conform to screen 53, USF 10A, our station #2. 0847: On station. 0915: BARTON returned to screen. Screen reoriented to form screen 54, USF 10A, our station #4. 0930: Changed base course to 180°T and PGC, 183°PSC. Received orders to take charge of screen, consisting of U.S.S. ZELLARS and U.S.S. WESTON, and to screen section #1, consisting of battleships U.S.S. NEVADA and U.S.S. TENNESSEE. Set screen 52 USF 10A, our station #2. 0940: Changed base course to 105°T and PGC, 108°PSC. 0959: Battleships entered firing area, changed base speed to 5 knots (46 R.P.M.) 1001: Changed base course to 015°T and PGC, 018°PSC. 1010: Changed base course to 195°T and PGC, 198°PSC. 1014: Changed base speed to 12 knots (111 R.P.M.) 1018: Changed base speed to 15 knots (140 R.P.M.) 1020: Changed base course to 130°T and PGC, 134°PSC. 1021: Changed course to 105°T and PGC, 109°PSC. Made daily inspection of magazines and smokeless powder samples; conditions normal.

S. E. ROBBINS, Lieut., USN

12-16
1200: Steaming as before. Maneuvering to maintain anti-submarine screen 52, USF 10A ahead of U.S.S. TENNESSEE and U.S.S. NEVADA. 1208: Changed course to 180°T and PGC, 183°PSC. Steaming on various courses at 20 knots (190 R.P.M.) to take station one. 1218: On station. Changed speed to 7 knots (64 R.P.M.) 1310: Changed formation course to 000°T and PGC, 005°PSC. Maneuvering on various courses at 20 knots (190 R.P.M.) to take station two. 1323: On station, changed speed to 7 knots (65 R.P.M.) 1335: Changed fleet course to 165°T and PGC, 174°PSC. Maneuvering on various courses at 20 knots (190 R.P.M.) to take station two. 1344: On station, changed speed to 7 knots (65 R.P.M.) 1412: Changed fleet course to 345°T and PGC, 347°PSC. Maneuvering on various courses at 15 knots (140 R.P.M.) to take station two. 1423: On station, changed speed to 7 knots (65 R.P.M.) 1425: Taking station to the northward of heavy ships at 3000 yards. U.S.S. WESSON taking station 3000 yards to the southward of heavy ships. 1435: On station. Patrolling station at 10 knots (92 R.P.M.) 1441: Changed fleet course to 090°T and PGC, 091°PSC. 1451: Changed fleet course to 165°T and PGC, 174°PSC. 1516: Changed fleet course to 345°T and PGC, 347°PSC. 1540: Changed course to 165°T and PGC, 174°PSC.

C. A. SMYLIE, Lieut., USN

16-20
1600: Steaming as before. 1632: Changed fleet course to 300°T and PGC, 305°PSC. 1642: Ceased present exercises. Took station ahead of U.S.S. TENNESSEE while recovering aircraft. 1648: Changed speed to 15 knots (140 R.P.M.) 1650: U.S.S. TENNESSEE completed recovering aircraft. Changed course to 225°T and PGC, 230°PSC. 1742: Changed course to 340°T and PGC, 344°PSC. 1749: Ceased screening U.S.S. TENNESSEE, maneuvering on various courses at various speeds to take station #9, in night retirement

APPROVED:

V. S. KIMBERGER, Comdr., U.S.N. COMMANDING.

EXAMINED:

Nelson E. SMITH, Lt.(jg), U.S.N.R. NAVIGATOR

TO BE FORWARDED DIRECT TO THE BUREAU OF NAVAL PERSONNEL AT THE END OF EACH MONTH

U.S. GOVERNMENT PRINTING OFFICE 1944 O - 617984

Drills began immediately.

At 1330 the General Quarters alarm sounded and the bridge announced that one of the carriers had furnished a plane towing a sleeve so that the escorting destroyers could prove to the Task Force Commander that they were up to the task of shooting down enemy aircraft.

It was not that easy, as the plane passed one destroyer and it opened fire, down went the sleeve on the first few salvos. When it came the ZELLARS turn, she did not disappoint or embarrass the Captain. The sleeve bit the sea on the first round of the main battery. The crew did not feel cocky but assured that if a Jap plane came within radar sight, it would wind up as a little flag painted on the side of the main battery gun director.

Each of the following days of travel was very eventful. The 24th, the ZELLARS had ship-to-ship mail duty. Due to security, all radio communications were forbidden. Ship-to-ship communications were controlled by signal lamps, signal flags and direct mail delivered by one of the destroyers to a group of ships in her part of the task force. There might be a dozen or more DDs doing mail duty at one time. The "mailman" would slide up alongside of the intended receiver and by high line send over the mail bag. Sometimes one crewman from one ship had a friend on the other ship and a lot of shouting would take place. It was always a friendly visit. Each 0 to 0400 day would always begin with "steaming as before" in a certain position of the task force. The course changed to conform to the task force requirements and speed changes. The watch section on the bridge was kept very busy maintaining the ship's position, speed and making sure that the ship did not get out of her assigned position by a single degree. If any ship did, a screaming blinker light would bring to attention the out-of-position offender from the task force commander and it was always a strong message.

GQ was sounded often as an unidentified aircraft would show up on the task force outer screen and all ships sounded the alarm. On the 26th, at 1120, a mine sweeper reported that it had sighted a torpedo passing astern, broaching on the surface. Torpedoes sighted by OOD and Commanding Officer. The mine sweeper subsequently reported sighting periscope and opened fire. The ZELLARS changed speed, came full left rudder to avoid torpedoes. Exercised crew at General Quarters. (Some exercise!) Torpedoes disappeared, having sunk. Possible sonar contact at 005 degrees T (true), maneuvering to develop contact.

The task force must have been getting closer to the target of Okinawa. It was the task force's routine that at a very early morning hour all ships were called to General Quarters. The ZELLARS was always on the ready with one watch set for a General Quarters situation. The main battery gun director, plot, one of the 5" guns manned and a selected 40MM gun crew at the ready.

The ship's log of March 27 reads,

> "At 0453 enemy aircraft in the area, went to GQ, many course changes and speed changes. Maneuvering radically on various courses and speed changes, enemy aircraft attacking formation. 0640 took aircraft on starboard bow under

CONFIDENTIAL

NAVPERS-134 (REV. 1-44)

DECK LOG—REMARKS SHEET

PAGE 210-45

UNITED STATES SHIP ___ZELLARS___   Wednesday 28   March, 1945

(Day) (Date) (Month)

0-4
0000: Steaming in company with Task Force 54 on base course 320°T and PGC, 335°PSC at speed 12.5 knots (116 R.P.M.), fleet axis 340°T and PGC, OTC in U.S.S. TENNESSEE, fleet guide in U.S.S. INDIANAPOLIS. Fleet formed up in cruising disposition 5RD with a thrity ship circular screen our station #8 with guide bearing 228°T, distance 10000 yards. Steaming on boilers #2 and #4, steaming split plant operation. Ship darkened. Material condition Baker set, condition of readiness II. 0045: Changed base course to 200°T and PGC, 207°PSC; changed speed to 13.5 knots (125 R.P.M.) Commenced zig-zagging in accordance with plan #6, USF 10A. 0122: Ceased zig-zagging. Changed base course to 230°T and PGC, 235°PSC. 0130: Changed base course to 155°T and PGC, 164°PSC. 0140: Commenced zig-zagging in accordance with previous plan. 0206: Ceased zig-zagging. 0330: Changed base speed to 15.5 knots (145 R.P.M.) 0331: U.S.S. MINNEAPOLIS, BENION, HALL, and PRESTON left formation to proceed independtly on duty previously assigned. Commenced reorienting screen for 27 ships. 0353: On station with guide bearing 233°T, distance 10000 yards.

S. E. ROBBINS, Lieut., USN

4-8
0400: Steaming as before. 0506: Changed fleet speed to 13 knots (120 R.P.M.) 0515: Exercised crew at General Quarters for morning alert, set condition Affirm. 0525: Commenced zig-zagging in accordance with Plan #6, USF 10A. 0543: Ceased zig-zagging, resumed base course. 0546: Changed disposition course to 180°T and PGC by simultaneous turn method on signal from OTC. 0615: Ships in screen to southward commenced firing on enemy aircraft reported to be a Val. 0617: Two Vals sighted bearing about 015° relative, distance 10000 yards. One shot down by screen. 0620: Second Val reported shot down. 0631: Changed disposition speed to 15 knots (140 R.P.M.) 0635: Changed course to 090°T and PGC, on signal from OTC. 0639: Changed course to 000°T and PGC, 0050PSC on signal from OTC. 0644: Changed course to 270°T and PGC, on signal from OTC. 0644: Secured from General Quarters, set condition Baker and coddition of readiness II. 0648: Changed course to 180°T and PGC on signal from OTC. 0651: Changed course to 135°T and PGC. 0709: Formation breaking up into Fire Support Units and proceeding to bombardment stations. Changed course to 190°T and PGC to close Fire Support Unit Three. 0717: Changed course to 220°T and PGC. 0719: Changed course to 200°T and PGC. 0720: Changed speed to 20 knots (190 R.P.M.) 0727: Changed speed to 10 knots (090 R.P.M.) 0728: Changed course to 135°T and PGC. 0730: Changed course to 170°T and PGC, 179°PSC. 0732: Changed speed to 15 knots (140 R.P.M.) 0735: Changed course to 160°T and PGC. 0745: Directed by ComDesRon 60 to join and screen Fire Support Unit Three, Section Two consisting of the U.S.S. NEVADA and U.S.S. TENNESSEE. Other ships in screen U.S.S. WESSON (DE-184), U.S.S. BARTON (DD-722), U.S.S. ABELE(DD-733) forming screen 54 (USF10A) ZELLARS in station #2, 0751: Changed disposition course to the left to 080°T and PGC on signal from OTC (CTF 54 in U.S.S. TENNESSEE).

C. A. SMYLIE, Lieut., USN

8-12
0800: Steaming as before. Changed speed to 10 knots (92 R.P.M.) 0810: Changed course to 000°T and PGC. Changed speed to 5 knots (46 R.P.M.) 0816: Took station 1000 yards astern U.S.S. TENNESSEE. 0836: Changed course to 180°T and PGC, 0855: Changed course to 000°T and PGC. 1030: Changed course to 180°T and PGC. 1045: Changed course to 230°T and PGC. 1050: Maneuvering on various courses and at various speeds screening U.S.S. TENNESSEE while redovering aircraft. 1105: Resumed normal patrol station astern of U.S.S. TENNESSEE. 1130: Made daily inspection of all magazines and smokeless powder samples; conditions normal. 1148: Changed speed to 20 knots (190 R.P.M.) Changed course to 270°T and PGC. 1150: Changed course to 290°T and PGC. Changed speed to 15 knots (140 R.P.M.) 1159: Changed course to 050°T and PGC.

Arthur LINDH, Lieut., USNR

12-16
1200: Steaming as before, on courses 000°T and 180°T screening north of U.S.S. TENNESSEE, changing courses by turn movements. 1445: Flash Red from SOPA, CTF 54, called crew to General Quarters; set condition Affirm. 1511: Secured from General Quarters; set condition Baker, condition of readiness II.

D. D. CLEVELAND, Lt.(jg), USNR

16-20
1600: Steaming as before. 1617: Changed base course to 180°T and PGC, 190°PSC. 1649: Changed base speed to 10 knots (92 R.P.M.) 1711: Changed base course to 330°T and PGC, 334°PSC. 1750: Received orders to proceed independently to form screening disposition for night retirement formation. Commenced maneuvering on various courses at various speeds, the Captain at the conn, the Navigator on the bridge. Proceeding to take station #7 in circular screen of 26 ships, fleet axis 000°T, fleet forming disposition 5RD. 1807: U.S.S. TENNESSEE designated as fleet guide. 1822: On station in screen. Set base

APPROVED

L. S. KINTBERGER, Comdr., USN   COMMANDING.

EXAMINED

Nelson E. SMITH, Lt.(jg), USNR.   NAVIGATOR

TO BE FORWARDED DIRECT TO THE BUREAU OF NAVAL PERSONNEL AT THE END OF EACH MONTH

U. S. GOVERNMENT PRINTING OFFICE 1944 O 617806

CONFIDENTIAL   PAGE 208-45

NAVPERS 138 (REV. 1-44)   DECK LOG—ADDITIONAL REMARKS SHEET

UNITED STATES SHIP _____ ZELLARS _____   Wednesday 28   March   , 1945
                                                (Day)   (Date) (Month)

ADDITIONAL REMARKS

course of 340°T and PGC, 343°PSC; set base speed of 13 knots (120 R.P.M.) 1924: Received orders to proceed to picket station #1. Changed speed to 20 knots (190 R.P.M.), changed course to 000°T and PGC, 006°PSC; commenced proceeding to assigned station. 1945: Enemy aircraft report closing the formation; went to General Quarters, set material condition Affirm.

                                    Nelson E. Smith LT(jg) USNR
                              for   S. E. ROBBINS, Lieut., USN

20-24
2000: Steaming as before. Maneuvering on various courses at various speeds while under air attack 2012: Commenced firing main battery at enemy aircraft. 2012½: Ceased firing having expended: 17 rds. 5"38 AA common projectiles, 16 rds. 5"38 AA common Special projectiles, 33 rds. 5"38 cal. flashless powder. Aircraft retiring. 2041: Secured from General Quarters, set condition Baker. 2045: All engines ahead flank, 25 knots (246 R.P.M.) Course 300°T and PGC, 305°PSC, to take picket station bearing 225°T distant 24000 yards from fleet center. 2057: Changed course to 290°T and PGC, 295°PSC. Changed speed to 12 knots (111 R.P.M.) On station. 2106: Unidentified surface radar target bearing 200°T, distant 21400 yards. 2115: Surface target identified as friendly. 2120: Changed course to 320°T and PGC, 325°PSC. 2133: Changed course to 270°T and PGC, 275°PSC. Changed course to 350°T and PGC, 355°PSC. Changed fleet speed to 15 knots (140 R.P.M.)

                                    Arthur Lindh
                              Arthur LINDH, Lieut., USNR

APPROVED: EXAMINED:

L. S. Kintberger   *Nelson E. Smith*
L. S. KINTBERGER, Comdr., U S N   Nelson E. SMITH, Lt. (jg), U.S.N.R.   NAVIGATOR
                    COMMANDING.

TO BE FORWARDED DIRECT TO THE BUREAU OF NAVAL PERSONNEL AT THE END OF EACH MONTH

fire. At 0641 ceased fire. 0720 secured from General quarters, expended 66 rounds 5" 38 common projectiles, 57 rounds 5" 38 AA special projectiles, 123 rounds mixed smokeless and flashless powder."

The ZELLARS had fired her first blast in anger and did well. There would be a great deal more.

March 28, 1945

General Quarters as usual at 0515. The main Task Force was broken up and the ZELLARS was assigned to a 27-group task unit, to be the main part of support for the invasion of Okinawa.

The ZELLARS had arrived off Okinawa and was doing her bit in the very beginning of the invasion of the first enemy soil. The task force broke up into firecontrol support units and proceeded to assigned bombardment stations. At 0745, the ZELLARS was directed to join screen fire support unit three, section two, consisting of the U.S.S NAVADA and the U.S.S. TENNESSEE. Other ships in the screen were the U.S.S. WESSON (DE 184), U.S.S. BARTON (DD 722), U.S.S. ABELE (DD 733) forming screen 54 (USF10A), U.S.S. ZELLARS (DD 777) in station #2. The ZELLARS was on station ready for her part of the fight that was sure to come soon.

At 2012 commenced firing main battery at enemy aircraft. At 2013 ceased fire, having fired 16 rounds of 5" 38 AA common special projectiles, 33 rounds 5" 38 rounds of flashless powder. Aircraft retiring. At 2045 pulled the stops out of the engine room and at flank speed (25 knots) assumed picket station 24000 yards from fleet center.

March 29, 1945

Early GQ, many course and speed changes. Zigzagging in accordance with plan #6, USF 19A and so on.

The 29th was the ZELLARS first salvo at the beaches and Okinawa in the Nagsuhi area, covering the underwater demolition team's efforts. At 0904 commenced firing main battery and 40MM battery at discretion at various shore installations. 1036 ceased firing at shore installations temporarily to repel air attack. 1050 resumed firing at shore installations.

1147 secured from General Quarters, set condition of readiness. Ammunition expended: 183 rounds 5" 38 AA common, one round of white phosphorous, 184 rounds smokeless powder, 372 rounds 40MM…

At 0615 ships in the screen to the south began firing on enemy planes reported to be two VALS sighted bearing about 15 degrees relative, distance 10,000 yards. One shot down at the screen. At 0620 the second VAL was shot down.

1404 received another order for fire support in station #6. Fired main battery and 40MM battery to starboard. Again fire support for underwater demolition teams. Another ammunition count. As evening closed in, the ZELLARS took up her picket station at 2112, commenced patrolling a nine-mile line off the southern coast of Okinawa. Again at 2228 hours called to fire support on beach targets with star shell illumination and bombardment of NAHA Airfield. More ammunition count.

As dawn broke on the 30 of March, the usual GQ and another enemy aircraft was seen on the radar scope. The crew was getting a little nervous with the constant GQ and little sleep. Few of the topside gun stations were left unmanned even though GQ may not have been in effect. The gunnery crews stayed close to their respective stations, ready to fire immediately should a Jap plane be noted. It was not unusual for the attacking planes to be just a few feet off the water, trying to sneak in under the radar and crash a ship.

March 30, 1945

Just before noon, with the ammunition and fuel getting on the low side, the ZELLARS dropped out of the support formation and headed for the supply anchorage of Kerama Retto. The anchorage was some 30 miles northwest of the main Island of Okinawa. They were made up of a number of small islands that formed a very comfortable and almost safe harbor. At 1321 the order was given to go alongside LST 227 for the purpose of rearming.

CONFIDENTIAL

NAVPERS-15M (REV. 1-44)

DECK LOG—REMARKS SHEET

PAGE 217-45

UNITED STATES SHIP _____ ZELLARS _____

Friday 30 March , 19 45
(Day) (Date) (Month)

0-4
0000: Steaming on course 010°T and PGC, 013°PSC patrolling station #8 in area D-3 west of Naha Town, Okinawa Jima, Nansei Shoto. Boilers #2 and #4 in use for steaming purposes, split plant operation. Speed 10 knots (92 R.P.M.) Patrolling a line bearing 010°T-190°T nine miles long approximately 4000 yards from Okinawa, conducting harrassing and interdiction fire on Naha Airfield and vicinity. Ships in company: 2 LCI(R) and 2 LCI(G). Ship is darkened in condition of readiness II, material condition Baker set. 0051: Changed course to 195°T and PGC, 198°PSC. 0100: Unidentified aircraft 211°T, 20 miles, closing. Ceased bombardment. 0135: Exercised crew at General Quarters, unidentified aircraft in vicinity. 0143: Changed course to 010°T and PGC, 013°PSC. 0153: Secured from General Quarters, set condition of readiness II, Lost air contact. 0201: Changed course to 005°T and PGC, 008°PSC. 0205: Sonar contact. 0207: Contact valued non-submarine. 0217: Resumed bombardment. 0226: Changed course to 010°T and PGC, 013°PSC. 0234: Changed course to 015°T and PGC, 020°PSC to avoid LCI. 0250: Changed course to 195°T and PGC, 198°PSC. 0315: Changed course to 185°T and PGC, 187°PSC. 0341: Changed course to 010°T and PGC, 013°PSC.

C. A. SMYLIE, Lieut., USN

4-8
0400: Steaming as before. 0427: Ceased interdiction fire on Naha Airfield. Ammunition expended: 49 rds. 5"38 AA common projectiles, 8 rds. 5"38 white phosphorous, 28 rds. 5"38 starshell projectiles, 85 rds. 5"38 flashless powder. 0429: Changed course to 029°T and PGC, 030°PSC. 0413: Changed course to 010°T and PGC, 011°PSC. 0515: All hands manned battle stations for morning alert. 0523: Changed course to 000°T and PGC, 005°PSC. 0600: Ceased patrolling station in area D-3, departed area. Course 330°T and PGC, 333°PSC. Changed speed to 20 knots (190 R.P.M.) to rejoin TF 54. 0630: Changed course to 270°T and PGC, 274°PSC. 0643: Secured all hands from General Quarters set condition watch. 0652: Maneuvering on various courses at various speeds taking screening station ahead of U.S.S. SAN FRANCISCO, distant 3000 yards, on course 160°T and PGC, 165°PSC. 0655: Changed speed to 15 knots (140 R.P.M.) 0715: Changed course to 190°T and PGC, 200°PSC. 0728: Changed course to 160°T and PGC, 170°PSC.

Arthur LINDH, Lieut., USNR

8-12
0800: Steaming as before. Changed base course to 090°T and PGC, 091°PSC. 0819: Changed base course to 000°T and PGC, 005°PSC, proceeding to area southwest of Naha Airfield while cruisers bombard, steaming on various courses at various screen speeds to northeast of U.S.S. SAN FRANCISCO. 1030: U.S.S. SAN FRANCISCO ceased bombardment, set course 240°T and PGC, 246°PSC enroute Kerama Retto. Steaming on various courses at various speeds to take station #3, screen 53, USF 10A. U.S.S. BRYANT in station #1, U.S.S. ABELE in station #2. 1105: U.S.S. SAN FRANCISCO, entering channel; screening to seaward. 1120: Stationed special sea details. 1130: Entered channel on course 010°T and PGC, 013°PSC, speed 5 knots (46 R.P.M.) Steaming through channel into harbor. 1150: All engines stopped, awaiting fueling and rearming assignments, using engines to maintain station.

D. D. CLEVELAND, Lt.(jg), USNR

12-16
1200: Lying to as before. 1321: In accordance with verbal instructions went alongside port side of LST-227 for purposes of rearming. 1323: Ship rolling heavily against LST, cast off lies and backed clear; minor hull damage to port side. 1329: Commenced lying to again, using engines as necessary. Awaiting assignment for fueling. 1424: In accordance with verbal instructions, commenced maneuvering on various courses at various speeds to berth K-16 to fuel from tanker, U.S.S. BRAZOS#4. 1549: On station astern of tanker, lying to awaiting permission to come alongside. 1555: Moored starboard side to port side of U.S.S. BRAZOS with six (6) five inch (5") manila lines doubled.

S. E. ROBBINS, Lieut., USN

16-18
1600: Moored as before. 1601: Secured special sea details. 1603: Commenced fueling ship. Draft forward 12'6", aft 14'4". 1707: Completed fueling ship. Draft forward 13'9", aft 14'6". Received 114506 gallons of fuel. Stationed special sea details. 1714: Cast off all lines. Underway from alongside U.S.S. BRAZOS in berth K-18, Kerama Retto, Nansei Shoto. Captain at the conn, Executive Officer and Navigator on the bridge. Set course 025°T and PGC, 025°PSC at 25 knots (246 R.P.M.) enroute to rendezvous with Task Group 52.2. Boilers #2 and #4 in use for steaming purposes, split plant operation. 1725: Secured all the special sea details. 1748: Changed course to 020°T and PGC, 021°PSC. 1751: Changed speed to 20 knots (190 R.P.M.) 1754: Changed speed to 15 knots (140 R.P.M.) Joining U.S.S. COLORADO, U.S.S. NEVADA, U.S.S. BRYANT, U.S.S. ABELE, and U.S.S. BUTLER for night retirement group #2. Standing by outside the screen awaiting orders. Changed fleet course to 073°T and PGC, 075°PSC. 1756: Changed fleet course to 023°T and PGC, 026°PSC. Changed fleet speed

APPROVED:

L. S. KINTBERGER, Comdr., U S N COMMANDING.

EXAMINED:

Nelson E. SMITH, Lt. (jg) U.S.N.R. NAVIGATOR

TO BE FORWARDED DIRECT TO THE BUREAU OF NAVAL PERSONNEL AT THE END OF EACH MONTH

U. S. GOVERNMENT PRINTING OFFICE: 1944 O - 617586

CONFIDENTIAL

NAVPERS 135 (REV. 1-44)

DECK LOG—ADDITIONAL REMARKS SHEET

UNITED STATES SHIP _____ZELLARS_____   Friday   30   March , 19 45
                                               (Day)   (Date)   (Month)

ADDITIONAL REMARKS

to 13 knots (120 R.P.M.)

_____
C. A. SMYLIE, Lieut., USN

__18-20__
1800: Steaming as before. Changed speed to 25 knots (246 R.P.M.) in order to take night radar picket station bearing 045°T from fleet center, distance 24,000 yards. Fleet course 000°T and PGC, 005°PSC. Fleet axis 030°T, speed 15 knots (140 R.P.M.) 1845: Sunset; darkened ship. 1927: Changed speed to 20 knots (190 R.P.M.) On radar picket station. Commenced zig-zagging according to plan #6, USF 10A.

_____
Arthur LINDH, Lieut., USNR

__20-24__
2000: Steaming as before. 2100: Changed base course to 310°T and PGC, 307°PSC. 2330: Changed base course to 233°T and PGC, 238°PSC.

_____
D. D. CLEVELAND, Lt.(jg), USNR

APPROVED:

_____
L. S. KINTBERGER, Comdr., U.S.N   COMMANDING.

EXAMINED:

_____
Nelson E. SMITH, Lt.(jg) U.S.N.R.   NAVIGATOR

TO BE FORWARDED DIRECT TO THE BUREAU OF NAVAL PERSONNEL AT THE END OF EACH MONTH

CONFIDENTIAL   PAGE **221-45**

NAVPERS-134 (REV. 1-44)   **DECK LOG—REMARKS SHEET**

UNITED STATES SHIP _____ZELLARS_____   Saturday   31   March , 19 45
                                                            (Day)   (Date)   (Month)

0-4
0000: Steaming in company with Task Force 54, formed in retirement disposition 5RD, OTC in U.S.S. TENNESSEE, TENNESSEE in fleet center. Escorts formed in 28 ship circular screen, fleet axis 000°, our station - picket #3, bearing 045°T distance 24000yards from fleet center. Formation steaming on base course 233°T and PGC, 238°PSC at base speed to 14 knots (129 R.P.M.) zig-zagging in accordance with plan #6, USF 10A. Boilers #2 and #4 in use, split plant operation. Ship darkened. Condition or readiness for war 2 set, material condition Baker set. 0045: Ceased zig-zagging. 0055: Changed base course to 180°T and PGC, 188°PSC. 0110: Commenced zig-zagging in accordance with plan #6, USF 10A. 0120: Ceased zig-zagging. 0127: Changed base course to 090°T and PGC, 094°PSC. 0137: Commenced zig-zagging according to previous plan. 0318: Radar contact on unidentified aircraft reported, bearing 107°T, distance 15 miles. Went to General Quarters, set material condition Affirm. 0346: Commenced steaming on various courses at various speeds, the Captain at the conn. Aircraft closing range. 0351: Commenced firing 5"38 battery at air target. 0353: Ceased firing, having expended 35 rounds of 5"38 AA common projectiles and 43 rds. of 5"38 AA special projectiles, and 78 rds. of flashless powder. Aircraft retired to westward, no damage noted.

                                            S. E. Robbins
                                          S. E. ROBBINS, Lieut., USN

4-8
0400: Steaming as before. 0408: Set condition Baker. 0410: Secured from General Quarters, set condition of readiness II. 0434: Ceased zig-zagging. Changed fleet course to 165°T and PGC, 177° PSC on signal from OTC. 0505: Changed course to 220°T and PGC, changed speed to 20 knots (190 R.P.M.) to rejoin formation. 0515: Changed course to 200°T and PGC, 212°PSC. 0522: Exercised crew at General Quarters for morning alert. Set condition Affirm. Maneuvering on various courses at various speeds to take station in screen. 0643: Secured from General Quarters, set condition of readiness II, condition Baker, sunrise, lighted ship. 0705: Unidentified aircraft. Exercised crew at General Quarters. Set material condition "Affirm", readiness II. Maneuvering while formation under air attack. 0717: Set condition Baker. 0722: Secured from General Quarters, set condition of readiness II. Set course 160°T and PGC, 174°PSC at 15 knots (140 R.P.M.) enroute fire support area. 0745: Changed course to 150°T and PGC, 155°PSC. Changed speed to 10 knots (92 R.P.M.) 0750: Changed speed to 5 knots (46 R.P.M.)

                                           C. A. Smylie
                                          C. A. SMYLIE, Lieut., USN

8-12
0800: Steaming as before. Mustered crew on stations; no absentees. 0816: Lit fires under #1 and #3 boilers. Cut in on main steam line at 0840. 0819: Maneuvering on various courses at various speeds in company with U.S.S. ABELE (DD-733) to close shore line of Okinawa Shima on western shore in vicinity of Hagushu Area to conduct covering operations for underwater demolition group. (TG 52.11) (CTG 52.11 in U.S.S. GILLIS (AVD-11)). 0837: Stopped all engines, ship heading 340°T and PGC, 345° PSC. 0844: Commenced firing main battery and 40 MM battery at targets of opportunity on the shore. 1107: Ceased firing all guns. Ammunition expended: 102 rds. 5"38 AA common with Mk 18 fuzes; 241 rds. 5"38 AA common with Mk 29 fuzes, 5 rds. 5"38 AA common, 10 rds white phosphorus (5 rds with Mk 29 fuzes, 5 rds with Mk 18 fuzes) Total rds. expended: 358. 358 rds. 5"83 smokeless powder. 5112 rds. 40 MM. 1120: All engines ahead 15 knots (140 R.P.M.) Came to course 215°T and PGC, ceased covering UDT operations, enroute patrol area Zebra #1 off southern Okinawa Shima. 1130: Made daily inspection of all magazines and smokeless powder samples: conditions normal. 1154: Secured from General Quarters, set condition watch II. 1155: Changed course to 180°T and PGC, 188°PSC. 1157: Changed course to 165°T and PGC, 173°PSC.

                                           Arthur Lindh
                                          Arthur LINDH, Lieut., USNR

12-16
1200: Steaming as before. 1220: On station patroling on North-South line for 5 miles, speed 10 knots (92 R.P.M.) reversing course every half hour, sound searching beam to beam. 1320: Secured boilers #1 and #3.

                                           D. D. Cleveland
                                          D. D. CLEVELAND., Lt.(jg), USNR

16-20
1600: Steaming as before. 1603: Received orders to proceed to patrol station W-1. Changed course to 305°T and PGC, 314°PSC, changed speed to 20 knots (190 R.P.M.), proceeding to newly assigned station. 1611: Changed course to 325°T and PGC, 332°PSC. 1625: Changed course to 350°T and PGC, 356°PSC. Changed speed to 15 knots (140 R.P.M.) 1632: Previous orders cancelled, received orders to proceed to South-eastern tip of Okinawa Shima for patrol duty. Changed course to 160°T and PGC, 168°PSC. 1650: Changed course to 090°T and PGC, 092°PSC. 1721: Radar contact of unidentified aircraft

APPROVED: EXAMINED:

L. S. Kimberger   _Nelson E. Smith_
L. S. KIMBERGER, Comdr., U S N   COMMANDING.   Nelson E. SMITH, Lt.(jg) U.S.N.R.   NAVIGATOR

TO BE FORWARDED DIRECT TO THE BUREAU OF NAVAL PERSONNEL AT THE END OF EACH MONTH

U. S. GOVERNMENT PRINTING OFFICE: 1944 O - 617088

CONFIDENTIAL

NAVPERS 132 (REV. 1-44)

DECK LOG—ADDITIONAL REMARKS SHEET

PAGE 219-45

UNITED STATES SHIP _____ZELLARS_____ Saturday 31 March , 19 45
(Day) (Date) (Month)

ADDITIONAL REMARKS

bearing 150°T, distance 21 miles. Went to General Quarters, set material condition Affirm. Changed speed to 20 knots (190 R.P.M.) 1759: Changed course to 278°T and PGC, 283°PSC. 1803: Secured from General Quarters, set condition of readiness for war II, set material condition Baker. 1825: Changed course to 310°T and PGC, 311°PSC. 1845: Changed course to 155°T and PGC, 158°PSC, changed speed to 15 knots (140 R.P.M.) 1906: Commenced steering on various courses at various speeds to take station #6 in screen 54, USF 10A. on column of battleships consisting of U.S.S. TEXAS and MARY*LAND, guide in TEXAS. 1947: On station, set base course 100°T and PGC, 106°PSC, base speed 16 knots (150 R.P.M.) 1952: Changed base course to 070°T and PGC, 074°PSC. 2000: Changed base course to 090°T and PGC, 090°PSC.

S. E. ROBBINS, Lieut., USN

20-24

2000: Steaming as before. 2011: U.S.S. MORRISON joining screen. Maneuvering to take station #4 of screen 54 USF 10A. 2037: On station. 2050: Changed base course to 060°T and PGC, 061°PSC. 2156: Changed fleet speed to 10 knots (92 R.P.M.) 2200: Changed base course to 090°T and PGC, 094°PSC. Maneuvering to take station #2 of an eight ship screen on circle 5. On station. 2302: Commenced zig-zagging in accordance with plan #6, USF 10A, on signal from OTC. 2356: Ceased zig-zagging, resumed base course.

C. A. SMYLIE, Lieut., USN

APPROVED:

J. S. KINTBERGER, Comdr., U.S.N COMMANDING.

EXAMINED:

Nelson E. SMITH, Lt. (JG) U.S.N.R. NAVIGATOR

TO BE FORWARDED DIRECT TO THE BUREAU OF NAVAL PERSONNEL AT THE END OF EACH MONTH

DECLASSIFIED
Authority NND 803052
by RGM date 10/18/

The sea was too rough and the ship had to back off and in the process, the ZELLARS received her first wound, one given by a friendly ship. It was some minor hull damage and was corrected, showing a patch of new paint.

If the ship couldn't "buy" ammunition, she still needed fuel. At 1555 moored starboard side U.S.S. BRAZOS for fueling. At 1707 completed fueling and immediately departed back to Task Group 52.2. At 1800 the ship took up her position for night radar picket duty. Sunset at 1845, darken ship, with hope that it would remain quiet just for one night.

March 31, 1945

March 31 was about the same. At 0351 the early morning wake up call of another Jap plane in the area, fired the main battery and scared it away, at least that is what the crew felt. 0522 dawn GQ. 0643 secured from GQ. 0705 GQ again with another Jap plane attacking Task Force. This was before breakfast and the very weary crew, seemed to have lost its interest, in eating.

Every morning from the first day of commission, the whole crew was mustered at 0800 regardless. It was interesting to see the ship's log, kept on the bridge by the OOD, and always read "no absentees." Where in the heck could any of the crew go?

It was obvious that the big day of invasion was near (April 1, 1945) for the momentum of shore bombardment really picked up. Most of the heavy stuff was aimed at strategic shore targets, or where targets had been. It was also suspected that the Japs had been sneaking some aircraft into the airfield late at night. For most of the remainder of the 31st, the ZELLARS shifted from one fire support area to another. Once to the north of NAHA and next to the south, then back again. At 1721 another Jap plane showed up on the radar at 21 miles but did not attempt to attack the Task Force.

The Hollywood movies had pictured the real heavy cannon fire whistling as they screamed overhead. NOT SO, as the ZELLARS lay close in to shore, several of the Battlewagons were laying further off and firing their 14 and 16 inch big guns directly over the ZELLARS' head. Coming toward the ship, there was no noise to speak of. As they closed over, there was a rattle like a freight train going downhill at maximum speed, more like a low thunder. As they passed over, one could see the dark projectile headed inshore to do its work.

April 1, 1945

Everyone around Okinawa and on the Island knew that the real invasion was not April fool's day. Days of heavy shelling and American aircraft from the carriers that stayed far from shore had been giving the whole area (all the islands) hell. The troop transports, LSTs and smaller equipment landing craft could be seen from one end of the Island of Okinawa to the other.

The battleships TEXAS, MARYLAND, and NEW MEXICO stood off shore about five miles and laid down one heck of a shore bombardment into the area where the main invasion troops were going to land. No one knew for sure just what was expected from the Japs on Okinawa. From the past island hopping every one was sure that it would be a knock-down fight for every inch of the island. (It turned out to be worse.) The U.S.S. TEXAS launched her SB2C spotting plane to observe the targets deep inside of the island in places that the force could not see. The plane would do fire support by directing the larger ships' fire inland where the ZELLARS 5" 3 8 guns could not reach.

Some new names were called for shore bombardment, like Kutaku Shima and others. Each one of the outlying islands got their share of attention from the many destroyers and even larger-gunned ships. There were so darned many ships that even though they could be identified, it was hard to keep track. "It's a battleship, it's a cruiser or one of the sister destroyers." There were no score cards. It seemed strange that no Jap aircraft made their presence all day. After all, this was the "big" day when the "stuff" was supposed to hit the fan. It was about 1915 before the task force received a flash "RED" of a Jap plane in the area. The task force settled in for the night, the ZELLARS took up her picket station and up to midnight, all was routine.

During the 0 to 0400 watch, things started to change. One would hope that the enemy might want to get a little sleep. At 0231 the GQ alarm made it's frightening sound. Most of the crew had been sleeping or trying to sleep, at or, near their gun station. At that time of the AM, with nerves already on edge, there was no sleep to rub out of their eyes. They jumped up in the ready 5" main battery, gunners grabbed the required projectile and powder; the 40MM crews stood by for they did not use the 40s or 20s during night combat due to the flash of the guns showing the Japs just where the ship was. The ZELLARS was on the target by full radar control.

There was a darkness of the night unlike any that the crew had ever seen. Using full radar control, flashless powder allowed the main battery to fire without being detected by the enemy. After some rapid firing of 66 rounds of special projectiles and powder, there was a bright flash toward the horizon on the starboard side.

The ZELLARS had recorded her first kill. There was no loud jubilation for the crew's deed, just relief that it was them, the crew of the Jap plane, and not their beloved ship. As the flames of the burning plane died down on the dark sea, men, human beings, had died this AM, and at the hands of the ZELLARS crew. This was war and that was the result of war. One group or country trying to take something very important away from another country. It was not going to happen to America.

There wasn't ever a dull moment on the ship. As soon as a fire mission where 40MM and 20MM guns were fired, restocking of all the "ready" ammunitions had to be done. Chains of sailors would line up and down in the designated magazine and lift the heavy 40MM cans (20 rounds per can) up to the main deck. From there the chain was broken into six to eight men, each with a handle of a can in each hand, staggering to the needed ready rack.

Chipping hammers and scrapers could be heard often as each spot of rust was cleaned down to raw metal, chromated and repainted when the under coating had dried. It was hard to understand where dirt would come from after being far out to sea where there was no dirt, but each day there was a film of dust and grime covering most of the ship. It came from the burning of heavy "bunker oil" that was laden with sulphur. Each time the ship fired the main battery, a thin cloud of dust would slowly float down from overhead and other hidden places. The grime from the burned oil was distributed about the aft part of the ship each time the engine room "blew" the boiler smoke tubes. It had a very strong acid, sulphur odor that choked anyone who might be aft of either stack. Usually the tubes were blown during the night due to the possibility of the smoke being detected by any enemy plane, submarine or ship.

April 3, 1945

On Tuesday April 3rd, 1945, the ZELLARS accounted for another Jap plane. At 0231 enemy planes were detected in the area and GQ was sounded. At 0316, in full radar control, the ZELLARS opened fire. Per the ship's log, "the plane was seen to burst into flames and crash into the water. The character of the plane was definitely determined by markings visible on wings in the light of the burning plane. Expended 66 rounds of projectiles and powder." Another small setting sun flag was painted on the gun director.

Most of the rest of the day was alongside an LST replenishing the ammunition. Near dusk, assumed position for night picket duty.

The support task force was growing. When the invasion first began there were only three battlewagons and only several cruisers and DDs. Now ships could be seen in every direction. The big friends the TENNESSEE, and TEXAS and the IDAHO were still present but along with them were the COLORADO, NEVADA, ARKANSAS and NEW MEXICO. Cruisers PORTLAND, SALT LAKE CITY, ST LOUIS, and the BILOXI. The little guys were the destroyers BEALE, BARTON, CALLAGHAN, HAMILTON, IRWIN, PORTERFIELD, PRESTON, PORTER, TWIGGS, LEUYZ, BENNETT, BRYANT, and of course, the ZELLARS. The task force had enough fire power to do just as they pleased.

The third Jap flag to be added to the gun director occurred again in the early morning hours of the 6th. This time it was a little earlier. At 0112 AM hours, radar picked up a target (bogie), fired 13 rounds and watched as the third Jap plane spun into the water close by.

It was time to go to the fuel supply again. The ship made her way into Kerama Retto and took on some 91000 gallons of bunker oil, then back to the station for GQ most of the day. There was always at least one enemy aircraft in the area causing the whole fleet to be real jumpy.

The ship-to-ship radio communications were reporting far too often that another ship had been hit by a suicide plane with many killed and wounded. Many of the Kamikaze-struck ships were our sister destroyers and this gave us very grave concern. It seemed that the Japs had learned that the destroyers were warning the fleet that planes from the Japanese mainland were on the way and decided to take as many of them out as they could. The DDs were always on the very outer edge of the Task Force and were sited first. The DDs had a sharp eye with their fire control radar and took a heavy toll of

NOB-SP—7-10-45—3M SETS OF 6

U. S. S. ZELLARS DD-777

HEADING:

Ø21340

CTF 51 SENDS ACTION TASK GROUP 54.1 X FIRING ASSIGNMENTS THREE APRIL X
TASK FORCE 52 COLORADO AND NEVADA X TASK FORCE 53 NEW YORK, WEST VIRGIN

MARYLAND, PENSA OLA, SALT LAKE CITY, BILOXI, EDWARDS, R P LEARY, NEWCOM
PORTERFIELD, PRESTON, ROOKS, ZELLARS, HALL X TASK FORCE 55 TENNESSEE, X

SAN FRANCISCO, BIRMINGHAM, ST LOUIS, C J BADGER, BEALE, BARTON, DALY, P
HAMILTON, SPROSTON, TWIGGS, CALLAGHAN, IRWIN X TASK GROUP 51.19 TEXAS

PENSACOLA, ISHERWOOD, LAFFEY, LAWS, LONGSHAW, MORRISON, PICKING KERANO
RETTO IDAHO, N VADA, ARKANSAS, NEW MEXICO WICHITA X TUSCALOOSA, SWEEP

SUPPORT UNIT EAST X MINNEAPOLIS AND WADSWORTH SWEEP SUPPORT UNIT WEST X
PORTLAND AND W D PORTER X INSTRUCTIONS SEPARATELY X NO RPT O EXCHANGE

WITH SCREEN DESIRED UNTIL ASSAULT SHIPPING AMMO EXHAUSTED

EXECUTIVE OFFICER

From:	CTF 51	Date: 3 APRIL 45	Originated by:	Released by:
		OP	SECRET	
Action To:	TG 54.1	Precedence:	Classification:	Radio.............
				Visual.............
				Mailgram

Information To:

Comdr Div		Capt	Exec	Gun	Eng	1st Lt	Comm	Supply	Nav	CIC	Radar	Sound	Torp	Medical	Office	OOD		

the suicidal-bent pilots. Throughout the day and into the evening there seemed to be anti-aircraft fire somewhere over the task force.

April 7, 1945

All day on the 7th, it was a bright sunny and busy time. Jap planes came in small numbers but almost constantly. Most of the anti-aircraft activity was on the opposite side of the fleet and did not cause problems for the ZELLARS. As large as the task force was, it seemed that the ship was scampering all over. The course changes and speed changes kept the bridge watch on the go at all times.

At 1846 the red flag went up again. The task force commander warned that a large group of enemy aircraft was approaching the fleet. The ZELLARS commenced firing at 1848 with main battery, 40MM and 20MM guns. Everyone on the ship knew when the 40MM began to fire the suicide planes were in close. But, when the 20MM started to fire, they were in far too close. The battleship U.S.S. MARYLAND took a direct suicide hit on top of her number three main battery mount. There was a large blast of flame as the plane hit and exploded. No word of the casualties but she did not slow down and stayed in formation.

Commander Kintberger was always a calm and quiet skipper. Something special was about to happen. He was all but dancing about the bridge. It was just after midnight and the 8th of April. The Task Force commander had ordered a select group of the supporting force to form up for a Jap Task Force; the last of their major warships that was headed south for Okinawa on a suicide dash. In the Jap force was an old enemy of the Captain, the mighty Jap battlewagon YAMATO. It was the largest battleship ever built and carried 18 inch main battery guns that threw a shell weighing over 3000 pound beyond a horizon.

The Captain had met this behemoth at Samar in the Leyte Gulf battle and had been part of sinking the HOEL, his last command. He would like nothing better than to get another crack at the big guy. (Some of the crew was not too sure.)

The quickly assembled strike force steamed away from Okinawa. The ship was alive with all kinds of emotions. As the sun began to show some light, the order was cancelled and the order was to return to the support task force at Okinawa. The crew learned later in the day, Admiral Halsey's Task Force 58 had intercepted the Jap force and destroyed all but one destroyer and a badly damaged cruiser. The mighty YAMATO, the ship that couldn't be sunk, was now on the bottom of the sea in Davy Jones locker.

The rest of the day was fire support to the beach and the ever present "red alert" of suicide planes in the area. The ship did have a new name to add to the list of target areas, Point Makiminato. The call from the beach was for star shell illumination to an assigned sector that was having some problems with Jap ground forces.

CONFIDENTIAL PAGE 250-45

NAVPERS-134 (REV. 1-44) DECK LOG—REMARKS SHEET

UNITED STATES SHIP _____ ZELLARS _____ Saturday 7 April, 1945
(Day) (Date) (Month)

0-4
0000: Anchored in 32 fathoms of water with 90 fathoms of chain to the port anchor bearing 176°T, 3300 yards from Makiminato Saki on the southwestern part of Okinawa Jima, Nansei Shoto. Boilers #2 and #3 in use for steaming purposes, split plant operation, jacking gear engaged. Ship is darkened, material condition Baker and condition of readiness II are set. Maintaining illumination with illuminating projectiles over enemy lines as directed by shore fire control party on the southern part of Okinawa. Firing one starshell every six minutes. Sonar search 360°. Ships present: various units of the United States Fifth Fleet.

C. A. SMYLIE, Lieut., USN

4-8
0400: Anchored as before. Ship went to General Quarters, presence of unidentified aircraft. 0415: Heaved in to 60 fathoms on the port chain. 0608: Secured from General Quarters, set condition of readiness II. 0614: Sunrise, lighted ship. 0745: Stationed anchor detail. 0749: Underway; steaming on various courses and at various speeds staying in area of last anchorage, awaiting orders to fire from shore fire control party.

Arthur LINDH, Lieut., USNR

8-12
0800: Steaming as before. 0800: Mustered crew on stations, no absentees. 0900: Made routine inspection of magazines and smokeless powder samples; conditions normal.

D. D. CLEVELAND, Lt.(jg), USNR

12-16
1200: Steaming as before. 1325: Proceeding to close the U.S.S. TENNESSEE (BB-43). 1338: All engines stopped. 1340: Captain left ship to attend conference aboard TENNESSEE. Lying to awaiting return of Captain; engines used as necessary to maintain proper heading. 1513: Captain returned aboard ship. Proceeding on various courses at various speeds to clear transport area enroute rendezvous with Task Force 54.

S. E. ROBBINS, Lieut., USN

16-18
1600: Steaming as before, set course 320°T and PGC, 329°PSC at 10 knots (92 R.P.M.) 1606: Changed course to 290°T and PGC, 299°PSC. 1609: Maneuvering on various courses at various speeds to effect rendezvous. 1625: Joined U.S.S. PICKNEY (CDG49), U.S.S. CHARLES J. BADGER, U.S.S. WILLIAM D. PORTER, as fourth ship in division column joining with Task Force 54. Set course 305°T and PGC, 307°PSC, set speed 13 knots (120 R.P.M.) 1637: Changed fleet course to 270°T and PGC, 279°PSC. 1647: Changed fleet speed to 8 knots (74 R.P.M.) 1651: Changed base course to 000°T and PGC, 005°PSC. Changed fleet speed to 12 knots (111 R.P.M.) 1658: Changed fleet course to 270°T and PGC, 279°PSC. Changed speed to 5 knots (46 R.P.M.) 1710: Changed course to 000°T and PGC, 005°PSC. Changed speed to 25 knots (246 R.P.M.) 1728: Changed course to 040°T and PGC, 041°PSC. 1729: Changed course to 000°T and PGC, 004°PSC. 1730: Changed speed to 12 knots (111 R.P.M.) 1731: Changed fleet course to 000°T and PGC, 004°PSC. 1730: Cut boiler #1 in on main steam line. 1746: Cut boiler #4 in on main steam line. 1753: Changed fleet course to 090°T and PGC, 094°PSC.

C. A. SMYLIE, Lieut., USN

18-20
1800: Steaming as before. 1846: All hands to General Quarters. Enemy aircraft approaching formation. Set condition Affirm. 1848: Commenced firing 40 MM and 20 MM guns at enemy aircraft. 1849: Ceased firing. Enemy aircraft crashed aboard U.S.S. MARYLAND. Ammunition expended 28 rds. 40 MM, 90 rds. 20 MM. 1912: Changed speed to 20 knots (190 R.P.M.) Changed course to 020°T and PGC, 022°PSC. 1915: Changed speed to 25 knots (246 R.P.M.) 1920: Changed course to 000°T and PGC, 004°PSC. 1930: Set condition Baker, secured from General Quarters, set condition of readiness II. 1944: Changed course to 090°T and PGC, 094°PSC. Changed speed to 15 knots (140 R.P.M.) 1952: Changed course to 180°T and PGC, 184°PSC.

Arthur LINDH, Lieut., USNR

20-24
2000: Steaming as before. 2118: Changed base course by turn movement to 270°T and PGC, 279°PSC.

APPROVED:

L. S. KITENBERGER, Comdr., U.S.N. COMMANDING.

EXAMINED:

Nelson E. SMITH, Lt.(jg), U.S.N.R. NAVIGATOR

TO BE FORWARDED DIRECT TO THE BUREAU OF NAVAL PERSONNEL AT THE END OF EACH MONTH

87

UNITED STATES SHIP   ZELLARS (DD-777)   Monday   8   April   1945
                                                     (Day)   (Date)   (Month)

00-04
0000 Moored portside to fuel dock, N.A.S., Pensacola, Florida with 5 six inch manila lines doubled up and one 1 3/4" wire rope aft. U.S.S. Douglas H. Fox (DD-779) moored outboard. Boiler #3 lit off for auxiliary steam, generator #2 furnishing power. SOPA in U.S.S. Ranger (CV 4). Ships Present: Units of the U.S. Atlantic Fleet. 0055 PAYNE, H. B., C.B.M., U.S.N., returned aboard being A.O.L. for a period of about 4 days and 17 hours and declared a P.A.L. 0145 Ensign N.A. Engelmann, U.S.N., MC PHERSON, Medford W., 291 90 18, WTlc, and COPE, Alfred Jackson, 358 37 78, SoM3c, USNR returned aboard from Shore Patrol Duty.

                                               Ens. A. F. KWISINSKY

04-08
0400 Moored as before. 0450 Lighted fires under boiler No.1. Commenced taking on fresh water. 0530 Secured from taking on fresh water, having received 2,830 gallons. 0648 Cut in boilers No.1 and 3 on main steam line. 0655 Stationed special sea details. 0716 U.S.S. Ranger underway. 0725 U.S.S. D. H. Fox underway from alongside. 0735 Underway to rendezvous with U.S.S. Ranger at buoy 1A. Captain at the conn, navigator on the bridge. 0741 Standing out Pensacola Bay using various speeds and courses conforming to channel. 0746 Passed buoy 19 abeam to port, distant 50 yards. 0759 Passed buoy 12 abeam to port, distant 60 yards.

                                               W. J. MC HUGH, Lieut., USNR

08-12
0800 Steaming as before. 0807 Secured special sea details. 0810 Passed buoy 1A abeam to port, distant 35 yards. Proceeding to anti-submarine screening station # 1, screen 52, USF1OB at 20 knots (185 RPM). Base course 180° T, fleet speed 15 knots. 0812 Pelican hook in forward boat falls parted, boat dragging in water. All engines were stopped. 0812½ All engines backing full. 0813 All engines stopped. Lying to in water to rescue JORGENSEN, D. J., 317 07 33, S1/c, USNR, caught in after falls when bow of boat dropped into water, and to recover boat. Injuries to JORGENSEN were contusions and abrasions of lower right leg. Treated by Medical Officer and confined to bed.

                                               W. J. MC HUGH, Lieut, USNR

08-12 (cont.)
0830 Lying to while hoisting Motor Whale boat aboard. 0842 Underway to rejoin U.S.S. Ranger (CV 4), on various courses and speeds. 0852 Mustered crew on stations. No absentees. 0947 Rejoined Carrier and took plane guard station #2, position 1200 yards on port beam of carrier. Flight course 230°T and pgc, 228 psc, flight speed 15 knots (136 RPM). 0952 Carrier ceased flight operations. Changed base course to 245° T and pgc, 242° psc. Carrier resumed flight operations. 1117 Made daily inspection of magazines and smokeless powder samples. Conditions Normal.

                                               C V. GEARIN, Lt., USNR

12-16
Steaming as before. 1257 Ceased flight operations, changed course to 040° T and pgc, 038° psc, speed 20 knots (185 RPM). 1320 Turned to course 220° T and pgc, 219° psc. resumed flight operations. 1325 Exercised crew at general quarters. 1404 Secured from general quarters, set condition "Baker". 1531 Ceased flight operations, turned to course 040° T and pgc, 038° psc.

                                               R. V. GAUTHIER, Lt., USNR

16-18
1600 Steaming as before. 1601 Turned to course 250° T, speed 19 knots (175 RPM). 1603 Carrier resumed flight operations. 1753 Carrier ceased flight operations. Changed course to 060° T and pgc, 056° psc. Changed speed to 9 knots (076 RPM). Escorts proceeding to anti-submarine screening stations as follows: Zellars 3050, Fox 3310.

                                               W. J. MC HUGH, Lt., USNR

18-20
1800 Steaming as before. 1820 Secured boiler #1. 1829 Sighted South pass Rear Range light bearing 300 T about 12 miles. 0930 Executed speed 9 knots (080 RPM).

                                               R. E. JAMISON, Ens., USNR

20-24
2000 Steaming as before. 2230 Changed base course 40° to the left to 020° T and pgc, 017° psc, in order to avoid ships bearing 054° T, distance 11,000 yards, and 063° T, distance 16,000 yards. 2313 Changed base course to 060° T and pgc, 056° psc.

                                               C. V. GEARIN, Lt., USNR

APPROVED: EXAMINED:

L. S. KINTBERGER, Comdr., U S N   COMMANDING.   W. M. TRUSHESKY, Lt. (jg) U.S.N.R.   NAVIGATOR

TO BE FORWARDED DIRECT TO THE BUREAU OF   THE END OF EACH MONTH

U. S. GOVERNMENT PRINTING OFFICE: 1944 O - 617966

CONFIDENTIAL

NAVPERS-134 (REV. 1-44)

DECK LOG—REMARKS SHEET

PAGE 256-45

UNITED STATES SHIP _____ ZELLARS _____ Monday 9 April , 19 45
(Day) (Date) (Month)

0-4
0000: Anchored in 38 fathoms of water with 90 fathoms of chain out on the port anchor on a bearing of 163°T distant 4500 yards from Point Makiminato Saki, western Okinawa Shima conducting fire support operations under CTB 53. Boilers #2 and #3 standing by for steaming purposes, jacking gear engaged. Ship darkened, material condition Baker, condition of readiness II. Firing illumination and harrassing fire as directed by shore fire control party and CTG 53. 0345: Shifted target to area #9 to give continuous star shell illumination. 0400: Ceased continuous illumination and resumed illumination and harrassing fire on western shores of Okinawa Shima.

Arthur LINDH, Lieut., USNR

4-8
0400: Anchored as before. 0500: Unidentified aircraft in area, called crew to General Quarters. Set condition Affirm. 0505: Stationed anchor detail. 0517: Underway, steaming on various courses at various speeds, remaining in fire support area #5. 0535: Secured anchor detail. 0630: Secured from General Quarters, set condition of readiness II, condition Baker.

D. D. CLEVELAND, Lt.(jg), USNR

8-12
0800: Steaming as before. 0812: All engines stopped; lying to in fire support area #5, using engines as necessary to maintain proper heading. 0834: Commenced firing main battery in accordance with instructions from shore fire control party. 1000: Manned main battery with General Quarters crew to enable firing of six gun salvos. 1010: Cut #4 boiler in on main steam line, let fires die under #3 boiler. 1102: In accordance with instruction from shore fire control party, checked fire. Ammunition expended: 346 rds. 5"38 AA common projectiles, 4 rds. 5"38 white phosphorous projectiles, and 440 rds. 5"38 smokeless powder. 1150: U.S.S. LONGSHAW reported for duty. Directed to relieve U.S.S. PORTER in fire support area #5. Made daily inspection of magazines and smokeless powder samples conditions normal.

for S. B. ROBBINS, Lieutenant, USN   Lt(jg)USNR

12-16
1200: Lying to as before conducting call fire as directed by shore fire control party. 1323: 2 LCM's alongside to transfer ammunition. 1350: Completed transfer of ammunition having received 484 rds. 5"38 AA common projectiles. 1415: ALGOOD, James H., 864 77 60, S1c, USNR suffered a lacerated tendon of the right thumb when cut by a knife while engaged in ship's work. Treated by the Medical Officer and returned to duty. 1427: Commenced firing main battery to port as directed by shore fire control party.

C. A. SMYLIE, Lieut., USN

16-18
1600: Steaming as before. 1640: Ceased shore bombardment. Ammunition expended: 54 rds. 5"38 AA common and smokeless powder. 1630: Released from CTF 53 and proceeding to report to CTF 54 for night retirement. cruising. 1650: Course 330°T and PGC, 335°PSC. Standard speed 13 knots (120 R.P.M.) Enroute rendezvous to form cruising disposition 5RD. In company with U.S.S. TENNESSEE (OTC, guide and CTF 54) U.S.S. WEST VIRGINIA, U.S.S. COLORADO, U.S.S. NEW YORK, U.S.S. TEXAS, U.S.S. NEW MEXICO, U.S.S. MINNEAPOLIS, U.S.S. PORTLAND, U.S.S. BILOXI, anti-submarine screen consisting of U.S.S. BARTON, U.S.S. IRWIN, U.S.S. PICKING (ComScreen and ComDesRon 56), U.S.S. PORTER, U.S.S. ROOKS, U.S.S. ZELLARS, U.S.S. TWIGGS, U.S.S. BENNION. 1750: On station #1 in circular screen guide U.S.S. TENNESSEE (2.5160 T from fleet center) bearing 174°T distant 8500 yards. Fleet course and axis 000°T, speed 13 knots (120 R.P.M.)

Arthur LINDH, Lieut., USNR

18-20
1800: Steaming as before. 1832: Commenced zig-zagging according to plan #6, USF (10A). Changed speed to 14.5 knots (134 R.P.M.) 1846: Sunset, darkened ship. 1857: Enemy aircraft in area, called crew to General Quarters. 1904: Took enemy plane under fire to port in full radar control. 1904: Ceased firing; no hits observed. 1847: Took enemy plane under fire to starboard in full radar control. 1849: Ceased firing; observed hit on enemy plane, crashed into the sea in flames, our hiting plane doubtful. Total ammunition expended: 111 rds. 5"38 AA common projectiles, 109 5"38 AA Special; and :, 220 rds. 5"38 mixed flashless and smokeless powder.

D. D. CLEVELAND, Lt.(jg), USNR

APPROVED: EXAMINED:

R. KNITBERGER, Comdr., U.S.N. COMMANDING.   Nelson E. SMITH, Lt.(jg), U.S.N.R. NAVIGATOR

TO BE FORWARDED DIRECT TO THE BUREAU OF NAVAL PERSONNEL AT THE END OF EACH MONTH

U. S. GOVERNMENT PRINTING OFFICE: 1944 O 617682

CONFIDENTIAL

NAVPERS 135 (REV. 1-44)

DECK LOG—ADDITIONAL REMARKS SHEET

PAGE 256-45

UNITED STATES SHIP **ZELLARS** Monday 9 April , 19 45
(Day) (Date) (Month)

ADDITIONAL REMARKS

20-24

2000: Steaming as before. 2000: Commenced firing to port on enemy aircraft. 2001: Ceased firing, expended the following ammunition: 49 rds. 5"38 AA common and 10 rds. 5"38 AA special projectiles, and 59 rds. 5"38 flashless powder. Enemy aircraft burst into flames and crashed on our port bow, bearing 310°T. 2035: Ceased zig-zagging, resumed base course, 000°T and PGC, 007°PSC. 2053: Secured from General Quarters, set material condition Baker, condition of readiness II. 2100: Changed base course to 270°T and PGC, 278°PSC. 2230: Changed base course to 180°T and PGC, 188°PSC. Stationed changed to #9, commenced toward proper station at flank speed. 2245: On station with guide bearing 308°T, distance 4000 yards. 2300: Changed base course to 090°T and PGC, 091°PSC.

Nelson E. Smith, Lt. (jg) USNR

S. E. ROBBINS, Lieut., USN

APPROVED:

L. S. Kintberger

L. S. KINTBERGER, Comdr., U.S.N COMMANDING.

EXAMINED:

Nelson E. Smith

Nelson E. SMITH, Lt. (jg), U.S.N.R. NAVIGATOR

TO BE FORWARDED DIRECT TO THE BUREAU OF NAVAL PERSONNEL AT THE END OF EACH MONTH

April 9, 1945

April 9 was again the same, GQ in the wee hours of the morning and enemy aircraft in the area. One unwanted break in the routine of the day, ship's crew member, James H. ALGOOD, suffered a serious cut to his thumb while doing ship's work and was treated by the ship's doctor and returned to duty.

Several different destroyers joined the task group, the U.S. PICKING, BENNION and the ROOK. Every new gun was most welcome.

At 2000, another Jap plane was splashed by the ZELLARS and crashed just off the port bow. The darned Japs were getting a little closer each time we shot one down.

The 9th, 10th and 11th were all but the same routine. The ZELLARS completed her assigned picket duty during the night and fleet security during the day, mixed with fire support to the beach.

April 12, 1945

Many "bogies" were in the area all during the day. It seemed that the ZELLARS was constantly going to GQ.

In mid morning, the ship was selected for delivering guard mail. Kinda like KP duty. The mail had been picked up from the Tennessee and the ZELLARS was passing it out to the other ships in the task group. As the selected ship to deliver mail, the ZELLARS would approach a ship from the stern and exchange high lines. A bag with the mail secured in it would be passed to the receiving ship and then the "mail man" would go on to the next mailbox. The mail delivery went on all morning. About 1400 the ship went to GQ another time but no Jap planes came close to the Task Group. The Task Group secured from GQ for about 4 minutes when GQ sounded again at 1445. The Task Group came under attack from a large number of very determined and aggressive Jap suicide pilots. The planes came from every direction. Four Jap Jill-type aircraft picked out the ZELLARS and began a concentrated attack.

Their approach was off the ZELLARS stern, port side. They were some 18000 yards out, about 15 feet above the water, when the ship's gunners began to pick them out. Traveling in excess of 250 knots, they closed the distance in a very short time. First, the 5" guns cut loose and almost at the same time the 40MMs, then the 20MMs. All firing was to port. The crew knew that the ship was in serious trouble when the 20MMs began to fire; their target was darned close The planes spread apart and two headed for the forward part of the ship with the two remaining targeting the area just aft of the number 2 stack. All guns on the port side were firing at all four targets. One of the forward planes was struck by the ZELLARS' gunners and burst into flames as it splashed into the sea. The forward most plane of the aft group hit the water next.

COPY OF
TEAMING ORDER
nd April '45

U. S. S. ZELLARS DD777

(021017)

IN CASE OF ENEMY CONTACT IF GENERAL SIGNAL BAKER
FORM 13 MADE BULLDOGS FORM TWO COLUMNS:

RIGHT COLUMN:
IDAHO
NEW MEXICO
TENNESSEE

LEFT COLUMN:
WEST VIRGINIA
TEXAS

COMMANDING OFFICER PORTLAND WITH MINNEAPOLIS AND
TUSCALOOSA TAKE STATION RIGHT THOUSAND YARDS AHEAD

OF BULLDOGS, CTU 54.2.4 WITH ONE HALF SEA HAWKS
TAKE STATION FIVE THOUSAND YARDS AHEAD OF BULLDOGS,

REMAINING SEA HAWKS UNDER CONDESRON 55, THREE
THOUSAND YARDS ASTERN BULLDOGS. WILL INTERPOSE AND

U. S. S. MONADNOCK

Heading:

121300/APR/45   VOICE P/L

ZELLARS (DD 777) UNDER ATTACK 1450N 3 JILLS 2 SHOT DOWN 3RD
SUICIDED AND EXPLODED ON SECOND DECK AREA OF PLOTTING ROOM X

3 JAP BODIES IN PLANE X 50 POUND BOMB THAT DID NOT EXPLODE BUT
THE TORPEDO WHICH IT WAS CARRYING EXPLODED X FOLLOWING DAMAGE ALL

FIRE CONTROL EQUIPMENT INOPERATIVE X GYRO AND CIC ROOM DEMOLISHED
X MOUNT 2 JAMMED IN TRAIN X SOUND GEAR DEMOLISHED X GALLEY DEMOL-

ISHED X DIRECTOR TRUMP DISPLACED ABOUT ONE INCH X FORWARD FIRE ROOM
BULKHEAD AND SECTIONS OF MAIN STEAM LINE RUPTURED X FORWARD FUEL

OIL SERVICE TANKS RUPTURED X NO APPARENT UNDERWATER DAMAGE X SIDE
PLATING ABOVE WATER LINE STARBOARD SIDE X 8 ENLISTED MEN MISSING X
P
PERSONNEL KILLED IN ACTION 3 OFFICERS 18 ENLISTED X WOUND IN ACTION
1 OFFICER 36 ENLISTED MEN X BT.....

FROM: ZELLARS (DD 777)							Priority	Routine	Deferred
TO: CTG -51.15									Radio
INFO:									Visual
									Mail
All Ofcrs	Div. Com.	Capt.	Exec.	O.O.D.	Eng.	65-E	omm. Supply Medical Yeo.	FILE	

The exact moment that the ZELLARS was struck by the JILL suicide plane, taken from the cruiser Portland. The heavy attack was from the ZELLARS main battery guns. With over 100 Japanese Kamikaze planes in the area, firing from the task group was everywhere. The low flying Jap planes created a real problem from "friendly fire."

At 1451, the remaining forward plane struck the ZELLARS under the number 2 5" gun and exploded into the upper handling room of mount two. The plane carried an 1100-pound torpedo slung under its right side, against the fuselage. Flaming airplane fuel cascaded over the port side and some of the flames were pulled down into the forward engineering spaces, burning the crew.

Other ships continued to fire on the Japanese planes just as the torpedo exploded on the ZELLARS' starboard side. It was difficult to understand how such a great ball of fire occurred and most of the crew was not aware of its size.

Regardless of the ship sailors serve on, they are all shipmates. The U.S.S. TENNESSEE was off the ZELLARS' port side and the lead command ship. She was the ship that generated the Task Group's mail. The TENNESSEE and her crew had to feel the ZELLARS' pain and watched helplessly as the ZELLARS was hit and burned. The ship that is somewhat a blur with smoke boiling from the suicide plane is the ZELLARS. (Photo from cruiser Portland.)

Photo taken from U.S.S. Portland April 12, 1945

Nakajima B6N Tenzan "Jill"

B6N1, B6N2

Origin: Nakajima Hikoki KK.

Type: Three-seat carrier-based torpedo bomber.

Engine: (B6N1) one 1,870hp Nakajima Mamori 11 14-cylinder two-row radial; (B6N2) 1,850hp Mitsubishi Kasei 25 of same layout.

Dimensions: Span 48ft 10¼in (14·894m); length 35ft 7½in (10·865m); height (1) 12ft 1¾in (3·7m); (2) 12ft 5½in (3·8m).

Weights: Empty 6,636lb (3010kg) (1, 2 almost identical); normal loaded 11,464lb (5200kg); maximum overload 12,456lb (5650kg).

Performance: Maximum speed (1) 289mph (465km/h); (2) 299mph (482km/h); initial climb (1) 1,720ft (525m)/min; (2) 1,885ft (575m)/min; service ceiling (1) 28,379ft (8650m); (2) 29,659ft (9040m); range (normal weight) (1) 907 miles (1460km); (2) 1,084 miles (1745km), (overload) (1) 2,312 miles (3720km); (2) 1,895 miles (3050km).

Armament: One 7·7mm Type 89 manually aimed from rear cockpit and one manually aimed by middle crew-member from rear ventral position, with fixed 7·7mm firing forward in left wing (often absent from B6N1); 1,764lb

Below: A formation of Nakajima B6N2 torpedo bombers, probably photographed by the radio-operator/gunner of another. Colours are dark green and pale grey, with black engine cowls.

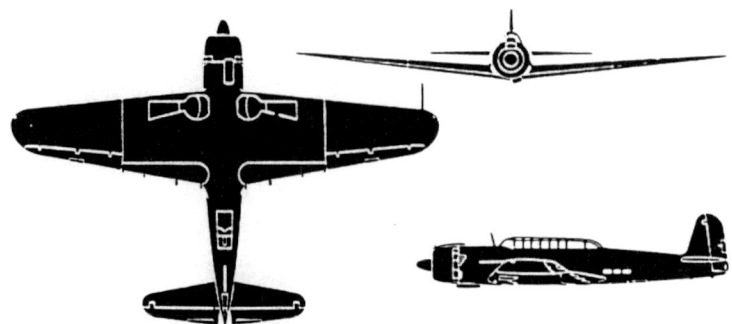

Above: Three-view of B6N2, without radar.

(800kg. 18in) torpedo carried offset to right of centreline. or six 220lb (100kg) bombs under fuselage.
History: First flight March 1942: service delivery (B6N1) early 1943: (B6N2) December 1943.
User: Japan (Imperial Navy).

Development: Named Tenzan (Heavenly Mountain) after a worshipped mountain in China. and code-named "Jill" by the Allies. the B6N was another conventional-looking aircraft which in fact was in many respects superior to the seemingly more advanced machines of the Allies (in this case the Grumman TBF and Fairey Barracuda). Designed as a replacement for B5N. Tenzan was slim and clean. with no internal weapon bay. The torpedo was offset. and to increase clearance on torpedo release the big oil cooler was offset in the other direction (to the left). The distinctive shape of the vertical tail was to minimise stowage length in the three-point attitude in carriers. Nakajima's big Mamori engine. driving a four-blade Hamilton-type propeller. suffered severe vibration and overheating. and though the B6N1 was kept in service it was replaced in production by the B6N2. The lower power of the proven Kasei was counteracted by the improved installation with less drag. and jet-thrust from the exhaust stubs. Tenzans went into action off Bougainville in the Marshalls campaign in June 1944. Subsequently they were heavily committed. many being later equipped with ASV radar for night attacks and ending in April-June 1945 with a hectic campaign of torpedo and suicide attacks off Okinawa and Kyushu. By this time the Imperial Navy had no operating carrier and hardly any skilled pilots.

When the large (over 125) group of Kamikaze's attacked the Task Group, each ship took a strong defensive position about the Task Group and more or less scattered so as to have the best firing position without hitting another ship in the Task Group. The ZELLARS was in the process of moving at her highest speed to gain the better position if there was such a place.

There wasn't a great deal a captain could do if his ship was selected by one of the attacking planes. If there were more than four or five planes coming in at ocean top level at high speeds, someone was going to get badly hurt, and this day, April 12, 1945, at 1451, it was the ZELLARS.

The formation was still under attack by scattered Kamikaze planes when the BENNION was ordered to go alongside the U.S.S. ZELLARS to aid in putting out fires and assisting in general.

From a personal log of Alvin H. Peters, FC2c of the U.S.S. Bennion DD 662.

The formation was still under attack by scattered Kamikaze planes when the BENNION was ordered to go alongside the U.S.S. ZELLARS to aid in putting out fires and assisting in general. As the BENNION closed on the ZELLARS, shouts were heard in the water and a man was seen struggling in a life jacket. He was too injured or dazed to swim to the ship and two of BENNION'S sailors jumped overboard quickly and brought him aboard. The rescued man was an officer from the ZELLARS who had suffered from burns on the head and shoulders which later proved to be fatal.

BENNION then proceeded alongside the ZELLARS and within a short time had the fires under control. Although the ship had been severely damaged in the vicinity of her wardroom and combat information center. She was navigable and proceeded to Kerama Retto with the loan of BENNION'S doctor and a pharmacist mate to administer emergency medical treatment.

Night of the 5th had several air attacks. One plane was hit and flew about 2 miles fully aflame until he crashed into the sea. Flew right over some of our ships but evidently he couldn't see well enough to crash dive them.

Morning of the 6th we were assigned to take some tanker transports to sea. Nine were in the group plus about 3 other cans and several DE's. Went out with them until about 2000 then turned back toward Okinawa, letting the DE's have them.

Received reports that five of our cans were hit by suicides and bombs! Newcomb, Leutze, Bush, Morris, Calhoune.

The Bush sank and the rest were seriously damaged. The Calhoune was the can that relieved us out on Radar Picket #2. That was the station 65 miles away from Okinawa. One can patroling.

On the 7th late in the afternoon word was passed about some of the Jap fleet coming down. The carriers of Task Force 58 launched immense air attacks of 350 planes at them.

We went into battle formation in case they'd come south. Six battleships, 3 carriers and 11 destroyers. We were all set to meet them. Reports came that our planes sank all including the Yomato, their big wagon; only three of their cans survived to go back toward home. Sure was a relief to hear that they nailed them so well with the air attacks. We had one bogey that crash dived on the fantail of the Maryland. Minor damage reported.

We're picketing around Okinawa the next few days.

On the 12th we had one of the biggest air raids we ever encountered! Were in formation with 17 heavy ships and about the same amount of destroyers. We were on the port quarter of the formation. About 50-75 bogeys were reported coming down from up north.

All of a sudden we saw a plane catch fire about ten miles out on our port side. Looking out we saw a large group of enemy planes coming for us. Some were in a dive - the zeroes came in low. Really was quick! We fired all our machine guns and really nailed them. Put 4 down for sure. All the port 40 M.M. were out of ammo. and there was one more low zeke coming directly at us! Our fantail and port 20 M.M. splashed him about 20 yards from the ship! Debris and water from the splash hit the ship. We all thanked God for our most fortunate outcome of the attack. One man on gun 43 was killed by another ships A.A. fire. He was full of shrapnel wounds. 4 more were injured and were transferred to the West Virginia later.

One of the planes that went by us hit a battleship - no damage. Another hit a can (777) and really smashed her - just below the bridge. We went alongside her to fight fire and to give them our doctor. Their doctor was killed. Sure was an awful sight. Men completely burned apart etc. etc.

We picked up one survivor that was thrown off the 777. He was screaming up ahead in the water. Was all burned and was really in a sad shape. Transferred him to West Virginia. Never want to see anything like it again. We were very lucky not to be hit. It was damn good shooting on our part that really helped. We were thankful.

-14 - USS BENNION (DD 662)

Nothwithstanding his own wounds, he got the more severely wounded removed, replaced his gun crew from the damage dontrol party and had his gun in action again before the completion of the attack.

The formation was still under attack by scattered Kamikaze planes when BENNION was ordered to go alongside USS ZELLARS to aid in putting out fires and assisting generally. As the ship closed ZE§ARS, shouts were heard in the water and a man was seen struggling in a life jacket He was too injured or dazed to swim to the ship and two of BENNION's sailors jumped overboard quickly and brought him aboard. The rescued man was an officer from ZELLARS who was suffering from burns on the head and shoulders which later proved to be fatal.

BENNION then proceeded alongside ZELLARS and within a short time had the fires under control. Although the ship had been severely damaged in the vicinity of her ward room and combat information center, she was navigable and proceeded to Kerama Rhetto with the loan of BENNION's Dr. Schmidt and a pharmacist's mate to administer emergency treatment. BENNION's casualties were transferred to the battleship WEST VIRGINIA that evening for treatment. Much to the sorrow of all hands, one of BENNION's crew died that afternoon of wounds received in action.

That night would have been an ideal night for an all-around rest but the war continued its relentless course. At 2045, combat information center reported bogies suddenly appearing ahead of the formation at close range. The ships of the group were soon brilliantly illuminated by aircraft flares and planes were heard overhead. As soon as the flares were dropped the formation changed course and shortly thereafter the sound operator reported torpedo noises. The course change probably caused the torpedoes to miss as they were heard to explode harmlessly at the end of their run.

The Japanese had apparently expended all available planes on the 12th as none put in an appearance during the next two days and BENNION was finally ordered to Kerama Rhetto for the long delayed gyro repairs which were satisfactorily completed in 24 hours.

BENNION found herself on radar picket station again on 15 April, 50 miles south of the beaches. This proved to be a quiet station except for the fact that night hecklers from Formosa passed over the station both proceeding to and returning from Okinawa On the following day, the Japanese launched a heavy attack with about 100 aircraft. Several of our ships were hit and USS PRINGLE, a close associate of BENNION's through several campaigns, was sunk.

After a two-day rest on anti-submarine patrol in the vicinity of the beachhead, BENNION was again assigned to a picket station

NAVPERS-124 (REV. 1-44)   **DECK LOG—REMARKS SHEET**   PAGE- 264-45

UNITED STATES SHIP _____ZELLARS_____   Thursday   12   April   , 45
                                                              (Day)   (Date)   (Month)

0-4

0000: Steaming on course 180°T and PGC, 186°PSC at fleet speed of 13 knots (120 R.P.M.) in company with Task Group 54 consisting of U.S.S. TENNESSEE (Guide and OTC, CTG 54), U.S.S. IDAHO, U.S.S. COLORADO, U.S.S. MARYLAND, U.S.S. NEW MEXICO, U.S.S. SALT LAKE CITY, U.S.S. TUSCALOOSA, U.S.S. BIRMINGHAM, U.S.S. ST. LOUIS, U.S.S. MOBILE in cruising disposition 5 RD. U.S.S. BEALE, U.S.S. DALY, U.S.S. HUTCHINS, U.S.S. BARTON (ComScreen and ComDesRon 60), U.S.S. BENNION in circular screen 6000 yards from fleet center. Fleet axis 000°T. U.S.S. ZELLARS in station #5. Ship darkened, material condition Baker, condition of readiness II. Boilers #1 and #4 on the line for steaming purposes, split plant operation. 0002: Changed course to 270°T and PGC, 276°PSC. Took station #1, guide bearing 180°T distant 6000 yards. 0145: Changed course to 180°T and PGC, 186°PSC. Took station #5, guide bearing 263°T distant 6000 yards. 0215: Changed course to 090°T and PGC, 095°PSC. 0322: Enemy aircraft in vicinity, called crew to General Quarters.

                                                   Arthur LINDH, Lieut., USNR

4-8

0400: Steaming as before. 0440: Changed base course to 160°T and PGC, 166°PSC, maneuvering to form cruising disposition 5 RV. 0504: Secured from General Quarters. 0558: Changed base course to 180°T and PGC, 186°PSC. 0609: Sunrise lighted ship. 0645: Changed base course to 000°T and PGC, 005°PSC, changed fleet speed to 10 knots (92 R.P.M.) 0730: Changed base course 180°T and PGC, 186°PSC.

                                                   D. D. CLEVELAND, Lt.(jg), USNR

8-12

0800: Steaming as before. Changed course to 000°T and PGC, 005°PSC. 0830: Changed base course to 180°T and PGC, 186°PSC on turn signal from OTC. 0903: Changed base course to 000°T and PGC, 005°PSC. Maneuvering on various courses at various speeds going alongside U.S.S. IDAHO for transfer of mail from IDAHO. 0946: Changed base course to 180°T and PGC, 186°PSC on turn signal from OTC. 0956: Came alongside starboard side of U.S.S. IDAHO. Maneuvering on various courses at various speeds. 0958: Commenced transferring mail. 1039: Completed transfer of mail. Increased speed to 20 knots (190 R.P.M.) enroute U.S.S. NEW MEXICO for transfer of mail to her, course 200°T and PGC. 1050: Maneuvering on various courses at various speeds to go alongside U.S.S. NEW MEXICO. Changed base course to 000°T and PGC, 005°PSC by turn signal from OTC. 1055: Alongside port side of NEW MEXICO. Maneuvering on various courses, speed 10 knots (92 R.P.M.) Commenced transferring mail. 1101: Completed transfer of mail to NEW MEXICO. Steaming on various courses, speed 20 knots (190 R.P.M.) enroute U.S.S. NEVADA. 1108: Maneuvering on various courses coming alongside NEVADA slowed to 10 knots (92 R.P.M.) 1105: Formed cruising disposition 5 VD on order from OTC. 1124: Commenced transferring mail to U.S.S. NEVADA. 1136: Completed transfer of mail to U.S.S. NEVADA. Maneuvering on various courses, speed 10 knots (92 R.P.M.) preparing to go alongside U.S.S. TUSCALOOSA. 1154: Alongside TUSCALOOSA starboard side to. Commenced transferring mail. 1159: Completed transfer of mail to TUSCALOOSA. Made routine inspection of magazines and smokeless powder samples; conditions normal.

                                                   Nelson E. SMITH, Lt.(jg), USNR

12-16

1200: Steaming as before. 1204: Coming under the stern of U.S.S. NEW YORK to transfer mail. 1224: Transfer completed. 1235: Coming under the stern of U.S.S. TEXAS to transfer mail. 1251: Transfer completed. 1300: Coming under the stern of U.S.S. SALT LAKE CITY to transfer mail. 1318: Transfer completed. 1320: Coming under the stern of U.S.S. PORTLAND to transfer mail. 1330: Discontinued transfer of mail. Unidentified aircraft reported 030°T distance 20 miles. Went to General Quarters; set condition Affirm. Maneuvering to take station in the screen. 1348: On station in screen. Set course 180°T and PGC, 186°PSC, speed 15 knots (140 R.P.M.). 1355: Unidentified aircraft 002°T, distance 28 miles, closing. 1431: Changed fleet course to 030°T and PGC, 031°PSC on signal from OTC. 1432: Set material condition Baker. 1435: Changed fleet course to 090°T and PGC, 091°PSC on signal from OTC. 1437: U.S.S. TENNESSEE designated disposition guide. 1439: Secured from General Quarters. Set condition of readiness II. 1444: Enemy aircraft in area went to General Quarters, set condition Affirm. Enemy aircraft shot down in flames approximately 15000 yards on port beam. Changed speed to 20 knots (190 R.P.M.) 1450: Three enemy torpedo planes sighted making a run on this vessel to port. Commenced firing main and machine gun battery to port to repel attack. Changed speed to 25 knots (246 R.P.M.) Two aircraft hit by AA fire and crashed into the sea. The third aircraft, approaching from 290° Relative about 15 feet above the water, crashed into the ship on the port bow at the base of five inch mount #2 (about frame 48). His torpedo released just prior to the crash slid across the main deck through the two forward wardroom staterooms and exploded at the edge of the main deck on the starboard side. Gasoline from the plane and the explosion of the torpedo threw flame which enveloped the forward part of the ship. A ruptured bulkhead in the forward fireroom and additional undetermined damage necessitated securing the forward fire room. All engines stopped. Repair parties fighting fires forward. 1500: U.S.S. BENNION came alongside port side to

APPROVED:

S. KINTBERGER, Comdr., U.S.N.   COMMANDING.   Nelson E. SMITH, Lt.(jg), U.S.N.R, NAVIGATOR

Authority NND 80 3052
BY RAM DATE 10/18/82

DECK LOG—ADDITIONAL REMARKS SHEET

PAGE

UNITED STATES SHIP _____ ZELLARS _____ Thursday 12 April 19 45

ADDITIONAL REMARKS

transfer Medical Officer and aid in fighting fires. 1515: All fires under control. Wounded removed from damaged area. 1540: Underway on port engine. Proceeding Kerama Retto Anchorage. Steering from After Steering Station, all compasses battle casualty.

C. A. SMYLIE, Lieut., USN

16-20

1600: Underway as before enroute Kerama Retto Anchorage, Nansei Shoto. 1616: Passed through anti-submarine nets, entered anchorage. 1625: Anchored in berth K-52 on orders from SOPA, CTG 51.15, in 24 fathoms of water with 75 fathoms of chain to the port anchor. Boiler #4 in use for auxiliary purposes. Secured special sea details, set port watch modified by nine (9) man armed sentry watch stationed forward, midships, and aft. 1700: The following casualties were sustained as result of enemy action at 1451, 12 April 1945: BARNES, Owen Calvin, 269384, Lieut.(jg), USNR, Diagnosis: Wound, fragment, shrapnel, right shoulder. Prognosis: Favorable. Disposition: Returned to duty. BIRD, Keith William, 324008, Lieut.(jg), USNR. Diagnosis: Burn, 2nd degree, forehead and right ear; wound, fragment, shrapnel, left thigh. Prognosis: Favorable. Disposition: Returned to duty. BROCKMAN, Earl Edward, 355494, Ensign, USN. Diagnosis: Avulsion, arms and legs. Prognosis: Fatal. Disposition: Died at 1451, 12 April 1945. Body transferred to U. S. Army Graves Registration Service for burial on Zamami Island, Kerama Retto, Nansei Shoto. CLEVELAND, Douglas Derr, 185345, Lieut.(jg), USNR. Diagnosis: Wound, fragment, shrapnel, right hand; Hemorrage, traumatic, left and right internal ear. Prognosis: Favorable. Disposition: Returned to duty. GUNTHER, Wilbert Martin, 328619, Lieut.(jg), USNR. Blown into the water by the explosion; picked up by U.S.S. WEST VIRGINIA aboard which vessel he died of 3rd degree burns. KINCAID, John Franklin, 140233, Lieut. (MC), USN. Diagnosis: Avulsion, complete. Prognosis: Fatal. Disposition: Died at 1451, 12 April 1945. Body transferred to U. S. Army Graves Registration Service for burial on Zamami Island, Kerama Retto, Nansei Shoto. ROBBINS, Spencer E., 165724, Lieut., USN. Diagnosis: Wound, shrapnel, fragment, head, arm, and leg. Prognosis: Favorable. Disposition: Transferred to U.S.S. GOSPER, (APA-170) for treatment. ROBINSON, John Parker, 355943, Ensign, USN. Diagnosis: Wound, fragment, shrapnel, left bicep. Prognosis: Favorable. Disposition: Returned to duty. SOUTHALL, Donald Lee, 333351, Ensign, USNR. Diagnosis: Wound, lacerated forehead. Prognosis: Favorable. Disposition: Returned to duty. ANDERSON, Robert Thomas, 877 83 23, SoM3c(T), USNR. Diagnosis: Amputation, traumatic, left leg. Prognosis: Serious. Disposition: Transferred to U.S.S. GOSPER (APA-170) for treatment. AVRETT, Willard Marshall, 359 87 35, FC1c, USNR. Diagnosis: Fracture, skull, compound. Prognosis: Probably fatal. Disposition: Transferred to U.S.S. GOSPER (APA-170) for treatment. BAKER, Harold Eugene, 671 73 55, S1c, USNR. Diagnosis: Wound, lacerated, right shoulder. Prognosis: Favorable. Disposition: Transferred to U.S.S. GOSPER (APA-170) for treatment. BELL, Leonard Allen, 313 41 27, F1c, USNR. Diagnosis: Wound lacerated left leg. Prognosis: Favorable. Disposition: Transferred to U.S.S. GOSPER (APA-170) for treatment. BERTELSON, William Kenwood, 960 90 09, S1c, USNR. Diagnosis: Wound, lacerated, both legs. Prognosis: Favorable. Disposition: Transferred to U.S.S. GOSPER (APA-170) for treatment. BIEBER, William John, 961 16 03, S2c, USNR. Diagnosis: Burn, 3rd degree, arms, legs, and body. Prognosis: Probably fatal. Disposition: Transferred to U.S.S. GOSPER (APA-170) for treatment. BILYEU, Jimmie McGill, 274 43 19, GM2c, USN. Diagnosis: Sprain, left ankle. Prognosis: Favorable. Returned to duty. BRADLEY, Andrew (n), 296 05 72, StM1c, USN. Diagnosis: Burn, 3rd degree, arms, face, trunk, and legs. Prognosis: Probably fatal. Disposition: Transferred to U.S.S. GOSPER (APA-170) for treatment. BREEN, Neil Peter, 603 91 49, MoMM3c, USNR. Diagnosis: Internal injuries. Prognosis: Serious. Disposition: Transferred to U.S.S. GOSPER (APA-170) for treatment. BROWN, Donald Joseph, 313 68 61, SoM3c(T), USNR. Diagnosis: Fracture, compound, left leg. Prognosis: Favorable. Disposition: Transferred to U.S.S. GOSPER (APA-170) for treatment. BURDETT, Charles Robert, 393 25 99, CCS(T), USN. Diagnosis: Burn, 3rd degree, legs, arms, and trunk. Prognosis: Fatal. Disposition: Died at 1700, 12 April 1945. Body transferred to U.S. Army Graves Registration Service for burial on Zamami Island, Kerama Retto, Nansei Shoto. BUSSE, Emmett Albert, 849 84 92, F1c, USNR. Diagnosis: Smoke Inhalation. Prognosis: Favorable. Disposition: Returned to duty. CADWELL, Harry Norwood, 317 13 60, S2c, USNR. Diagnosis: Burn, 3rd degree, arms and face. Prognosis: Favorable. Disposition: Transferred to U.S.S. GOSPER (APA-170) for treatment. COLEMAN, Henry Stokes, Jr., 644 30 03, SK1c, USNR. Diagnosis: Wound, lacerated, stomach. Prognosis: Serious. Disposition: Transferred to U.S.S. GOSPER (APA-170) for treatment. CRAIG, David Simpson, 891 03 84, S1c, USNR. Diagnosis: Blast, concussion, atmospheric. Prognosis: Fatal. Disposition: Died at 1451, 12 April 1945. Body transferred to U. S. Army Graves Registration Service for burial on Zamami Island, Kerama Retto, Nansei Shoto. CREIGHTON, John Luther, 826 84 71, StM1c, USNR. Diagnosis: Smoke inhalation. Prognosis: Favorable. Disposition: Transferred to U.S.S. GOSPER (APA-170) for treatment. CUSTER, Dallas Howard, 317 13 34, S2c, USNR. Diagnosis: Burn, 2nd degree, right hand and both legs. Prognosis: Favorable. Disposition: Returned to duty. DANKERT, Fred John, 961 03 92, S2c, USNR. Diagnosis: Blast, concussion, atmospheric. Prognosis: Fatal. Disposition: Died at 1451, 12 April 1945. Body transferred to U. S. Army Graves Registration Service for burial on Zamami Island, Kerama Retto, Nansei Shoto. ENSLEY, John Radcliff, 619 24 45, PhM3c, USNR. Diagnosis: Avulsion, complete. Prognosis: Fatal. Disposition: Died at 1451, 12 April 1945. Body transferred to U. S. Army Graves Registration Service for burial on Zamami Island, Kerama Retto, Nansei Shoto. ERICKSON, Lester Oswald, 638 03 25, BM2c, USNR. Diagnosis:

APPROVED:

L. S. KINTBERGER, Comdr., U.S.N.   COMMANDING

EXAMINED:

Ison E. SMITH, Lt.(jg) U.S.N.R.   NAVIGATOR

PAGE _____
NAVPERS 18 (REV. 1-44)

DECK LOG—ADDITIONAL REMARKS SHEET

UNITED STATES SHIP _____ ZELLARS _____ Thursday 12 April 19 45
(Day) (Date) (Month)

ADDITIONAL REMARKS

Burn, 2nd degree, back and neck. Prognosis: Favorable. Disposition: Returned to duty. FERRELL, James Willard, 677 20 69, Flc, USNR. Diagnosis: Avulsion, complete. Prognosis: Fatal. Disposition: Died at 1451, 12 April 1945. Body transferred to U. S. Army Graves Registration Service for burial on Zamami Island, Kerama Retto, Nansie Shoto. FLETCHER, Arthur Longstreet, 668 15 91, EM1c, USNR. Diagnosis: Avulsion, complete. Prognosis: Fatal. Disposition: Died at 1451, 12 April 1945. Body transferred to U. S. Army Graves Registration Service for burial on Zamami Island, Kerama Retto, Nansie Shoto. GEDMAN, Stanley (n), 212 43 28, CTM, USN. Diagnosis: Burn, 3rd degree, complete. Prognosis: Serious. Disposition: Transferred to U.S.S. GOSPER (APA-170) for treatment. GIERER, Robert Walter, 873 31 38, Slc, USNR. Diagnosis: Fracture, compound, left leg. Prognosis: Serious. Disposition: Transferred to U.S.S. GOSPER (APA-170) for treatment. GOLDBERG, Herman Jerry, 624 87 69, 3EM1c, USNR. Diagnosis: Wound lacerated, right eye. Prognosis: Favorable. Disposition: Returned to duty. GOREE, William Aaron, 381 74 76, Slc, USN. Diagnosis: Burn, 3rd degree, right hand. Prognosis: Favorable. Disposition: Transferred to U.S.S. GOSPER (APA-170) for treatment. GRAY, Robert Alven, 945 35 74, Slc, USNR. Diagnosis: Burn, 3rd degree, complete. Prognosis: Fatal. Disposition: Died at 1451, 12 April 1945. Body transferred to U. S. Army Graves Registration Service for burial at Zamami Island, Kerama Retto, Nansie Shoto. HAJICEK, Henry George, 961 20 24, S2c, USNR. Diagnosis: Burn, 3rd degree, arms and face. Prognosis: Favorable. Disposition: Transferred to U.S.S. GOSPER (APA-170) for treatment. HARTIGAN, Matthew Donald, 853 23 87, S2c, USNR. Diagnosis: Burn, 2nd degree, right arm. Prognosis: Favorable. Disposition: Returned to duty. HAWES, Donald Mayo, 924 06 59, ScM3c, USNR. Diagnosis: Blast, concussion, atmospheric. Prognosis: Fatal. Disposition: Died at 1451, 12 April 1945. Body transferred to U. S. Army Graves Registration Service for burial on Zamami Island, Kerama Retto, Nansie Shoto. HARRIS, Charles Franklin, 669 34 84, EM2c, USNR. Diagnosis: Fracture, compound, skull. Prognosis: Probably fatal. Disposition: Transferred to U.S.S. GOSPER (APA-170) for treatment. HOPSON, Wayne William, 888 03 07, ScM3c, USNR. Diagnosis: Ruptured eardrum. Prognosis: Favorable. Disposition: Returned to duty. HORIST, Joseph Anthony, 853 48 42, FC3c, USNR. Diagnosis: Avulsion, complete. Prognosis: Fatal. Disposition: Died at 1451, 12 April 1945. Body transferred to U. S. Army Graves Registration Service for burial on Zamami Island, Kerama Retto, Nansie Shoto. HUGHES, Charles Evans, 849 38 08, Flc(EM), USNR. Diagnosis: Avulsion, complete. Prognosis: Fatal. Disposition: Unable to find body, identification only found. HUMRICHOUSE, Roy LaVern, 662 30 72, Slc, USNR. Diagnosis: Burn, 3rd degree, hands. Prognosis: Favorable. Disposition: Transferred to U.S.S. GOSPER (APA-170) for treatment. JONES, William Francis, 650 46 54, TM2c, USNR. Diagnosis: Avulsion, abdomen. Prognosis: Fatal. Disposition: Died at 1451, 12 April 1945. Body transferred to U.S. Army Graves Registration Service for burial on Zamami Island, Kerama Retto, Nansie Shoto. KAWULA, Julius Ferdinand, 622 17 40, Slc, U3NR. Diagnosis: Wound, lacerated, leg. Prognosis: Favorable. Disposition: Transferred to U.S.S. GOSPER (APA-170) for treatment. KEANE, Clair Victor, 973 08 91, S2c, USNR. Diagnosis: Blast, concussion, atmospheric. Prognosis: Fatal. Disposition: Died at 1451, 12 April 1945. Body transferred to U.S. Army Graves Registration Service for burial on Zamami Island, Kerama Retto, Nansie Shoto. KIEFERLE, Frank Morris, 945 38 32, S2c, USNR. Diagnosis: Burn, 3rd degree, complete. Prognosis: Serious. Disposition: Transferred to U.S.S. GOSPER (APA-170) for treatment. KING, Alfred Owen, 756 05 33, Slc, USN. Diagnosis: Blast, concussion atmospheric. Prognosis: Fatal. Disposition: Died at 1451, 12 April 1945. Body transferred to U.S. Army Graves Registration Service for burial on Zamami Island, Nansie Shoto. KRAMER, John Aberhardt, 368 47 07, BM1c, USN. Diagnosis: Blast, concussion atmospheric. Prognosis: Fatal. Disposition: Died at 1451, 12 April 1945. Body transferred to U.S. Army Graves Registration Service for burial on Zamami Island, Kerama Retto, Nansie Shoto. KROMBAR, Emmett John, 810 40 55, Flc, USNR. Diagnosis: Wound, lacerated scalp. Prognosis: Favorable. Disposition: Returned to duty. LEE, William Lavaral, 964 47 87, S2c, USNR. Diagnosis: Burn, 2nd degree, both hands. Prognosis: Favorable. Disposition: Returned to duty. LEVITZ, Eugene Jerry, 563 64 89, BFlc, USNR. Diagnosis: Burn, 3rd degree, face, arms and back. Prognosis: Favorable. Disposition: Transferred to U.S.S. GOSPER (APA-170) for treatment. LIBK, Eddie Loren, 357 20 02, Slc, USNR. Diagnosis: Sprain, right ankle. Prognosis: Favorable. Disposition: Returned to duty. LISTON, John Walter, Jr., 393 76 66, Slc, USN. Diagnosis: Blast, concussion atmospheric. Prognosis: Fatal. Disposition: Died at 1451, 12 April 1945. Body transferred to U.S. Army Graves Registration Service for burial on Zamami Island, Kerama Retto, Nansie Shoto. LOVO, Floyd Robert, 879 13 89, RT2c, USNR. Diagnosis: Back injury. Prognosis: Serious. Disposition: Transferred to U.S.S. GOSPER (APA-170) for treatment. MARMON, Chester Garfield, 961 14 31, Slc, USNR. Diagnosis: Avulsion, complete. Prognosis: Fatal. Disposition: Died at 1451, 12 April 1945. Body transferred to U. S. Army Graves Registration Service for burial on Zamami Island, Kerama Retto, Nansie Shoto. MC LEOD, Richard Eugene, 250 57 71, GM3c, USN. Diagnosis: Amputation, right leg. Prognosis: Serious. Disposition: Transferred to U.S.S. GOSPER (APA-170) for treatment. MERRIMAN, Jack Lewis, 888 30 56, Flc, USNR. Diagnosis: Avulsion complete. Prognosis: Fatal. Disposition: Died. Body could not be found, identification only found. MOHR, John Richard, 815 24 96, FC(R)3c(T), USNR. Diagnosis: Avulsion, complete. Prognosis: Fatal. Disposition: Body could not be found, identification only found. MOORE, Howard James, 860 76 67, Slc, USNR. Diagnosis: Blast, concussion atmospheric. Prognosis: Fatal. Disposition: Died at 1451, 12 April 1945. Body transferred to U. S. Army Graves Registration Service for burial on Zamami Island, Kerama Retto, Nansie Shoto. MURPHY, Raymond John, 961 19 26, S2c, USNR. Diagnosis: Blast, concussion, atmospheric. Prognosis: Fatal. Disposition: Died at 1451, 12 April 1945. Body transferred to U. S. Army Graves Registration Service for burial on Zamami Island, Kerama Retto, Nansie Shoto. NAVA Juan Longoria, 624 17 20, SC1c, USNR. Diagnosis: Burn, 3rd degree, complete. Prognosis: Fatal. Disposition: Died at 1451, 12 April 1945. Body transferred to U. S. Army Graves Registration Service, for burial on Zamami Island, Kerama Retto, Nansie Shoto. PEDEGANA, William John, 890 15 05, RM3c, USNR. Diagnosis: Sprain of the back. Prognosis: Favorable. Disposition: Returned to duty. PITTS, Elvin Esthler, Jr., 658 09 60, Cox, USNR. Diagnosis:

APPROVED:

L. S. KINTBERGER, Comdr., U.S.N.
COMMANDING.

EXAMINED:

SMITH, Lt. (jg) U.S.N.R. NAVIGATOR

103

UNITED STATES SHIP	ZELLARS	Thursday	12	April	1945
		(Day)	(Date)	(Month)	

ADDITIONAL REMARKS

Avulsion, complete. Prognosis: Fatal. Disposition: Body could not be found, identification only found. PORTER, Paul Wayne, Jr., 975 62 80, MaM3c, USNR. Diagnosis: Wound, fragment, shrapnel, left cheek. Prognosis: Favorable. Disposition: Returned to duty. POTTER, Paul Leslie, 973 08 31, S2c, USNR. Diagnosis: Burn, 3rd degree, complete. Prognosis: Fatal. Disposition: Transferred to U.S.S. GOSPER (APA-170) for treatment. REA, Earl Franklin, 942 41 95, S1c, USNR. Diagnosis: Fracture, compound, left leg. Prognosis: Serious. Disposition: Transferred to U.S.S. GOSPER (APA-170) for treatment. ROACH, Billy Joe, 356 75 70, FC1c, USN. Diagnosis: Avulsion, complete. Prognosis: Fatal. Disposition: Body could not be found, identification only found. ROHLFER, Kermit "Q", FC2c, 613 17 84, USNR. Diagnosis: Fracture, compound, skull. Prognosis: Probably fatal. Disposition: Transferred to U.S.S. GOSPER (APA-170) for treatment. SEAIS, Fred (n), 887 37 35, StM2c, USNR. Diagnosis: Smoke inhalation. Prognosis: Favorable. Disposition: Transferred to U.S.S. GOSPER (APA-170) for treatment. SHULMAN, Lester Michael, 814 90 18, MM3c(T), USNR. Diagnosis: (Unknown). Prognosis: Probably fatal. Disposition: Missing in action. SIMS, John Burnett, 633 31 45, ScM2c, USNR. Diagnosis: Wound, lacerated, both legs. Prognosis: Favorable. Disposition: Transferred to U.S.S. GOSPER, (APA-170) for treatment. SIRES, Charles Alfred, 888 23 02, RdM3c(T), USNR. Diagnosis: Wound, lacerated, left hand. Prognosis: Favorable. Disposition: Transferred to U.S.S. GOSPER (APA-170) for treatment. SOMMERFIELD, Raymond Joseph, 611 81 79, B2c, USNR. Diagnosis: Wound, fragment, shrapnel, left arm and leg. Prognosis: Favorable. Disposition: Returned to duty. THOMPSON, Ernest Richard, 861 92 13, S2c, USNR. Diagnosis: (Unknown.) Prognosis: Probably fatal. Disposition: Missing in action. THOMPSON, Wilfred Clarence, 971 77 68, S1c, USNR. Diagnosis: Wound, fragment, shrapnel. Prognosis: Favorable. Disposition: Returned to duty. TRAEGER, Casper Winston, Jr., 842 83 11, ScM2c(T), USNR. Diagnosis: Fracture, compound, right leg. Prognosis: Favorable. Disposition: Transferred to U.S.S. GOSPER (APA-170) for treatment. VON HINKEN, Frederick Herman, Jr., 710 63 90, FC3c, USNR. Diagnosis: Wound, lacerated scalp. Prognosis: Favorable. Disposition: Transferred to U.S.S. GOSPER, (APA-170) for treatment. WADE, Clarence Wilbur, 372 21 79, SC3c, USNR. Diagnosis: Fracture, compound left femur. Prognosis: Favorable. Disposition: Transferred to U.S.S. GOSPER (APA-170) for treatment. WALLACE, Walter (n), 637 25 28, St2c, USNR. Diagnosis: Burn, 3rd degree, complete. Prognosis: Fatal. Disposition: Died at 1451, 12 April 1945. Body transferred to U. S. Army Graves Registration Service for burial at Zamami Island, Kerama Retto, Nansie Shoto. WHITE, Roy Clayton, 840 80 29, GM3c, USNR. Diagnosis: Burn, 3rd degree, both hands. Prognosis: Favorable. Disposition: Transferred to U.S.S. GOSPER (APA-170) for treatment. WATT, Samuel Vance, 648 22 20, Y1c, USNR. Diagnosis: Fracture, compound, skull. Prognosis: Probably fatal. Disposition: Transferred to U.S.S. GOSPER (APA-170) for treatment. WHITLOW, Glen Edward, 293 02 28, F2c, USNR. Diagnosis: Smoke inhalation. Prognosis: Favorable. Disposition: Transferred to U.S.S. GOSPER (APA-170) for treatment. WILLIS, Orville Hannaford, 201 24 93, BM1c, USN. Diagnosis: Blast, concussion, atmospheric. Prognosis: Fatal. Disposition: Died at 1451, 12 April 1945. Body transferred to U. S. Army Registration Service for burial at Zamami Island, Kerama Retto, Nansie Shoto. WOLF, Paul Joseph, 961 04 04, S2c, USNR. Diagnosis: Fracture, compound, skull. Prognosis: Probably fatal. Disposition: Transferred to U.S.S. GOSPER (APA-170) for treatment. WOOTEN, Fred Junior, 680 49 21, S1c, USNR. Diagnosis: Blast, concussion, atmospheric. Prognosis: Fatal. Disposition: Died at 1451, 12 April 1945. Body transferred to U. S. Army Graves Registration Service for burial at Zamami Island, Kerama Retto, Nansie Shoto. WYATT, Chester Lawerence, 883 89 40, S2c, USNR. Diagnosis: Blast, concussion, atmospheric. Prognosis: Fatal. Disposition: Died at 1451, 12 April 1945. Body transferred to U. S. Army Graves Registration Service for burial at Zamami Island, Kerama Retto, Nansie Shoto. WYCKOFF, Harold Roger, 382 32 61, ScM2c(T), USN. Diagnosis: Fracture, compound, both legs. Prognosis: Favorable. Disposition: Transferred to U.S.S. GOSPER (APA-170) for treatment. YOUNG, William Lamar, 893 40 06, S1c, USNR. Diagnosis: Dislocation, left knee. Prognosis: Favorable. Disposition: Transferred to U.S.S. GOSPER (APA-170) for treatment. The following damage was sustained as a result of enemy action, 12 April 1945: Mount 2 jammed in train, adjacent powder hoist and rotating rack damaged and jammed. Compartments A-409-& A-411, A-410, A-404M, A-405M, A-503A, B-0103M, B-0101E, A-101CLM, A-305L, A-303BL, A-205L, A-204-5L partially or completely flooded. Compartments A-307-E, A-207-1L, A-207-3A, A-102-L, A-101-L, A-103-L, . , A-105, A-106-T, and A-101-CLM completely or essentially demolished; all equipment contained therein destroyed. Compartments B-1-1, B-1-3, B-101-L, B-102-E, B-105-E, A-101-CLM, A-205-L, A-206-C, A-305-CL, A-3-F, A-4-F, A-505-F, A-507-F, A-509-F, A-5-VF damaged to various extents. Longitudinals:

NUMBER	LEVEL	FRAME	FRAME	REMARKS
2 Port	Maindeck		at 60	Buckled
1 Centerline	Maindeck		at 60	Parted
2 Starboard	Maindeck		at 60	Buckled
3 Starboard	Maindeck	60 to	73	Buckled
4 Starboard	Maindeck	60 to	75	Buckled
5-7-6-8 Starboard	1st platform and maindeck	56 to	72	Buckled or missing
Sheer Strake	Maindeck	54 to	73	Buckled or missing
12½ Starboard		65 to	68	Holed
13 Starboard		62 to	68	Missing
13½ Starboard		60 to	72	Missing
14 Starboard		54 to	72	Missing

APPROVED:

T. S. KIMBERGER, Comdr., U.S.N. COMMAND:

EXAMINED:

Glen E. SMITH, Lt. (jg)., R.

104

DECK LOG — ADDITIONAL REMARKS SHEET

UNITED STATES SHIP _____ ZELLARS _____ Thursday 12 April , 19 45
                                                    (Day)   (Date) (Month)

ADDITIONAL REMARKS

Number	Level	Frame	Frame	Remarks
₵ Plus 1-2-3-4 Starboard	1st platform	60 to	72	Buckled

Frames; and Decks:

Frame number	Level	From	To	Remarks
60 to 72	First Platform	Centerline	Skin	Missing or buckled
48	Maindeck	At Centerline		Possibly damaged
58 to 74	Maindeck	Centerline	Skin	Missing or buckled
46 to 52	Maindeck	Centerline Supporting #2 barbette		Warped
41½ to 75	Superdeck	Full Width		Missing or badly damaged
75½	Maindeck	Stbd. Skin	Long'l 5 Stbd.	Twisted
79	Maindeck	Stbd. Skin	Long'l 5 Stbd.	Twisted

Bulkheads: 1. All bulkheads on or above maindeck between frames 41 and 72. 2. All bulkheads enclosing A-206-C and B-1-3 buckled. 3. Bulkheads enclosing fuel tanks A-3-F, A-4-F, A-505-F, A-507-F, A-509-F, and A-5-VF ruptured or bowed. 4. Bulkhead 60 between second platform deck and maindeck from centerline to starboard skin. 5. Bulkhead 72 between second platform deck and maindeck from centerline to starboard skin. 6. Bulkhead along longitudinal 5 starboard between main and superstructure deck forward of frame 90. 7. Bulkhead along longitudinal 5 port between main and superstructure deck forward of frame 80. 8. Sheet metal bulkheads and vertical stiffeners in Laundry (B-109-E), Sick Bay (B-108-AL) and Engineer Office. Shell plating: Frame 56 to 72, starboard skin, from longitudinal 13 starboard up to sheer strake missing; probably must be replaced down to longitudinal 12 starbbard. No significant underwater damage apparent but a slight crack, not located, is believed to be in starboard skin in compartment A-409-M. Other and miscellaneous damage as follows: Extensive wiring damage throughout afflicted area. Director off roller path. Additional damage undetermined. Computer probably beyond repair. Gyrocompass beyond repair. QGA Sonar Console units and chemical recorder demolished. Fathometer and Loran Gear damaged. Dead Reckoning Tracer and Analyzer damaged. Pit Log damaged beyond repair. Piping and ventilation systems throughout damaged area to be replaced. Degaussing cable out between frames 60 and 72 starboard and oil soaked both port and starboard in compartment A-205-L. Diesel Generator and all equipment in A-307 demolished. Scullery and equipment demolished. Many radio and radar units damaged. Brickwork damaged in numbers 1 and 2 boilers. 1919: DE-185 alongside to port. Moored starboard side to with six (6) six inch (6") manila lines doubled.

Arthur LINDH, Lieut., USNR

20-24
2000: Anchored as before.

D. D. CLEVELAND, Lt.(jg), USNR

APPROVED:

L. S. KINTBERGER, Comdr., U S N   COMMANDING.   Nelson E. SMITH, Lt.(jg), U S N R.   NAVIGATOR

USS ZELLARS (DD777)

OKINAWA, APRIL 12, 1945

Sunset and evening star, and one clear call for
May there be no moaning of the bar,
When I put out to sea.

AVRETT, WILLARD M.	FC1c	359-87-35	USNR
BIEBER, WILLIAM J.	S2c	961-16-03	USNR
BRADLEY, ANDREW.	StM1c	296-05-72	USNR
BROCKMAN, EARL E.	Ens.	355494	USN
BURDETT, CHARLES R,	CCS.	393-25-99	USN
COLEMAN, HENRY S.	SK1c.	644-30-03	USNR
CRAIG, DAVID.S.	S1c.	891-03-84	USNR
DANKERT, FRED J.	S2c.	961-03-92	USNR
ENSLEY, JOHN R.	PhM3c.	619-24-45	USNR
FERRALL, JAMES W.	F1c.	677-20-69	USNR
FLETCHER, ARTHUR L.	EM1c.	668-15-91	USNR
GEDMAN, STANLEY.	CTM.	212-43-28	USN
GRAY, ROBERT A.	S1c.	945-35-74	USNR
GUNTHER, WILBERT M.	LTjg.	328619	USNR
HARRIS, CHARLES F.	EM2c.	669-34-84	USNR
HORST, JOSEPH A.	FC3c.	853-48-42	USNR
HAWES, DONALD M.	SoM3c.	924-06-59	USNR
HUGHES, CHARLES E.	F1c,(EM).	849-38-08	USNR
JONES, WILLIAM F.	TM2c.	650-46-54	USNR
KEANE, CLAIR V.	S2c.	973-08-91	USNR
KINKAID, JOHN F.	LT (MD).	140233	USN
KING, ALFRED O.	S1c.	756-05-33	USN
KRAMER, JOHN A.	BM1c.	368-47-07	USN
LISTON, JOHN W.	S1c.	393-76-66	USN
MARMON, CHESTER G.	S1c.	961-14-31	USNR
MERRIMAN, CHESTER L.	F1c.	888-30-56	USNR
MOHR, JOHN R.	FC(R)3c.	815-24-96	USNR
MOORE, HOWARD J.	S1c.	860-76-67	USNR

MURPHY, RAYMOND J.	S2c.	961-19-26	USNR
NAVA, JUAN L.	SC1c.	624-17-20	USNR
PITTS, ELVIN E.	Cox.	658-09-60	USNR
POTTER, PAUL L.	S2c.	973-08-31	USNR
ROACH, BILLY JOE.	FC1C.	356-75-70	USN
ROHLFER, KERMIT G.	FC2c.	613-17-84	USNR
SHULMAN, LESTER M.	MM3c.	814-90-18	USNR
THOMPSON, ERNEST R.	S2c.	861-92-13	USNR
WALLACE, WALTER.	St2c.	637-25-28	USNR
WATT, SAMUEL V.	Y1c.	648-22-20	USNR
WILBANKS, DWIGHT H.	F1c.	973-15-36	USNR
WILLIS, ERVILLE H.	BM1c.	201-24-93	USN
WOLF, PAUL J.	S2c.	961-04-04	USNR
WOOTEN, FRED J.	S1c.	680-49-21	USNR
WYATT, CHESTER L.	S2c.	883-89-40	USNR
YOUNG, WILLIAM L.	S1c.	893-40-06	USNR

We Remember Them

At the rising of the sun and at it's going down,
we remember them.

 At the blowing of the wind and in the chill of the winter,
 we remember them.

At the opening of the buds and in the rebirth of spring
we remember them.

 At the shining of the sun and in the warmth of summer,
 we remember them.

At the rustling of the leaves and in the beauty of autumn,
we remember them.

 At the beginning of the year and at it's end,
 we remember them.

As long as we live, they too will live; for now they are a part of us,
we remember them.

 When we are wary and in need of strength,
 we remember them.

When we are lost and sick at heart,
we remember them.

 When we have joy we crave to share,
 we remember them.

When we have decisions that are difficult to make,
we remember them.

 When we have achievements that are based on theirs,
 we remember them.

As long as we live, they too live; for they are now a part of us,
we remember them.

sylvan kamens & jack riemer

USS ZELLARS (DD777)

Ship's Crew, Wounded on April 12, 1945

BARNES, ARTHUR H.	S1c	378-78-82 USNR
BARNES, OWEN CALVIN	Lieut (jg)	269984-USNR.
BIRD, KEITH WILLIAM	Lieut (jg)	324008-USNR
CLEVELAND, DOUGLAS	Lieut (jg)	185345-USNR
ROBBINS, SPENCER E.	Lieut.	165724-USN
ROBINSON, JOHN P.	Ens.	355943-USN
SOUTHALL, DONALD L.	Esn.	333351-USNR
ANDERSON, ROBERT T.	SoM3c	877-83-23-USNR
BAKER, HAROLD E.	S1c	671-73-55-USNR
BELL, LEONARD A.	F1c	313-41-27-USNR
BERTLESON, WILLIAM K.	S1c	960-90-09-USNR
BILYEU, JIMMIE M.	GM2c	274-43-19-USN
BREEN, NEIL P.	MoMM3c	603-91-49-USNR
BROWN, DONALD J.	SoM3c	313-68-61-USNR
BUSSE, EMMITT A.	F1c	849-84-92-USNR
CADWELL, HARRY N.	S2c	317-13-60-USNR
CREIGHTON, JOHN L.	StM1c	826-84-71-USNR
CUSTER, DALLAS H.	S2c	317-13-34-USNR
ERICKSON, LESTER O.	BM2c	638-03-25-USNR
GIERER, ROBERT W.	S1c	873-31-38-USNR
GOLDBERG, HERMAN J.	StM1c	624-87-69-USNR
GOREE, WILLIAM A.	S1c	381-74-76-USN
HAJICEK, HENRY G.	S2c	961-20-24-USNR
HARTIGAN, MATHEW D.	S2c	853-23-87-USNR
HOPSON, WAYNE W.	SoM2c	888-03-07-USNR

HUMRICHOUSE, ROY L.	S1c	662-30-72-USNR
KAWULA, JULIUS F.	S1c	622-17-40-USNR
KDEFERLE, FRANK M.	S2c	945-38-32-USNR
KROMBAR, EMMETT J.	F1c	810-40-58-USNR
LEVITZ, EUGENE J.	SFic	563-64-89-USNR
LISK, EDDIE L.	S1c	357-20-02-USNR
LOVO, FLOYD R.	RT2c	879-13-89-USNR
MCLEOD, RICHARD E.	GM3c	250-57-71-USN
PEDEGANA, WILLIAM J.	RM3c	890-15-05-USNR
PETTERSON, VERILYN H.	F1c	306-69-94
REA, EARL F.	S1c	942-41-95-USNR
SALDANO, CENERO	52C	619-42-61
SEALS, FRED.	STM2c	887-37-35-USNR
SIMS, JOHN B.	SoM2c	633-31-45-USNR
SIRES, CHARLES A.	RdM3c	888-23-02-USNR
SOMMERFIELD, RAY.	B2c	611-81-79-USNR
THOMPSON, WILFORD C.	S1c	971-77-68-USNR
TRAEGER, CASPER W.	SoM2c	842-83-11-USNR
VON HINKEN, FRED H.	Fc3c	**710**-63-90-USNR
WADE, CLARENCE W.	SC3c	372-21-79-USNR
WHITE, ROY C.	GM3c	840-80-29-USNR
WHITLOW, GLEN E.	F2c	293-02-28-USNR
WYCKOFF, HAROLD R.	SoM2c	382-32-61-USN

20 OF THE 45 SHIPMATES THAT WERE WOUNDED. Left to right, back row. First enlisted man, Mat HARTIGAN S2c, fifth Harold BAKER Slc, sixth, Les ERICKSON, BM2c, ninth, Dallas CUSTER S2c, tenth, Lt. (jg) K.W. BIRD. None of the shipmates in front row were identified.

The ZELLARS had her own ***PURPLE HEART*** gang. The only thing to be real proud of was that they were survivors of April 12.

From officers to seamen, no rate or rank missed the devastating blast of the Kamikaze. As written earlier, a number of shipmates died after leaving the ship. Those who were wounded and moved to the hospital ships could not be photographed.

A newspaper clipping used the word "hero" in addressing outstanding deeds preformed by many shipmates. In looking back to April 12, 1945, there were so many life saving efforts by the whole crew that the word "hero" would apply to many.

Regardless, the medical emergency aid Lt. (jg) BIRD gave was of an extraordinary measure. The ship's doctor, Lt. J. F KINKAID, MD, had been killed along with PhM3c John ENSLEY. The remaining medical service was the Chief Pharmacist mate, Carl HIRST in the aft emergency medical space of the aft Chief quarters, and another PhM2c, W.L. GOGAN stationed amidships.

HEROES — Lt. (jg) K. W. Bird, left, saved lives by performing surgical operations when ship's surgeon was killed. Comdr. L. S. Kintberger, right, commanding officer

Lt. (jg) Bird removed a badly mangled leg from a shipmate, which had to take great courage and nerve. He did what had to be done in order to save a life.

Lt.(jg) Bird had also been wounded and still, like many other wounded, was more concerned about others who were more seriously hurt. The true measure of a shipmate and very fine officer.

The ammunition handlers whose GQ duties were to hand powder and projectiles up from the magazine hoist into the ready barbet of the mount were either killed outright or suffered serious burns. The torpedo tore thru the forward officers' quarters, the officers' wardroom and exploded on the starboard side just above the scullery.

As the torpedo exploded on the starboard side, it dismantled the officers' wardroom killing everyone stationed there. The ship's scullery, along with the starboard 20MM guns and crews, on the sheer strake deck just aft of mount two, starboard side, simply just disappeared.

Shredded steel tore about the ship killing and wounding a number of the crew from bow to stern. Shipmates whose GQ station was aft of the number 2 stack had legs cut and TM2c JONES was cut in half by flying metal. There wasn't a secure place on topside of the ship. It was a great wonder that many more of the crew were not killed or wounded.

Below the main deck, along with the scullery, the plotting room hatch and bulkhead were smashed, the main battery computer and stable clement all were totally damaged. In the plotting room all but one firecontrolman were killed, including the firecontrol officer, Ensign F.C BROCKMAN. The lone survivor was Fred VON HINKEN, FC 3/c. He had serious wounds about his legs and was in great shock.

Below the scullery deck, the emergency power generator was torn from it's stand and turned about 90 degrees. The lone electrician's mate in the room was slightly wounded and covered with diesel oil. The bulkhead leading into the crews' mess deck was blown out of shape and driven into the crews' mess.

The intensity of the blast to the plotting room was so great that several of the firecontrolmen completely disappeared. JOHN MOHR'S, FC3c, only remains were his dog tags. He had to be standing just inside of the hatch in front of the computer when the explosion took place.

On the port side of the bridge, the sheer strake deck, the two 20MM guns and crew were blasted and sprayed by the burning Jap plane's fuel as they attempted to man their GQ station. GM MURO was about half way up the ladder when the plane hit. It blew him to the bottom of the ladder onto the

main deck. The side of the ship from the back of mount 2 to the outer bulkhead of 40MM gun mount 42 was blackened from the fire. The weather break saved more crew members from being burned.

Part of the forward boiler room bulkhead was also torn away exposing the high pressure line and the main fuel supply storage. Much of the ship's connecting electrical wiring was shredded and out of service. The outer hull had been torn out down to within several inches of the water line. Another couple of inches and all the crew would have gotten wet.

Several crew members inside of mount 2 were also burned. The 5" gun was jammed pointing outboard toward where the oncoming Jap planes were first seen. (It remained stuck there.) Gas fire from the plane covered almost all of the port side from mount 1 5" gun, back to the weather break below the 40MM gun mount 42.

The officers, ward room was the ship's number 1 medical emergency support station and as such, had the ship's medical doctor, a 3rd class pharmacist mate and the main body of the damage control party. As the explosion took place, everyone in the ward room was killed. Lt KINKAID, MD, Phm 3/c ENSLEY, BMI/c KRAMER and all others.

Standing in the hatchway, where the plotting room hatch had been, looking out through shredded steel main beams of the starboard outer hull, the islands of Kerama Retto seemed to be out of place in the middle of such an anchorage of death and disaster for our Navy ships. It was very difficult to

understand how the ship was so badly wounded from one blast. Down at the foot of this mess, was the remains of the emergency diesel generator.

As the Jap planes were coming in, crewmen on the port side, seeing what was about to happen, all ran thru the midships' passageway to the starboard side. As they reached the starboard side, some ran forward and some ran aft. All who ran forward ran straight into the torpedo blast and were killed or badly wounded. Where the weather break had been was a torn blackened scene of ripped metal overlooking a gaping burning hole in the deck.

The ship's outer hull, starboard side, was blown away down to about one foot of the water. All the devastation was not up forward. Back on the aft torpedo tubes, WILLIAM JONES TM2/c was cut in half by a piece of one of the starboard 20MM guns' base mount that had traveled over the ship and struck him as he attempted to secure himself under his tubes. Leonard BELL, F1/c, a 20MM gunner on the starboard side just aft of mount 43 was struck about the legs by flying metal and received serious wounds.

Paul GOWEN, GM 3/c, Darold JORGENSEN, S1/c, P.K. WATSON, GM 1/c and several others laid BELL on a 20MM ammunition ready box and rendered first aid. It was stated that BELL's greatest concern as he lay there wounded was, "Are we sinking?"

As all the forward fire fighting and damage control effort was going on, there was one more Jap plane determined to hit the wounded ZELLARS. It had a course toward the very stern and changed its mind, winging almost over the stern, in it's attempt to hit the ship in the area of the number 2 stack. P.K. WATSON had made his way up to two 20MM guns alongside the number 2 stack and as he said later, "I sent the SOB to Jap hell." He took over one of the 20MMs and downed the plane just a few hundred yards from the ship. Had the Jap plane hit where it seemed he was aiming, it would have killed some 40 to 50 more crew.

As the ship was hit, all power was lost and no guns had power to operate except the 20MM. Without a word being said or a command being given, all crewmen who could leave their GQ stations went to work fighting the fire, rescuing the wounded and retrieving those of the crew that had been killed. It seemed that the ship had dead and dying all over the stern. Shipmates carrying a friend to the stern for medical aid, and others with tears in their eyes, gently holding the body of a special friend, moved cautiously to the stern.

On the bridge the same struggle was going on. Harold BUCK, TM 1/c, was on the port side of the bridge. As he saw that the plane was going to hit the ship, he quickly went to the starboard side just as all hell broke loose. Smoke and flames bellowed up on both sides of the bridge. "I was aware that a man was wounded and moaning beside me. I and, I think, TM 1/c KENNEDY put him in the Captain's sea cabin and gave him morphine."

They then left to give help down on the main deck. They grabbed fire hoses and moved forward, fighting the fire on the port side. Per BUCK, he remembers the Captain leaning over the bridge and yelling "put that fire out." Next, he found Chief torpedoman STANLEY GEDMAN on the deck next to the torpedo shack badly burned and wounded. He made him as comfortable as he could. And also remembers passing where the galley had been and saw the doors torn off the oven and trays of baking chicken scattered all over the deck. It was a long, long day.

ROGER HAYES, QM 2/c watched as the suicide plane came screaming toward his position, He could see the ZELLARS, 40MM rounds going into the Jap plane's cockpit and he was sure the plane's crew had been killed. After the plane hit, he left the bridge and went below to the chart house. There he found DON BROWN, SOM 3/c, with a broken leg and bleeding. Struggling, he piggy backed Brown down the port ladder which had been badly damaged and was blown out and very hot. He carried BROWN to the fantail for medical aid, made sure he was in good hands with CPM HIRST. HIRST asked HAYES if he had been wounded. HAYES had blood on his back and head,. It was BROWN's blood.

Every crewman that could did everything to help with the wounded. A 2nd class from engineering, with hand badly burned, sat in the aft officers passageway mixing plasma. When asked if another crewman could do that for him, he gruffly replied, "this is may job, go get your own." There were not just a few so-called "heroes," every man on the ship as far as the ship was concerned, was more than a hero.

BARNES, SI/c, left his mount 43 gun director station because of the loss of power, and rushed up the port side to the burning area. Just forward of the weather break he joined Gunnersmate 1/c KUZMICH, who was attempting to roll the engine of the Jap plane over the port side. One of the Jap crewmen was molded to the cylinders, which made for one horrible site. Even with BARNES help, the engine was too heavy to roll over. Another crewman from the forward part of the ship lent a hand to dispose of the gruesome piece of airplane junk. As the remains of the plane hit the water, KUZMICH noted that BARNES had some blood on his forehead and commented, "Did you get hit? You have some blood on your head." BARNES had a thin cut along the bridge of his nose to the center of his forehead and had not felt any pain. He was not aware of having been hit and felt that he had most likely bumped into a sharp piece of torn metal during the removal of the Jap plane's engine.

BARNES was very concerned for his friend WILLIAM BIEBER, SI/c, who was one of the ammunition passers for the barbet of mount 2. After helping remove the Jap plane engine, he went forward where the suicide plane had hit and found BIEBER standing just forward of the mount. His shirt, face, hands and arms were burned but he showed no more serious wounds. It was a great shock to learn later in the day that he had been transferred to the hospital ship where he had died.

Shipmates confirmed that he had escaped the burning gas and exploding ammunition only to charge back into the burning hell to rescue several of his shipmates who shared the same duty. It was later learned that he had received the Navy Cross for giving his life trying to save his shipmates. He had ingested very hot flames that burned his lungs so badly that it was impossible for him to breathe. He was married and had small children. His action was one of the most significant deeds of heroism that one person could give to another.

The ZELLARS regained power and struggled into the Anchorage of Kerama Retto. The real hard work began. A landing craft came along the ship's stern and the ZELLARS crew, with many tears, began off-loading their dead shipmates onto the craft. Army Graves Registrations would take the remains to be buried on Zamami Island, part of the Kerama Retto group. The number of shipmates killed onboard was 36. A number of the wounded who were transferred to the hospital ship died later. (The final number of shipmates killed was 44.)

Special watches had to be set due to Jap's swimming out to the ships in the anchorage, climbing on board and killing some of the crew. This had happened before the ZELLARS became part of the "ships' hospital." All of the wounded ships were anchored in close to the beaches of the island. The rest of April 12 was a somber time for all left on board. The ZELLARS tied up alongside DE. 185. The ZELLARS' galley was a mess and the DE generously provided meal service. The ZELLARS provided some of the food stores and also some of the galley help.

As the night of April 12 came to a close, small groups of the remaining crew gathered topside, on the fantail, on the 01 deck near the two quad 40MM guns, and down on the main deck near the depth charge "K" guns. They found it difficult to control their pain in losing so many of their special shipmates. They would linger for a few moments and as they attempted to make some sense of the problem, and were not too successful, would slowly join another group that was doing much the same. It seemed that each different group that moved about the ship, would receive some comfort from the different faces and were grateful that they could share the same pain. One would slowly walk up the starboard side of the ship to midship, cross through the midship passageway to the port side, back to the stern, meeting other shipmates doing the same. Walking off the anger or the hurt or whatever. The hollowed look on each man's face expressed his personal loss. It did not explain the loss, just expressed it.

Not many of the crew slept that night.

April 13, 1945

April 13 began a rough and difficult day of recovery. No one assigned a crew member to a certain task. Cleanup was everyone's responsibility and where hands were needed they just appeared. The greatest task was on the starboard side. The gaping hole in the deck had to have all the jagged torn metal material removed. The outer hull, or where the torn part of the outer hull had been, had to be trimmed so that repairs could be made. A very important space, the galley, had to be put back in some kind of order so that the crew could be fed. There was a mountain of heavy cleaning to be done.

The photo on the following page shows part of the open main deck and the second deck down to the emergency diesel room, details the extent of the damage to the starboard side of the ship. The open part of the forward boiler room shows how close the blast came to rupturing the main high pressure steam line which could have doomed the ZELLARS. It is estimated that if it had ruptured, it would have blown past the water line, flooding all the forward boiler room.

The twisted flange of metal lying against the side of the bridge was part of the deck where two 20MM guns and crews had been. All were lost.

Down the deck, about where the welding tank stands, is where the starboard weather break was and just past the break, the torpedo shack.

The straight edge of the outer hull on bottom left is about 10 to 12 inches above the water line.

One of the results of the explosion was the twisting of the port ladder leading up to the sheer strike deck, the two 20MM guns, CIC, Commodore's cabin, and the inside ladder to the bridge.

The open hatch is at the weather break going forward to the bow. Remember, the ladder is on the port side of the ship and the blast was on the starboard side. The ladder is outside of the officers' ward room.

It was mentioned that part of a 20MM gun base was exploded over the ship and cut TM 2/c JONES in half. He was stationed on the aft torpedo tubes. The piece that struck Jones came from this 20MM gun base of the starboard guns (right).

CONFIDENTIAL

NAVPERS-134 (REV. 1-44)

DECK LOG—REMARKS SHEET

PAGE _271-45_

UNITED STATES SHIP _____ ZELLARS _____ Saturday 14 April , '45
(Day) (Date) (Month)

0–4
0000: Moored in Kerama Retto, Nansei Shoto, Berth 56, portside to U.S.S. MULLANY bow to stern
with six (6) manila lines doubled. Boiler #3 steaming for auxiliary purposes. Ships is darkened, armed sentries posted on bow, midships, and fantail. SOPA Commander, Task Group 51.15.

Nelson E. SMITH, Lt.(jg), USNR

4–8
0400: Moored as before. 0608: Sunrise, lighted ship. Secured armed sentries.

B. D. FREEMAN, Ens., USN

8–12
0800: Moored as before. 0840: Mustered crew at quarters; no absentees. 1128: Called crew to
General Quarters, enemy planes in the vicinity. Set condition Affirm. Made routine inspection of
magazines and smokeless powders samples; conditions normal. 1145: Set material condition Baker.
1150: Secured from General Quarters, set condition of readiness III.

J. P. ROBINSON, Ens., USN

12–16
1200: Moored as before. 1446: BUSSEE, Emmett Albert, 849 84 92, Flc(MM), USNR transferred to
U.S.S. GOSPER, (APA-170) for medical treatment, with pay accounts and health records. Diagnosis:
Internal injuries in line of duty; type undetermined.

Herman SCHAEFFER, Jr., Ens., USN

16–20
1600: Moored as before. 1609: ARF-95 alongside to starboard to remove diesel generator from forward diesel generator compartment. 1636: Diesel generator clear of ship and aboard ARF-95. Recovered body of WILBANKS, D. A., Flc(MoMM), 973 15 36, USNR. Location and condition of body indicates
subject man died at 1451, 12 April 1945. Death due to enemy action. 1702: ARF-95 cast off from
alongside. 1852: Sunset, darkened ship. 1922: Called crew to General Quarters. Enemy aircraft
in vicinity from SOPA, CTG 51.15. 1932: Commenced making smoke. 1943: Ceased making smoke.

A. J. RITTER, Lt.(jg), USNR

20–24
2000: Moored as before. 2016: Secured from General Quarters on all clear from SOPA, CTG 51.15. Set
armed sentry watch on bow, midships, and fantail.

K. W. BIRD, Lt.(jg), USNR

APPROVED:

L. S. KINTBERGER, Comdr., U.S.N   COMMANDING.

TO BE FORWARDED DIRECT TO THE B

EXAMINED:

Nelson E. SMITH, Lt.(jg), U.S.N.R.   NAVIGATOR

EL AT THE END OF EACH MONTH
U. S. GOVERNMENT PRINTING OFFICE : 1944 O - 617800

April 14, 1945

On April 14, the forward diesel generator was lifted out of the ruins of the forward generator compartment. (See photo on following page.) As the heavy piece of equipment was lifted, the body of Dwight A. WILBANKS F1c MoMM 073-15-36 was found. Ship's log reads, "Transferred to U.S. Army Graves Registration Service, Kerama Retto."

While the ship was under repair in Kerama Retto anchorage, it was constantly a General Quarters situation. Sleep was almost non-existent. Most of the crew tried to find some rest near their GQ station. They would curl up on the heavy canvas gun covers of their respective gun mounts and just doze, waiting for the next alarm to sound. It usually wasn't long in coming

DECLASSIFIED
Authority _NND 803052_
BY _RAM_ NARS, 9th _10/18/82_

CONFIDENTIAL

NAVPERS-13M (REV. 1-44)

DECK LOG—REMARKS SHEET

PAGE _273-45_

UNITED STATES SHIP _____ZELLARS_____ Sunday 15 April , 19 45
(Day) (Date) (Month)

0-4
0000: Moored in Kerama Retto, Nansie Shoto, Berth 56 portside to U.S.S. MULLANY. Bow to stern with six (6) manila lines doubled. Boiler #3 steaming for auxiliary purposes. Armed sentries posted on bow, midships, and fantail. SOPA: Commander, Task Group 51.15. Ship is darkened.

W. M. Krushesky
W. M. KRUSHESKY, Ens., USNR

4-8
0400: Moored as before. 0610: Sunrise; lighted ship. Secured sentries. 0700: Body of WILBANKS, Dwight Arthur, F1c(MoMM), USNR, 073 15 36 transferred to U. S. Army Graves Registration Service, Kerama Retto.

Owen C Barnes
Owen C. BARNES, Lt.(jg), USNR

8-12
0800: Moored as before. 0825: Mustered crew at quarters; no absentees. 1015: Made routine inspections of magazines and smokeless powder samples; conditions normal.

M L Marlow
M. L. MARLOW, Ens., USNR

12-16
1200: Moored as before.

D. L. Southall
D. L. SOUTHALL, Ens., USNR

16-20
1600: Moored as before. 1835: Held Church services. 1852: Sunset; darkened ship. 1913: Went to General Quarters, enemy aircraft in area from SOPA, CTG 51.15.

Sheldon E Bernstein
Sheldon E. BERNSTEIN, Ens., USNR

20-24
2000: Moored as before. 2030: Secured from General Quarters. 2052: Went to General Quarters on Flash Red from SOPA, CTG 51.15. 2207: Secured from General Quarters, set armed sentries on bow, midships, and fantail.

Weldon E. Smith
Weldon E. SMITH, Lt.(jg), USNR

APPROVED:

H Kintberger
L. S. KINTBERGER, Comdr., U.S.N. COM
TO BE FORWARDED DIRECT TO T

EXAMINED:

Weldon E Smith
Weldon E SMITH, Lt. (jg), U.S.N.R. NAVIGATOR
EL AT THE END OF EACH MONTH
U. S. GOVERNMENT PRINTING OFFICE: 1944 O - 617888

DECLASSIFIED
Authority NND 803052
by RGM NARS, Date 10/18/82

CONFIDENTIAL

NAVPERS-134 (REV. 1-44)

DECK LOG—REMARKS SHEET

PAGE 275-45

UNITED STATES SHIP _____SELLARS_____   Monday   16   April , 19 45
                                                           (Day)   (Date)   (Month)

0-4
0000: Moored in Kerama Retto, Nansei Shoto, Berth 56 portside to U.S.S. **MULLANY**, bow to stern with six (6) manila lines doubled. Boiler #4 steaming for auxiliary purposes. Ship is darkened. Armed sentries posted on bow, amidships, and fantail. SOPA, CTG 51.15.

                                                     B. D. FREEMAN, Ens., USN

4-8
0400: Moored as before. **0606:** Sunrise; lighted ship, secured sentries.

                                                     Nelson E. SMITH, Lt.(jg), USNR

8-12
0800: Moored as before. **0821:** LCT-1371 alongside to starboard, bow to bow. **0825:** Commenced taking fresh water aboard. **0850:** Mustered crew at quarters; no absentees. **0918:** Completed taking on water having received 6000 gallons. **0919:** LCT-1371 cast off. **0940:** Called crew to General Quarters. Enemy aircraft in vicinity. **1021:** Secured from General Quarters. Made routine inspection of magazines and smokeless powder samples; conditions normal.

                                                   Herman SCHAEFFER, Jr., Ens., USN

12-16
1200: Moored as before. **1543:** Commenced testing smoke screen generator. **1550:** Completed test of smoke screen generator.

                                                   W. M. HRUSHESKY, Ens., USNR

16-20
1600: Moored as before. **1837:** Went to General Quarters, enemy aircraft in vicinity. **1853:** Sunset; darkened ship. **1959:** Secured from General Quarters. Set armed sentry watch on bow, midships, and fantail.

                                                   D. L. SOUTHALL, Ens., USNR

20-24
2000: Moored as before.

                                                   Sheldon E. BERNSTEIN, Ens., USNR

APPROVED   EXAMINED:

L. S. KITENBERGER, Comdr., U.S.N.   COMMANDING   Nelson E. SMITH, Lt. (jg) U.S.N.R.   NAVIGATOR

TO BE FORWARDED DIRECT TO THE BU   L AT THE END OF EACH MONTH

U. S. GOVERNMENT PRINTING OFFICE 1944 O 617804

CLEAN UP, All hands turn to.

Finally, the major cleanup, where some of the repair work could begin, was done. The major problem was to close the gaping holes in the starboard side and the main deck plates.

Carl CROSBY, S1/c, who had served as a deck hand from the beginning, was a certified welder. Why this had not come to the attention of the damage control gang there is no explanation. He was immediately "drafted" into the gang. The lone sailor leaning over the outer hull plate with welding hood on is "BING." He claimed that he was getting fresh air, but everyone was so tired from lack of sleep, it looked more like resting. He did an outstanding job of assisting the repair ship crew in getting the ship's wounds repaired enough for travel back to the States for final repair. On the main deck, one can see through to where the officers' ward room had been. The port side. Mount #2 is turned to port where it was jammed when the ZELLARS was hit by the suicide plane. *(Note Crosby's personal history on page 166.)*

As the shredded steel members were cut away and new steel in place, there seemed to be a different bond among the crew members. Everyone wanted to help wherever possible. There was no shortage of volunteers for each effort that was underway. Shipmates stood by as the twisted steel was cut away so that they could dispose of the unwanted metal.

———

As the ZELLARS and a number of other wounded ships lay at anchor in the anchorage, the nights brought additional fear. Almost every night, Jap planes would sneak in and drop bombs in the area. Each ship that had a smoke generator would light them off and fill the anchorage with heavy diesel-smelling smoke. The smoke must have covered the area reasonably well, for the Japs dropped their bombs off target. During the weeks that the ZELLARS was at anchor, no ship in the anchorage was hit, several very near misses, but no hits.

It seemed like years before the blasted places were closed. The galley was the first service to be restored because it was needed most. A means for washing the trays and dishes was also devised. Just like the marines and soldiers on the beach, clean garbage cans were set where the scullery had been and as each shipmate passed on his way above deck, he simply washed his tray in hot water, along with the cutlery and cups.

The chiefs "dined" with the crew in the crews' mess and the officers' ward room was somewhat rebuilt so that they had a place for meals and meetings.

Patches on the starboard side of the bridge were welded over the many holes, Mount #2 was left sitting pointing out to port just as the Jap plane put it. The basic topside housekeeping was left as is and very little painting and scraping and was done. As the few weeks passed the ZELLARS became a sad-looking ship with the patches in place and battle scarred stains about her midships on both sides. It was very obvious that she had been in harms way, received battle damage, and suffered a great deal.

April 21, 1945

On April 21, during the repair period, with the Kerama Retto Island so close, the Captain allowed small groups of adventurous crew to take the motorwhale boat and do some of their own invasion. It was special to just stand on solid ground. A few pieces of leftover war junk were collected but no real item that could be called a souvenir was found.

On a visit to the temporary burial site of our shipmates at Kerama Retto, one of the crew was able to visit one of the Jap prisoner camps. He recorded a photo of the enemy behind barbed wire, looking somewhat happier than those who

One of the crew took this photo of the enemy during a visit to a Japanese prisoner camp.

Two "comfort girls" walk in a nearby camp.

fought to their death in the struggle for Okinawa.

Even though members of the crew felt good about killing such enemies, the taking of any human life was disturbing to them. Still it was a choice of them or us.

Somewhat of a surprise, in a nearby camp were several so-called "comfort girls" that had benefits."

It was learned that the "girls" were Korean and had been conscripted some time ago and sent to a number of different Japanese-held islands before arriving in the Okinawa area.

They seemed very happy to be recaptured with a promise of being returned to their homeland.

During the long and heart-breaking hours of the cleanup from the damage done by the suicide plane, the Captain always seemed to be near, encouraging the crew and offering his support. It was not unusual for him to just stop by and ask questions about events of the day or, "Is everything going OK with you?"

The cigar, half-smoked or chewed, or his favorite pipe was part of his presence. During the cleanup, as the crew shoveled and swept, washed and cleaned and, in some cases, cut away the torn, twisted and mangled steel parts of the ship, he was there standing watch with pained expression on his face. This was his ship that was badly wounded and he felt a deep personal loss. There was a greater concern for the loss of so many of his crew as he made his way from one working place to another. He was our Captain and each shipmate knew it.

Steve MORGAN, GMlc, Harold BUCK TMlc and Ted KENNEDY TMlc, take a moment to reflect on the past few days and catch a breath of fresh air in front of the torpedo shack. The blackened bulkhead and burned deck is in small contrast to what was toward the bow starboard side. The hatch to the torpedo shack was completely blown off and the weather break just disappeared. Toward the bow, was a gaping 35-foot-long hole down to the water line, left by the exploding torpedo/bomb.

Page 83

<u>CONFIDENTIAL</u>   5 June 1945

Subject: War Diary for period of 1 April 1945 to 30 April 1945.
- -

                    2000   26° 02 N   127° 33 E

Sunday 8 April 1945.

    0720 Directed to proceed independently. Threat of surface attack broken
up by Task Force 58's air attacks. Reported to CTF 55 for fire support
mission. 0726 Ordered to relieve U.S.S. HARDING in vicinity of Makiminato
Saki. 0756 Relieved U.S.S. HARDING as fire support ship. Lying to. 1105
Commenced firing indirect fire with air spot as directed by shore Fire Control
Party. 1405 Enemy aircraft reported in area went to General Quarters. 1422
Aircraft passed clear, secured from General Quarters. 1810 Enemy aircraft in
vicinity, went to General Quarters. 1915 Secured from General Quarters. 1925
Commenced firing starshells for illumination of enemy lines. 1930 Anchored.
4500 yds. from Makiminato Saki.

Position   0800   26° 17-40 N   127° 42-12 E
Monday 9 April 1945.
    0500   Radar contact on unidentified aircraft went to General
Quarters. 0517 Underway in fire support area. 0630 Secured from General
Quarters. 0834 Commenced firing main battery at shore targets as directed by
Shore Fire Control Party.   1640 Ceased bombardment. Expended 400 5"/38 cal
AAC projectiles, 4 5"/38 cal White Phosphorous projectiles, 404 rds 5"/38
smokeless powder. Directed by CTF 53 to report to CTF 54 to screen night
retirement group. 1750 On station in screen retiring to northward. 1857
Enemy aircraft in area went to General Quarters. 1904 Commenced firing main
battery in full radar control at aircraft. 1905 Ceased firing aircraft
retiring out of range. 1947 Commenced firing main battery in full radar control at air target. 1849 Ceased firing plane burst into flames and crashed
into the sea as a result of combined AA formation. Expended 111 5"/38 cal
AAC projectiles, 109 5"/38 cal AAC projectiles (VT fuze), 220 rds 5"/38
flashless powder. 2000 Commenced firing main battery in full radar control
at enemy aircraft 2001 ceased firing aircraft burst into flames and crashed
into sea off our port bow. Expended 49 5"/38 cal AAC projectiles, 10 5"/38
cal AAC projectiles (VT fuze) no other ships fired at aircraft. 2053
Secured from General Quarters.

Position   0800   26° 19-10 N   127° 40-45 E

                   1200   26° 17-20 N   127° 40-20-E

                   2000   26° 55 N   127° 32 E

CONFIDENTIAL   5 June 1945

Subject: War Diary for period of 1 April 1945 to 30 April 1945.
- -
Tuesday, 10 April 1945.

0030 Headed southward for objective area. 0634 Detached from TF 54 and
ordered to proceed to fire support sector #7 by CTF 53. 0720 Went to General
Quarters unidentified aircraft. 0734 Secured aircraft friendly. 0850 Arrived
in assigned area. Lying to. 1059 Commenced firing main battery at targets
designated by shore fire control party on the northwest coast of Okinawa. 1733
ceased bombardment expended 33 5"/38 cal AAC projectiles, 4 5"/38 cal white
phosphorous projectiles, 37 rds 5"/38 cal smokeless powder. Commenced patrolling a five mile line parallel to the coastline   at 10 knots.

Position   0800   26° 38 N   127° 50-45 E

                  1200   26° 44 N   128° 04 E

                  2000   26° 46-30 N   128° 04-15 E

Wednesday, 11 April 1945.

0903 Relieved on station by U.S.S. ROOKS. Enroute transport area off
Hagushi Beaches. 1014 Enemy aircraft in area went to general quarters. 1049
Lying to in transport area for transfer of patient to hospital ship. 1052
Secured from General Quarters. 1121 Underway for Kerama Retto for logistics.
1208 Orders changed. Proceeding to Hagushi Beach area for further orders
from CTF 53. 1344 Went to General Quarters enemy aircraft in area. 1358
Secured from General Quarters. 1435 Ordered to take on ammunition from LST.
1451 state of sea made going alongside impractical, proceeding to anchor
1831 Anchored off Zampa Nisaki. 1718 Underway to join TF 54 for night retirement. 1810 On station in anti-aircraft disposition retiring to westward.
Heavy enemy air attack expected.

Position   0800   26° 41 N   128° 05 E

                  1200   26° 18 N   127° 26 E

                  2000   26° 05 N   127° 33 E

Thursday, 12 April 1945.

Patrolling in company with TF 54 to the westward of transport area.
0302 Enemy aircraft approaching, went to General Quarters. 0504 Aircraft
retiring, secured from General Quarters. 0903 Designated to effect transfer
of official mail from flagship to other ships in formation. 1330 Discontinued
mail transfer. Large group of enemy aircraft approaching area. Proceeding
to station in screen. 1340 On station. 1349 Secured from General Quarters.
1444 Observed enemy aircraft shot down by C.A.P. about 15000 yards on port

Page #7

CONFIDENTIAL   5 June 1945

Subject: War Diary for period of 1 April 1945 to 30 April 1945.
- -

beam. Went to General Quarters. Increased speed to 20 knots. 1450 three
torpedo planes believed to be Jills, sighted about 4000 yards distance on
port side making coordinated attack. Planes were only 15 feet or so above
the surface so did not make radar contact until time of sighting and then
on SG radar. Two of the aircraft were hit by AA. fire and crashed but the
third approaching from about 300° relative crashed into the base of five
inch mount number two. His torpedo released just prior to the crash slid
across the main deck through wardroom country and exploded on the starboard side. 1515 Fires under control and wounded under treatment. 1540
Underway proceeding Kerama Retto anchorage. 1625 Anchored Kerama Retto.

13 April - 30 April 1945.

     1458 on 13 April the ZELLARS moored alongside U.S.S. MULLANY in berth
K-56 Kerama Retto for temporary repairs by U.S.S. ENDYMOIN (ARL-9) moored
in nest, before returning to rear area for final repairs. During the period
of 13-30 April the ENDYMOIN cut away the damaged sections and installed new
strength members and plating. Temporary messing facilities for officers and
men were also installed. Under the direction of ComTask Group 51.15 (SOPA
Kerama Retto) and ComDesRon Two (ComDesPacRep, Kerama Retto) the ship distributed spare parts, parts from damaged gear and surplus ammunition to supply
the needs of the operating ships in the area. Everyday at least once a day
and often as many as three or four times the ship was called to General
Quarters by an alert from SOPA. Several ships in the area were damaged
during this time but no direct attacks were made on the ZELLARS. The greatest
danger appeared to be from the AA. fire of our own ships in the harbor. On
30 April the ZELLARS, her temporary repairs completed, got underway from
alongside the ENDYMOIN at 0730 and fueled from the U.S.S. BRAZOS (AO-4) from
0844 - 0941. Upon completion of fueling provided and anchored in berth K-60
Kerama Retto at 1046 awaiting sailing orders.

L. S. KINTBERGER

DD777/A9

068

Fleet Post Office,
San Francisco, California.

CONFIDENTIAL   30 September 1945.

Subject: War Diary for period of 1 May 1945 to 31 May 1945.
- -

18 May 1945 - 23 May 1945.

  Refueled and proceeded at 1645 en route Pearl Harbor, T. H.

24 May 1945.

  Moored in middle loch Pearl Harbor, T. H. at 0909.

25 May 1945.

  Underway at 1001 in company with U.S.S. FLETCHER (DD-445) OTC and
U.S.S. SIGOURNEY (DD-643) en route San Pedro, California for final repairs
to battle damage.

26 May 1945 - 30 May 1945.

  En route Pearl Harbor, T. H. to San Pedro, California.

31 May 1945.

  0851 Moored at N.O.B., San Pedro for arrival ceremony. 1133 underway en route Ammunition Depot, Seal Beach, California. 1233 Moored to
pier U.S. Naval Ammunition Depot, Seal Beach. Commenced unloading.1551
All ammunition off the ship. 1606 Underway from U.S. N.A.D., Seal Beach.
1649 Anchored in Los Angeles Harbor. Shifted operational and administrative control to Commander Western Sea Frontier.

                                    L. S. KINTBERGER.

April 26, 1945

Shouts were heard from the aft part of the ship. Several sailors had been looking out toward the island beach when some 35 to 40 Jap soldiers came walking down the beach with hands raised. Several of the crew manned the aft 20MMs and swung them into place, pointing at the Japs. It was all the other crew members could do to keep them from firing on the Jap surrendering party. Shorty after, an Army LCI picked them up and took them to a safer place.

May 4, 1945

On May 4th, the ZELLARS went into the floating dry dock (ARD-13) to have her lower sonar (sound) unit removed. Radio had announced that another major Jap suicide attack had occurred the day before (May 4) and that two destroyers had been sunk and others damaged. The ARRON WARD really took a pounding. As the ZELLARS stood by, the ARRON WARD was towed into the anchorage. She was a junkyard from her bridge to the fantail. Her hull on the stern had been breached and she was down by several feet at the stern. It was very difficult to see how any of the topside crew could have survived, but some did.

May 5, 1945

As the ship's log read, "left drydock at 09:00. Had another night raid last night. One bomb came very close."

A new tempo came over the ship. May 7; word was passed to get underway for an anchorage called Hagushi Beach, Okinawa. Regardless of where the ship went, General Quarters was sure to follow. It seemed that the ship was always going to GQ, with enemy planes in the area. Sometimes they were reported as friendly but still GQ made everyone very nervous.

May 8, 1945

On a bright morning of May 8, 1945 at 0910, word was passed, "up anchor set special sea detail." The ZELLARS was headed home. Her first destination was Saipan, in the Marinas Islands. First the ship had to rendezvous someplace off Point Bolo and meet convoy OKS-3. The convoy was made up of other ships that had taken a suicide plane and was headed home for repairs just like the ZELLARS. The U.S. ANNEARUNDEL (APA-76), the U.S.S. BASS (APD-124), U.S.S. PICKNEY (APH-3) U.S.S, CROUTER (DE-11). The ship's log for May 8 reads, "1013, on station speed 13 knots (120 RPM), course 195-T. A short time later speed was changed to 14 knots, convoy speed."

As each evening's sunset spread it's beautiful colors across the sea, each crew member could not help but be grateful that he had survived and was going home. Each evening's display assured him that the death and devastation was being left further behind with each turn of the ship's screws.

L346   0312Ø5/MAY/45   ~~UNCLASSIFIED~~

CTF 51 SENDS ACTION COM5THFLT X SPECIAL SUMMARY COMMENCIG ABOUT 1820 AN ESTIMATED TWENTY TO TWENTY FIVE ENEMY PLANES APPROACHED FROM THE SOUTHWEST IN FOUR RAIDS APPARENTLY FROM FORMOSA OR CHINA

X CAP SPLASHED FOUR X FOUR SHOT DOWN BY FOLLOWING SHIPS(2 BY AARON WARD(DM 34) X 1 BY LCS 25 X 1 BY LCS 831 X 9 ENEMY SUICIDES AS FOLLOWS X FIVE HIT AARON WARD(DM 34) X AT LEAST ONE EACH CRASHE] THE FOLLOWING

SHIPS X LCS 25 X LSM 195 X MACOMB(DMS 23) AND LITTLE(DD303) AND LSM 195 SUNK X AARON WARD(DM 34) IN SERIOUS DANGER OF SINKIG ALL SHIPS HIT HERE IN RP 10 EXCEPT MACOMB WHICH WAS IN P 9 X BT,....

NOTE

COPY OF TEAMING ORDER 2nd April '45

U. S. S. ZELLARS DD777

(021017)

IN CASE OF ENEMY CONTACT IF GENERAL SIGNAL BAKER FORM 13 MADE BULLDOGS FORM TWO COLUMNS:

RIGHT COLUMN:
IDAHO
NEW MEXICO
TENNESSEE

LEFT COLUMN:
WEST VIRGINIA
TEXAS

COMMANDING OFFICER PORTLAND WITH MINNEAPOLIS AND TUSCALOOSA TAKE STATION RIGHT THOUSAND YARDS AHEAD

OF BULLDOGS, CTU 54.2.4 WITH ONE HALF SEA HAWKS TAKE STATION FIVE THOUSAND YARDS AHEAD OF BULLDOGS,

REMAINING SEA HAWKS UNDER CONDESRON 55, THREE THOUSAND YARDS ASTERN BULLDOGS. WILL INTERPOSE AND

U. S. S. MONADNOCK

Heading:

121300/APR/45   VOICE P/L

ZELLARS (DD 777) UNDER ATTACK 1450N 3 JILLS 2 SHOT DOWN 3RD SUICIDED AND EXPLODED ON SECOND DECK AREA OF PLOTTING ROOM X

3 JAP BODIES IN PLANE X 50 POUND BOMB THAT DID NOT EXPLODE BUT THE TORPEDO WHICH IT WAS CARRYING EXPLODED X FOLLOWING DAMAGE ALL

FIRE CONTROL EQUIPMENT INOPERATIVE X GYRO AND CIC ROOM DEMOLISHED X MOUNT 2 JAMMED IN TRAIN X SOUND GEAR DEMOLISHED X GALLEY DEMOL-

ISHED X DIRECTOR TRUMP DISPLACED ABOUT ONE INCH X FORWARD FIRE ROOM BULKHEAD AND SECTIONS OF MAIN STEAM LINE RUPTURED X FORWARD FUEL

OIL SERVICE TANKS RUPTURED X NO APPARENT UNDERWATER DAMAGE X SIDE PLATING ABOVE WATER LINE STARBOARD SIDE X 8 ENLISTED MEN MISSING X P

PERSONNEL KILLED IN ACTION 3 OFFICERS 18 ENLISTED X WOUND IN ACTION 1 OFFICER 36 ENLISTED MEN X BT.....

FROM: ZELLARS (DD 777)		Priority	Routine	Deferred
				Radio

May 12, 1945

Saturday, May 12, just 4 days after leaving Okinawa, the ZELLARS arrived in Saipan. At 1150 anchored in the safe harbor in 45 fathoms of water, port anchor in birth #L-31. Secured special sea detail, secured main engines." The ship was still in dangerous water and set mount 44 at readiness.

The ship's log for May 12, 12-16 hours note that for the first time in a long while (from Ulithi to Saipan) some of the crew just had to rest and were caught sleeping and shirking their duties, and had to stand before the Captain for Captain's Mast.

May 15, 1945

May 15 found the ZELLARS underway for the island of Eniwetok and then on to Pearl Harbor. Crossed the International Date Line on May 21; arrived Pearl Harbor on the 24th. The Commander of Destroyers Pacific gave the ship one heck of a beer party. It was the first time since April 12, that the crew shared smiles.

May 25, 1945

Departed Pearl Harbor on May 25 for Long Beach Naval Shipyard for major repairs and leave for the crew.

If anyone had taken notice, the returning crew did not look like the same young men that had, not so long ago, departed the shores of our country. They had gone and found how harmful it could be. Their faces showed the pain and loss of the many friends they had left behind, buried on a lonely island so far away. They were older in experience, much older.

The sea miles from Pearl Harbor seemed to pass ever so slowly. As the ZELLARS passed the first outbreak of the Los Angeles harbor and entered the Long Beach Naval Shipyard, she was greeted by a number of the press and several Hollywood entertainers. Fresh milk in pint-size cartons was tossed from the dock to the crew that lined the ship's starboard side. Slowly the ZELLARS moved toward the mooring side of the dock, lines were passed, the ship and her remaining crew were home.

The once sleek destroyer now showed her battle scars. Her number 2 5" gun mount still trained to port just as the suicide attack left it and the main battery gun director also pointed toward the attack. Along the starboard side amidships, the temporary patch down to the water line had been painted but still had the marks of the wound. The starboard side of the bridge was still pock-marked from the torpedo blast, with black burned bulkheads alongside the bridge, where the entire crews of the 20MM guns had just disappeared.

The ZELLARS was not the polished "Tin Can" that she was used to being. Even though her hull and bulwarks were battle stained, she and her crew were very proud of the short time she had stood before our enemy and accounted for herself.

The crew standing at ease by divisions lined the starboard side as the ship docked.

Even though the ZELLARS was at dockside, there was a lot to do before leave and the repair of the ship could begin. All ammunition and explosives had to be off-loaded. The following day, a short trip across the harbor to Seal Beach Naval Weapons Depot brought an ammunition lighter alongside, and most of the day was spent removing the explosives. When everything was safe, she reentered the shipyard and leave began for two sections. Some went to the East coast, others to the middle of our country and a good representation along the West coast.

The remaining members of the crew were housed in some very poor barracks. They were cold and had no heat. The outer walls were covered with tar paper but they did have windows. The regular Navy "chow hall" was a short walk and the food was very good.

The task of the shipyard began with some of the crew assisting with the removal of the patches that had been placed over the damaged area. It was amazing how fast and well the shipyard workers dismantled all the torn area and began replacing everything that needed replacing. Some of the replacement equipment was of a newer model than the ones removed. The new 40MM guns had a "pickle" mode that allowed for the trainer to command both the pointer and the trainer operation. There were better radar and sonar systems and a new firecontrol computer.

One big surprise was a soft ice cream-making machine, (the ship's own Foster Freeze) an item that the ship had never had before. It was placed on the starboard side just as the crew left the mess deck going to the new scullery. Ice cream was not a daily affair but more like a treat. Each shipmate received about two scoops at a time; still it had "home" all over it.

As the first shipmates returned from their leaves, the section that manned the ship's repair received their turn. A number of replacement sailors had reported aboard and the empty bunks were slowly filled.

August 1945

About mid-August, the ZELLARS had her original look back and the repair shakedown period came next. Much of the planning was directed for her return to the war which had closed upon the mainland of Japan. Some of the anxiety and remembrance of the ship's last visit to the war zone was not to be looked on with any amount of pleasure. Before the ZELLARS began her second shakedown, thank God the war came to an end and a different mood took over the ship.

A number of the "plank owners" who had been in the Navy for some time, had enough points for separation from the Navy and happily went home. For many of the remaining crew, it was sad to see such specially-bonded friends leave, but also happy that they would be with their families.

For the older crew members there was a real job at hand. Almost all of the replacement sailors were new in the Navy and had no sea duty. It was up to the "old salts" to shape up the new crew.

After the Navy yard acceptance of the repair work and some short sea trials just off the Long beach coast, the ZELLARS departed for San Diego and a more formal shakedown period. It was no different than the first shakedown. Emphasis was on ASW and antiaircraft drills. The ZELLARS would go out in the early AM and return just before dark. The new men were settling in nicely but there was a sorta us/them feeling among the plank owners. The plank owners had worked very hard to make the "Z" into one of the very best destroyers in the Navy. They had sweated, bled and some died in making her a very proud ship. The new guys would have to prove that they could hold up their responsibility to the ship before full acceptance. As the training progressed, every one of them stood their ground and became an equal part of the ship. The crew was one again.

October 8, 1945

On October 8, 1945, the ZELLARS slipped anchor and headed south to Panama City and the canal. Few of the crew had been thru the "big ditch" and had liberty in the Canal Zone. Part of the crew had liberty in Panama City, on the Pacific side and the other half in Coco Solo which was on the

Atlantic side. Some of the antics of the local people were a real eye opener. The beer was real cold and natives friendly; some of them too friendly.

She was to become part of the Atlantic fleet. Her first stop was the Naval Shipyard in Brooklyn, New York. Many of the crew had not been in that part of our country but took in many of the sites. Navy Day found the ZELLARS anchored up the Hudson River where President Truman was supposed to pass up and down the long line of ships. At night, each ship would turn on their search light and swing it around in the cold of the night. The arc-fired light gave off a blue cone of light and drew a great deal of attention.

The first "duty" that was assigned to the ZELLARS was as escort for the new and impressive aircraft carrier MIDWAY, CVG 41. The ZELLARS was very familiar with the Aircraft carriers of WWII, but the MIDWAY was huge in comparison. She had single mount 5" guns all along each side just below the flight deck, carried many more aircraft, and could cruise at a greater speed. The ZELLARS followed at the Midway's stern for plane guard duty down to Guantanamo Bay Cuba for the carrier's shakedown. All the way south, the carrier conducted air operations and regular seamanship training.

Guantanamo was just a service base manned by the Navy and a bunch of Marines. The closest city was "GITMO CITY" just outside of the gate. Many of their local inhabitants were employed at the base. Gitmo City had a cigar factory that made the great Cuban cigars, One of the crew was dating a very lovely lady in new York whose father smoked cigars. The factory made a cigar called Royal Havana Whites. In New York, they sold for a dollar each and at the factory, a penny each. He made many great points with the father by giving him several boxes of 50 cigars.

The carrier's shakedown was a little different. Her torpedo bombers launched training torpedoes at the ZELLARS, with the depth set to go under the ship. AS the torpedo spent it's fuel and ended it's run, it would float to the surface and the ZELLARS would send her motorwhale boat to pick it up and bring it alongside the ship where it would be hoisted on board for recycling. The weather in the Caribbean was always warm and very pleasant.

After completing the cruise with the Midway, the ZELLARS docked in Norfolk and caught up on some minor service needs.

January 1946

In early January, the Midway's sister ship, The FRANKLIN D. ROOSEVELT, CVB-42, received her shakedown orders along with orders for the ZELLARS for her escort. Back down to Guantanamo Bay Cuba. After several weeks of rushing around trailing on the ROOSEVELT'S stern for plane guard detail, the group received orders to cruise down to Rio de Janeiro. It was a great cruise. On the way south, the ZELLARS stopped in Puerto Rico for fuel and again in Reciefe, Brazil.

Rio was a delight. The city was just cleaning up from their carnival activities and it was still full of the celebrants. The people were most friendly and welcomed the U.S. Navy ship's visit. During a day of flight operations with the President of Brazil on the carrier, two F4 Corsairs were lost with crew as the carrier gave a demonstration for the Brazilian president. The ZELLARS was off her stern and try as she could, the two pilots were not found.

Upon the return to the United States, the ZELLARS was ordered to Pensacola Florida for the purpose of escorting the carrier RANGER, again standing off her stern watching the new student pilots practice the art of carrier landings.

April 8, 1946

The weather was perfect for the routine of each day. Out in the early morning to meet with the carrier, plane guard all day, then back into the harbor of Pensacola. Just routine, but not quite! On Monday April 8, 1946 while proceeding out for the day's duty (0812) the motorwhale boat was on the bay and coming along the port side to bring it onboard. The crew had performed the operation many times without any problems. The stern pelican hooks had been attached and tension applied to the boat falls that would lift the boat out of the water.

As the take up began, and the whale boat was about two feet out of the water, the bow boat fall pelican hook parted, dragging the boat into the water. DAROLD JORGENSEN, S1/c, the coxswain, had his foot caught between the pelican hook and the frame and gunnel of the whale boat. With all engines stopped, the boat handling crew rescued Jorgensen from his very painful position. "Jorgie" suffered some very painful contusions to his foot and leg. The ship's doctor treated his wound and ordered him confined to bed. He was later transferred to the hospital for repairs.

April 22, 1946

A different assignment was to the Naval Academy on April 22. The ZELLARS had the honor of a summer cruise for a number of Midshipmen that lasted until August.

After her adventure with the future Naval officers, the next stop was for basic overhaul and repairs and another shakedown at Cosco Bay, Maine.

October 6, 1946

With the world settling down to a peaceful time, there still was a need for constant training. The new emphasis was on improved anti-submarine warfare. Beginning on October 4, 1946, she was assigned to the Submarine Force, Atlantic, and served as a target ship for submarines conducting torpedo training.

January-February 1947

January and February 1947, the ZELLARS was part of the first major fleet tactical exercise since fleet problem XXI At the successful completion of that exercise, she reported back to Norfolk on March 17 and for the next four months, operated along the middle Atlantic and New England coast.

July 21, 1947

The first real peace-time overseas deployment for the ZELLARS came on July 21, 1947. What a treat it had to be, off to Europe with all expenses paid. First she visited Plymouth England and really enjoyed the hospitality of the local people. For the next 30 days, the ship made the rounds to various ports and received the same great treatment. Some of the crew had relatives in the area and first time friendships were made.

September 1947

In early September 1947, the ship looked out to port and had their first chance to view the great rock of Gibraltar and began a three-month cruise of the Mediterranean. In the short time, she visited Soudha Bay, Crete; Taranto, Naples; Venice, Salerno, and Trieste in Italy, then on to Tangiers on the African Coast. Again the ship made many new friends and learned more about different peoples. This was the first 6th fleet deployment for the ship and everyone enjoyed the new experience.

December 1, 1947

On December 1, 1947 there was a very brief stop in Boston. For three months, another refresher training cruise to Guantanamo Bay, Cuba.

The ZELLARS reentered Norfolk Naval Shipyard on April 20, 1948 and remained there for six weeks preparing for another deployment, once more to the 6th fleet. June found the ship thru Cape Hatteras and deep waters with a course set for the Mediterranean. It was a short stay in the Med and she returned to Norfolk in early October. For the next two years, she was part of the 2nd fleet, conducting fleet operations out of Norfolk; a somewhat boring duty.

June-August 1950

The World was not satisfied with the status quo. In June 1950, the North Korean communist forces decided to break the peace and invaded the Republic of South Korea. In a fast move south, the communists were at the doorsteps of Seoul, South Korea before the United Nations could respond.

The ZELLARS departed Norfolk in August 1950 and headed for the Far East. She and her division mates arrived in Yokosuka, Japan early in October.

What a departure! Some five years had passed since the ZELLARS was conducting shore bombardment off Okinawa, a territory of Japan, shooting down the remains of her air force, killing her ground troops and here she was tied up to one of the docks in a major shipyard of her former enemy, and enjoying it.

The ship was provisioned and immediately set sail for Korean waters. Her tour of duty would be for nine months during which time she would perform a number of different missions. Her primary duty was something she had learned during WWII, "Shore bombardment." The "Z" was assigned gunfire support for the United Nations troops ashore and coastal surveillance. In addition, she also provided antisubmarine protection for the larger American warships against an underwater potential threat that never materialized.

The ZELLARS in Korea

As soon as the ZELLARS arrived on station in October 1950, she took part in the opening of Wonsan harbor. Late in November the Chinese intervened in the conflict, driving the United Nations troops into a southern retreat. The ZELLARS supported the retirement of the South Korean division down the east coast, then provided gunfire support to the Marines in the defensive perimeter around Wonsan, while the 3rd Infantry Division was evacuated by sea. In mid-December the warship moved north from Wonsan to Hungnam to provide gunfire support during the evacuation of another coastal enclave held by retreating United Nations forces.

The ZELLARS remained in Korean waters for another six months after the November-December evacuations and ranged both coasts of Korea delivering gunfire support of the ground troops and interdicting costal logistics.

July 1951

Having earned four battle stars for her Korean duty, she returned back to the United States in July of 1951 and resumed duty with the Atlantic fleet. Upon her return, the ZELLARS began a concentrated retraining of her ASW capability. For the next eight years, the ship had five extended cruises to Europe and the Mediterranean waters and exercises in the western Atlantic and Caribbean sea.

Late 1959-December 1965

By late 1959, the "ZELLARS" was beginning to show her age. It was time for a major overhaul. She entered Norfolk Naval Shipyard to begin a mark 11 fleet rehabilitation and modernization overhaul and alteration. The addition of more up-to-date equipment would add years to her projected service life and greatly enhance her ASW capability.

Now, she became an aircraft carrier, almost. The most noticeable change was the addition of a flight deck and storage area for an ASW helicopter. The modifications were completed in June 1960; and the ship moved south to a new home port, Mayport, Florida. Between June 1960 and December 1965, the ZELLARS made five deployments to European waters. Four of those assignments consisted of duty in the Mediterranean with the 6th fleet and the remaining one involved a midshipman summer cruise to northern European ports.

NOTE: During one of the Med cruises, after a great deal of steaming, the ship developed a crack in the hull of the aft engine room just outboard of the starboard propeller shaft and close to the number 2 main feed pump foundation. The ship's hull actually cracked open where one could see daylight from the main deck down to the water line when the ship rolled to port, continuing under the ship and up to the main deck to the port side. The cause of the hull failure was later determined to be a very slight hull warp deflection due to sitting in dry dock so long during the FRAM conversion (see BJ. Reynolds' personal history).

1967-October 9, 1969

The ZELLARS duties with the 2nd fleet in the Western Atlantic and the Caribbean consisted for the most part of training and yard over hauls. Her most important "break" was highlighted by the participation in the Cuban quarantine in the fall of 1962 and an occasional duty supporting the Polaris missile test program.

The ZELLARS would spend the whole year of 1966 in the Western Atlantic, only breaking her training routine between Mid-May and Mid-September for regular overhaul at the Boston Naval Shipyard. More than half of 1967 was taken up by NATO exercise Operation Matchmaker 111, an experiment designed to determine what problems might rise from combined operations of ships of various nations and to test solutions to those problems.

The operation began in mid-January 1967 and lasted until mid-August. It took the ZELLARS on her first trip to the West Indies, then across the Atlantic to waters around northern Europe, and finally to the coast of New England and Canada. "What a great trip."

The ZELLARS sailed once again, back to the Med. The deployment consisted of the usual unilateral and multinational training exercises and goodwill port visits, lasting until September 27, 1968 when she tied up at Newport once again. Following eight months of operations out of Newport, she began her last visit to the Mediterranean and the end of her career.

The warship returned to Newport on October 9, 1969 and, one month later, moved to New York where she became a Naval Reserve training ship.

The ZELLARS' self esteem began to change.

Within the ship's structure, she began to notice a different attitude among the reserve crew. There was not the special attention that she had been used too. After months of going to sea on short training exercises, the feeling of not being cared for crept into her tired and well-used structure. Not just neglect, but the once-in-a-while sailors did not have the time to really make the great ship wanted.

Few and fewer men served my needs and after some 16 months I really knew that my time was running out. Days, I would sit tied to a lonely dock with just a handful of sailors wandering about my decks. My fuel tanks held a minimum of fuel, the ammunition magazines were empty, and the once-busy galley stoves were cold. In the boiler rooms, the fires were out and I could feel the cold where fires had turned water into steam. The engine rooms were also quiet. Where once the rumbling sound of the screws turning that sped me on my way, there was now nothing but stillness. No crew scampering around looking at the gages and answering the telegraph for the desired number of turns on the propeller shaft. I was now completely alone.

"There was no longer the call from the bridge to single up all lines or the call for all ahead slow as I would pull away from a dock and get underway to some great sounding new adventure. It was all gone, I was slowly dieing. The last pangs of my long life were assured as the long blue ribbon of the commissioning pennant slowly fluttered down to the bridge. I was no longer."

On March 19, 1971 the ZELLARS DD 777 was struck from the Navy records.

Reflecting back to her beginning, instead of great expectations of serving her country and the finest young men of that time, she now began to wither and measure the life being drained from every bulkhead, compartment and deck. Stains began to form in many places. Rust would not be far behind.

Epitaph

The ZELLARS earned one battle star during WWII and four during the Korean War. It is estimated that some 5000 sailors served aboard her during her life time. They served her well and she gave each of them a special experience that many of them would view as an important part of their life and future.

THANK YOU ZELLARS, DD 777, for the service you rendered to all those men and your country.

USS ZELLARS (DD777)

PAUL GOWEN

ENLISTED: OCTOBER 1943

BOOT CAMP. SAN DIEGO, CA.

ASSIGNED TO ZELLARS: SEPTEMBER 1944

RATING: GM3c

PLACES VISITED: San Diego, CA; Seattle, WA; Pearl Harbor, Hawaii; Ulithi; Okinawa; Panama Canal; Guantanamo Bay, Cuba; New York City; New Port News, VA; San Francisco, CA.

I finished high school the end of August 1943 with the express purpose of enlisting in the Navy and volunteered the first week of October, 1943. It took me that long to convince my parents that in a period of eight weeks I would have to submit to the draft. The person in charge at the Draft Board declared that if I would enlist as a selective volunteer, he would assure me a spot in the Navy. Otherwise, I would have to take what the Draft Board needed at the time, which could have meant any branch of the service. A group of us from South Texas, traveled to San Diego to start Boot Camp. Having always kept my body in good physical condition, Boot Camp training was not to difficult. I contracted "Cat Fever" about half-way through training camp, which was the flu as we know it today, and my classmates left me. I then applied for Gunnersmate school and was accepted.

Upon completion of this school I was assigned to a training facility just north of San Diego, training armed guard crews. The day I arrived there I put in for a transfer to sea duty. The first people to visit me were an Officer and GM1c enticing me to volunteer for the Submarine Service. It did not take me long to decide that I was not fit for underwater duty. I am just a little claustrophobic, which is like saying that a woman is just a little bit pregnant. So it was not difficult for me to say no.

My transfer came through as we made up ship's crew at Treasure Island. (I do not know if that was considered Oakland or San Francisco.) As I recall, the crew makeup took about six weeks, at least that is how long that I was there. I was fortunate to have the oldest of my siblings and her family living in San Francisco. My liberties took me to her house every evening and then to the "Stage Door Canteen," in downtown San Francisco. I would spend the night with my family and return to Treasure Island the next morning. Mama could not understand why I never became homesick. I had to tell her that I was always too busy. The morning that we pulled out of San Francisco, I almost missed the train due to a faulty alarm clock. We really had to scramble to get me back to the base.

My fondest memories of the troop train ride to Seattle was of the forest's of the Pacific Northwest, the cobalt blue lakes and the warmth of the people that met us at each stop along the way. In particular, the folks at Klamath Falls, Oregon. For a kid born and reared in South Texas, and until I joined the Navy had been no farther from home than San Angelo, Texas, this was an exciting trip. Mountains, forests, lakes — forget the square wheels, hard bunks and inconvenience of the train — this was a trip to remember..

Who can forget the beauty of the Straits of Juan De Fuca and the waters of Puget Sound? The night in the fog when we nearly rammed a fishing boat, the pitching of the ship as we entered the Pacific Ocean that gave way to the rolling seas, as we took off cold weather gear and replaced it with dungarees. Do I remember that it took us seven days to get to Pearl Harbor? I was amazed at the change in the color of the sea as we made our way around Diamond Head and entered COMDESPAC staging area. Another lesson was in the making of competition among ships crews to be the best in the fleet.

Seamanship and gunnery exercises would be taking place with our sister ships. Adjustments to the body for watch duty was a major change. I was always ready to lie down and catch some shut eye. Most of the time, it was too hot to sleep below, even when you diverted air from the blower onto your bunk.

Does anyone remember that the Gunnery Officer and Assistant Gunnery Officer were confined to quarters for having "borrowed" a Jeep? Or was this just a story making the rounds? Perhaps that is one reason we had such a skilled gunnery crew.

As we became a sharply trained crew and joined the fleet, one could sense the camaraderie and mutual respect that we all had for one another. The skipper, Commander KINTBERGER, would stop by my gun mount (Mount 44) and ask strategic questions. I thought that he was the smartest man that I had ever encountered. And he was, except for my father. At the time I was not aware that he had lost the HOEL DD 533, six months prior to assuming command of our ship. It was a pleasant surprise at our first full dress inspection to recognize the NAVY CROSS that he wore. Even a country boy was aware of the significance of such an honor, but I did not learn the story of the sinking of the HOEL until we started having reunions.

I carried a guitar aboard which got sat on. Do not remember which one of the crew repaired it for me. Had to be a carpenter's mate. I bunked in the next-to-last compartment aft. Between me trying to sing and craps games going on, this compartment became a popular spot. A lot of money changed hands the first of each month. I never gambled and only took a small amount of money each pay day. Surely did get raucous at those times. The pay that I received was spent on cigarettes and candy. You can see where my priorities lay at that time.

Many things made up the cruise to Ulithi in the Carolinas: An Albatross landing on the fantail, flying fish landing on deck, and a shark surfacing alongside while we were in chow line that must have been forty feet long. Also, the efflorescence of the night sea, circular rainbows in rain storms and St. Elmo's fire at night in these same storms, a torpedoman drunk in the middle of the day from mixing torpedo juice with Kool-Aid, seas as smooth as glass and porpoises as far as you could see for 360 degrees.

Our arrival at the staging area at Ulithi, where as far as the horizon, in all directions, there were ships of every description. The water was so clear you could see every pebble on the bottom. Yet big draft ships were everywhere. It was amazing to me.

We joined Task Group 58 and became one of the USS FRANKLINS' support ships. Through binoculars I would watch aircraft landing and taking off for hours. I have always been a flying enthusiast. We picked up several pilots that were unable to land on the flight deck. Upon transfer back to the FRANKLIN we received twenty-five gallons of ice cream, which meant about one scoop per person, at least that is all I remember getting each time. Those big ship sailors must have led the good life. When we were pitching and rolling, they just glided with ease. Think of the meals that they must have gotten, being served ice cream, boy howdy! I suspect that our skipper was a lot more tolerant of our dress code, though.

The last thirty years of my working life I was associated with a friend and boss who was an SB2C pilot on the FRANKLIN. He remembered the time that a hawser parted while we were refueling, which sprayed fuel oil from my gun mount aft. My friend was waiting in line to take off when the Kamikaze hit the FRANKLIN. His aircraft was flipped over, whereupon he dropped out onto the deck and an explosion blew him overboard.

I spoke of trying to get some shut-eye earlier. I was so fatigued, as was everyone, during the bombardment of the village of Naha and other targets on Okinawa. Even though the main battery may have been firing, or Battleships and Cruisers were firing over us, it was no problem to go to sleep any time that we were relieved. I remember seeing the butt ends of sixteen-inch projectiles on their way to a target. Life magazine published a photo of the butt ends of a broadside from a Battleship, but I saw it first hand. I am sure that others saw this too.

The life of Foot Soldiers and Marines on the beach must have been miserable. We at least had dry beds and warm meals, instead of wet ground and dry rations. We supplied ammunition and supplies to ground troops on one occasion that I remember. The Coxswain of the landing craft that made this run was filthy and hungry. His eyes were sunken so far in his head that it was hard to see his eyeballs. He greatly appreciated a hot bath and warm meal.

April 12, 1945.

Like most of the first crew, I was less than twenty years old at the time, and an act of carnage was to take place that has remained with me to this very day. Each generation has grown up bearing scars of life. These experiences surely have a profound effect on maturation. History has borne out this claim many times. The facts may be a little fuzzy at times, but the horror of that fateful afternoon is still very real.

Those of you that have attended any of the reunions have had the opportunity to read transcripts from the daily log, or one of the copies of a diary that was kept by a member of the torpedo gang. These writings enable one to get a better picture of the sequence of events leading up to the point of action, along with a description by the writer of his recollections. I hope that each of the "PLANK OWNERS" as well as those of you who came later will someday either attend a reunion or secure a copy of these documents.

It is not my intention here that the crews that followed us be overlooked, for they, too, are as much a part of the ZELLARS' history as those of us that sailed on the first cruise. Our crew shares with those of you who sailed later the responsibilities that shipmates share with one another for their lives and safety.

From the days of pounding the island prior to the invasion on April 1st, until mid afternoon of the 12th, we'd had very little sleep. But the klaxon sounding General Quarters had a way of energizing a person in what today would be described as an adrenaline high, regardless of the complete fatigue. Seems we had just secured from General Quarters. I had not gone below, but was still around my gun mount. I was Gun Captain of the Quad 40MM on the port side aft. (Mount 44) with a superior gun crew. I thought it strange we had secured from General Quarters earlier, with so much activity in the area.

After we had entered the forward war zone a machinist mate told me that as long as the main battery was firing he was not particularly worried. When the forties came on line he became a little nervous, but when the twenties began he was sure enough scared.

The aircraft attacking that afternoon were already in the forties range when the gun crew was assembled. We began firing immediately. The Japanese warriors (Kamikaze we were to later learn meant Divine Wind), were determined not to return home to give their lives for their Emperor. The main battery concentrated on the closest aircraft which was furthermost aft and downed it.

Mount 44 directed its fire on the aircraft in the middle of the group of three. We took this one out and swung our fire to the target that ultimately hit the ship. The aircraft was taking direct hits but was so close that it did not explode prior to hitting the ship.

As gun captain, my position on the gun mount was between the two sets of barrels. Of the twelve men that made up the mount 44-gun crew, I do not remember the exact position of each man except DWIGHT LEVERTON. Dwight was pointer; he instinctively followed the tracer burnout projectiles to the target. He was very calm, stayed with his target until it was destroyed, and undoubtedly saved many lives on the aft portion of the ship. For this I am eternally grateful.

We were running at 20 knots; the explosion shook the entire ship. We shuddered and stopped dead in the water. Fire, smoke and explosions continued. Strange as it may seem, I did not duck but saw the impact of the aircraft and the accompanying explosion, fire and smoke firsthand as did each pointer and gun captain on the port side.

Upon the explosion of the aircraft and it's bomb/torpedo (to my mind it was a bomb, but has been variously described as a torpedo because of the type of aircraft carrying it) a massive amount of shrapnel filled the air, taking with it many lives and severely wounding many shipmates. I saved a lethal piece of shrapnel that fell into my gun tub. Fortunately, none of the gun crew on mount 44 were injured. Just behind my mount and outside the gun tub, a torpedoman, W.F. JONES, TM2c, was cut in two by flying debris.

We lost all power upon impact. In the confusion of the smoke and fire, P.K. WATSON, GM1c, observed another aircraft attacking from the stern, diving toward the ship. He manned a 20MM to ward it off; mount 44 swung around to take up the fight. I do not remember any other guns firing at this target. Without power it became a manual operation and we were unable to catch up with the target that strafed the deck and ultimately splashed off the port bow. The aircraft went into the water with 20MM holes in the fuselage where the pilot sat, courtesy of P.K. WATSON.

As fire and smoke engulfed the forward part of the ship and until the standby aft generator began supplying power, there were no pumps to supply damage control parties with water pressure to fight the fire. There were many heroes that afternoon, not the least of them was a destroyer that came alongside to aid in putting out the fire. This maneuver took great courage on the part of the crew of our sister ship. A memory that has stayed with me throughout the years, is that the aircraft that attacked us were traveling at a speed of at least two hundred MPH and the distance closed very rapidly. Yet, it seemed that the action was taking place in slow motion.

All others were too busy concentrating on their tasks. The afternoon suddenly became evening as if we had lost three hours. I can still visualize the grief and shock on the faces of my shipmates as we rescued bodies of the dead and tended the wounded. Losing our Doctor and S1c k Bay created a major problem. Chief HIRST and WILLIE GOGAN did a marvelous job administering to the surviving wounded. An MD came aboard from another ship to aid in caring for the wounded. Continued training allows one to perform from rote to complete a task for which he has been trained.

Those same shipmates that revealed their innermost feelings on seeing the dead and wounded, were very callous when extricating the bodies of the pilot and crew of the aircraft that took so many of our shipmate's lives. Loss of friends because of combat action and propaganda accompanying war can do that to you.

As we entered the Kerama Retto anchorage harbor, a signalman came to me with a message from a high school classmate asking of my condition. He was aboard the net tender at the harbor entrance. Another high school classmate was on the crew of the floating drydock, which we entered for repairs. In war time to run into friends in faraway places is not unusual, however two schoolmates in less than twenty-four hours seems out of the ordinary. We were able to visit about other classmates in the Pacific theatre of war.

My family had been lifelong friends with a family whose daughter was a reporter on a San Antonio daily paper. Upon my arrival home for some R and R, she wrote up an account of my homecoming. The San Antonio papers have always been delivered to Corpus Christi, approximately 150 miles south of San Antonio. The story of my homecoming was read by the family of shipmate JUAN NAVA SC1c who was killed that afternoon. Juan's mother and wife drove up to San Antonio and brought with them Juan's baby son. This child who had become a police officer in Los Angeles attended the Portland reunion. I was able to visit with him and relate the story of his mother, grandmother and his visit to me that summer day.

Juan had a gregarious personality, the sort of fellow who tried to please you in whatever way he could He was a favorite of many of us. Many nights he gave me a loaf of bread to eat with sardines, cheese and other items we pilfered while loading supplies. Looking back I am certain the supply officer was cognizant of these thefts, but said nothing about it.

Some of you may remember those long midnight watches when I would sing through the communication phones to keep us all awake. Juan and I at other times sang Mexican Corridas.

As a parent and grandparent, I can understand the desire of a mother, father or widow to visit with a survivor of a tragedy where they had lost a loved one thousands of miles from home. It could be very comforting to have the benefit of talking to one who had been in daily contact with the loved one. There were not many details that I could give them without adding to their sorrow, so I did not relate the grizzly details.

We returned to the States, completed repairs and cruised with the fleet to New York for Navy Day, October 1945. While in New York we received replacement crewmen. One of the new crew had been in my Boot Camp company in San Diego. He, along with others, would comment what a peculiar odor the ship had. All of us had gotten used to the odor, but it surely was obvious to the new crewmembers.

Returning Home

The voyage to Pearl Harbor and subsequently to Long Beach for repairs after we were hit, was slow and tedious and without excitement. But at least no one was shooting at us. The weather was perfect for a ship that might not have survived a storm. While temporary repairs were adequate, I am not sure we could have taken the stresses that we had encountered in the Typhoon where we skirted the edges, earlier in the spring of 45.

After repairs and shake down, mercifully President Truman had the courage to employ the Atomic bomb. I was not looking forward to returning to the war zone. I realize today the courage of Captain KINTBERGER. To have placed himself and crew in life threatening positions so many times, without a doubt a hero's action. And to think that we would be heading back into harms way was frightening. Of course all of us would have done so, but with strong thoughts of survival. I do not think that I could have been a career military person. Fortunately there are people that do not have my mindset, and are career military. To them, all of us owe a great deal. They keep the United States safe for democracy.

Several of us were sent to fire fighting school while we were in San Diego. This school lasted about a week. When we returned to the bay, the ZELLARS was gone. Someone in charge was able to see that a fast-sea going tug, with us aboard, chased down the ZELLARS. We threw our gear aboard the ZELLARS and at the right moment jumped from one vessel to the other.

New York and Navy Day 1945 was about as good as it could get for all sailors. Again the Stage Door Canteen was a popular place. I was still too young to purchase liquor, but that did not discourage enterprising young men from getting too much to drink. And I had done so one night and ended up at the Canteen. While dancing with a hostess I began to rock just like being aboard, adjusting for the roll of the ship. This queen stopped, stepped back and said, "what's the matter with you?"

Shake down cruise with the largest Carrier of its day, the USS FRANKLIN D. ROOSEVELT, was another chapter in my life. The Gunnery officer and P.K. Watson pestered me to ship over, even offering me GM1c All the while my papers were being processed for discharge. When we arrived in New Port News with the FDR, I left the ship, heading to Houston, Texas and Camp Wallace for discharge. My active Naval career came to its end, but not my continued interest in the Navy.

A final interesting memory. The FDR was being pushed into her berth in New Port News by tugs. As we approached our pier just across the slip, the wash from the tugs threw us into the pier, ripping up quite a number of piling, some of which became entangled in our screws. You could hear the skipper all over the ship screaming to back down. That was my exit from the ZELLARS.

I made lifetime friends while in the Navy. Our reunions seem more like family reunions. After all, we are an extended family unit that just happened to share a battle experience together. I am wiser for the experience. Most certainly my life since surviving the attack on our ship has made me cognizant of the joy of life. Each day brings new memories and I have no fear of death, for I have already looked it in the eye.

PAUL GOWEN, GM 3c, Plank owner

USS ZELLARS (DD777)

HOWARD B. WALTERS

ENTERED NAVY: MAY 11, 1944

BOOT CAMP: FARRAGUT, IDAHO

COMPANY: 560

ASSIGNED TO ZELLARS: OCTOBER 1944

LENGTH ON ZELLARS: 2 YEARS

RATING: S1C

PLACES VISITED: Farragut, Idaho; San Francisco, CA; Seattle, WA; Honolulu, Hawaii; South Pacific, Mog Mog, Ulithi; OKINAWA; Panama Canal; New York; Guantanamo Bay, Cuba; Norfolk, VA; Pensacola, Fl; Rio De Janeiro, Brazil.

I entered the Navy shortly after I became 18. The reason, I wanted to do my share and fight for my country. My dad fought in France in WWI. My brother was to go on and fight with Patten's 3rd Army at the battle of the Bulge. Our family was always proud of America.

Special Memories

I still remember the morning we entered Pearl Harbor for the first time. A beautiful sunny day and I was so impressed by the different shades of blue and green reflecting from the sea. I also remember the few liberties we had in Honolulu. I could always be found swimming at the beach at the Royal Hawaiian Hotel, or eating pineapple sundaes at the USO. Liberty was only from 0800 to 1600.

My duty station was in the radio shack. CECIL HILL (now deceased), TOMMY THOMPSON (now deceased), and BOB HODGE were nice friends. It was wonderful to see them at the reunions.

My general quarters station was on mount 44. PAUL GOWEN was the Gun Captain. As a PLANK OWNER the memories of the ZELLARS means a lot to me. There were seven or eight of us from the

Pudget Sound area so we frequently would talk of home. I was an ammo passer to LEN WESTNEDGE. Its great seeing PAUL, DWIGHT LEVERTON and DAROLD JORGENSEN at our reunions.

The return to the states after we had been hit was glorious. The Long Beach welcome was great. Spending VJ night in Long Beach was certainly exciting. I was just going out the gate (1600) at the shipyard when President Truman announced the end of the war with Japan.

When we went to New York, and marched in the first post-war Navy Day parade, it was great — right down 5th Avenue. We were the closest Navy crew to the speakers' stand where Mayor Fiorello La Guadia (The Little Flower) gave his speech. Liberty in New York was great. I remember going to the movie theaters off Times Square. They always had a "big band" playing. Also, I saw the Dorsey's, Louie Armstrong, Cab Calloway, and Lionel Hampton.

Our trip to Rio was exciting. We docked right downtown - the end of the Praca Mara. I remember that the British frigate HMS AJAX was docked in front of us. She was very active in the sinking of the Graf Spee in either Paraguay or Uruguay.

Ensign BIRD was my division officer. I'm glad I was able to see him at the 1993 Charleston reunion. He is now deceased. Also Ensign SCHAEFER. I was able to locate him in 1990. He and his wife Phyllis joined us at the Norfolk reunion.

How exciting and beautiful it was when our ZELLARS sailed into Pearl Harbor, Hawaii at 1230 on January 31, 1945. It was a brief stopover on our way to the Pacific War Zone. After a six-day cruise from Seattle where the ZELLARS was constructed, the warmth of the Hawaiian sun with the majestic blues and greens of the sea ever present, was a real treat to this eighteen-year-old sailor. In contrast, the remembrance of the December 7, 1941 attack on the fleet at Pearl Harbor was so ever prominent in my mind.

Many hours were spent at sea in the Hawaiian Islands during the next thirty days for gunnery practice, and joint exercises with such ships as the carrier FRANKLIN, BATANN, GUAM, and TICONDEROGA. There was even time for two liberties in Honolulu for this young sailor (0800 to 1600 only during the war). Liberty included swimming at famous Waikiki Beach.

At 0630, March 3, 1945 we sailed from Pearl Harbor with three carriers, one cruiser and eight destroyers. Destination unknown. On March 4, which was my nineteenth birthday, we were told our destination was Ulithi in the Caroline Island group. We fueled with the USS FRANKLIN and the USS INTREPID enroute. Arrived Ulithi at 0800, March 13, 1945. Ships of the British Navy arrived also during the period we were there. They formed Task Force #57. On one occasion we were able to have a fun beach party at a small island called Mog Mog. In less than a month, many of our shipmates who swam and laughed in the water that day would be killed in action. I have group pictures taken at Mog Mog that day which I treasure.

At 0630, on March 21, we sailed from Ulithi with Task Force #54. The force consisted of ten battleships, twelve cruisers, twenty-six destroyers and four APD's. Twelve hundred miles from our destination, but no location name was announced. At sea on March 22, we were told that our destination was Okinawa, located approximately three hundred miles south of Japan. Prior to April 1, Easter Sunday, invasion date of Okinawa, the island of Kerama Retto was invaded and secured. The island was to become a supply and refueling base, also a temporary repair base for our damaged ships. This island was located twenty miles west of Southern Okinawa.

We arrived at our destination at 0700 on March 24. The plan of the day for March 24 and 25 set the tone of our mission. The daily plan sheet carried the signature of our executive officer — Ltcmdr. R.R. DUPZYK. Quote: item #7

KILL JAPS   KILL JAPS   KILL MORE JAPS

There was still one week remaining until the invasion of the main target, Okinawa. On March 26 our troops landed on Kerama Retto. The base was captured with little resistance. During the remaining days prior to "Love Day" as it was referred to, the battleships and cruisers bombarded Okinawa. We screened the capital ships, patrolled on picket duty, covered and protected underwater demolition teams, and also participated in bombarding the island with our 5-inch guns.

On March 27, GQ sounded at 0500. Our first real enemy action. Attacked by four Jap planes — "Irvings," light bombers. I watched as the first Jap plane was shot down, and shortly after, saw the second plane knocked down after making a bomb run. USS DORSEY, DMS-I, was hit. The third plane shot down crashed on the deck of the USS BILOXI. The forth plane headed for us, but turned and dropped his bomb by one of the battleships. We lost the USS HALLIGAN, DD 584 on March 29.

The invasion of Okinawa began at 0830 on Easter Sunday, April 1, with the 10th Army Corp. and the 3rd Marine Amphibian Corp. hitting the beaches. Light resistance. In the period until organized resistance ended on June 21, 1945, fighting had claimed the lives of some seven thousand American soldiers and Marines.

Naval casualties in the protracted sea-air battles offshore were also heavy. Close to five-thousand sailors died, and five-thousand more were wounded, a total far exceeding the losses suffered in any previous US Naval campaign. Seventy-thousand Japanese soldiers died fighting on Okinawa, along with the loss of eighty-thousand Okinawans, most of them civilians.

At 0230 on April 3, GQ sounded. We shot down our first Jap plane, either a Betty or Sally. On April 6, at 0100 GQ sounded again. We shot down our second Jap plane. A Betty.

Japanese air attack began in earnest on the afternoon of April 6. They continued through the next day when hundreds of planes, many of them Kamikazes, struck at the fleet. The attacks were against our Task Force 54, and the carrier Task Force 58. TF58 was chasing the Jap battleship YAMATO and accompanying ships when the YAMATO was sunk by our carrier planes.

The fleets' anchorage at Kerama Retto began to fill up with mangled, blackened ships of our fleet. I remember one afternoon on April 7 when the battleship MARYLAND was a very short distance in front of us off the coast of Okinawa. A Jap Zeke dived on her, and was hit by our shells and crashed into her number-3 turret, which was 16 inches. It bounced off the heavy mount like a ball. A later report stated that the MARYLAND received minor damage. Kamikaze activity was increasing daily.

On the morning of April 12, 1945, the USS ZELLARS DD 777 had delivered guard mail to the ships of the fleet. Shortly after noon I had been talking to DAVE CRAIG, who was also from Tacoma, Washington. We had been assigned to the same boot camp company at Farragut Idaho. Dave was 38, and had been drafted. He stated "I'll never make it home again to see Point Defiance Park and my family."

In less than an hour, at 1330, GQ sounded. Secured at 1345. I had not had time to reach my compartment when GQ sounded again at 1350. Fleet was under a massive air attack by Jap Jill-torpedo planes. I raced to my battle station, which was mount 44, aft 40MM on the port side. We were attacked by three Jills. Our port batteries shot down two of the Jills, and the third one, "suicided" into us hitting the base of our five-inch mount two. The plane's bomb, or torpedo, skidded across the main deck and exploded on the starboard side causing major damage. This damage included blowing out thirty-one feet of our side. We had major fires in the forward part of the ship. I was passing ammo. I remember glancing in the distance and seeing two Jap Jills make a torpedo run on a battleship. I saw the leading plane shot down, and as soon as I saw the second plane shot down there was a big rumble, and flames and smoke raced after us. I was passing ammo to the loader furiously. To this day I don't know how I was able to see the above listed attack on the battlewagon. The exact time we were hit per the ships log was 1451.

I remember turning my head to the after torpedo tubes, located directly behind our gun mount, shortly after we were hit. WILLIAM JONES, TM2c had been at his battle station on the tubes. I was shocked to see that he had nearly been cut in two. The 20MM gun stanchion had been blown away from the bridge and it had flown back and hit him. It killed him instantly.

MIKE SHYLMAN, MM 2/C, from New York, was an older fellow I befriended. Before we sailed from the Puget Sound area I had a chance to go home to Tacoma for Christmas. It was only twenty miles away. Mike had mentioned he had no place to go so I brought him to my family home. His battle station was at the 20mm station below the bridge, on the starboard side, just above where the bomb exploded. His body was never found.

As the damage control parties fought the blazes, and attempted to control them from spreading, many of the wounded were brought aft on the portside deck below our gun mount. Hearing the moans, and sometimes screams was so painful to many of us who were fortunate to survive. I can still visualize and hear ANDREW BRADLEY, STM 1/C, a neat black American sailor from Alabama. He was burned terribly over most of his body. He was screaming, "I can't see, I can't see!" This shipmate died shortly after. Shortly after we were hit I saw four men who were blown into the water. One was

Ensign GUNTER. We later learned he had been picked up by the USS WEST VIRGINIA but had died of third degree burns.

Later on I saw DAVE CRAIG'S body. As I mentioned, he was also from Tacoma. His premonition had come true. He had been killed by blast concussion. He had been near the area of explosion. He had very blonde hair. When I saw him his face had been charred black, but not one of his blonde hairs had even been singed.

Damage control parties continued fighting fires in the forward part of the ship. More dead and wounded were brought aft. The expression on the crew's faces was one of disbelief. I had not been fearful in the previous smaller actions. On April 12, I learned what fear was. I'm sure a large percentage of the crew did also.

The officers' wardroom during the GQ conditions was to be the infirmary. The blast wiped out the wardroom. Our Dr. Kincaid, and the young pharmacist mate from Colorado were both killed. The DD 692 came alongside and their doctor came aboard the ZELLARS to do what he could with the many wounded, assisted by our own Chief Pharmacist Mate CARL HIRST. I still remember crew members on the DD 692 just shaking their heads in disbelief after seeing our damage.

I had the pleasure of meeting and talking to this doctor from the DD 692 at our ZELLARS reunion in Portland, Oregon in 1988. He was a resident of Portland.

The attack continued against the fleet for a short while after we had been hit. The ZELLARS' deck log for April 12, 1945 stated: "All fires under control by 1515. Wounded removed from damaged area. 1540: Underway on port engine. Proceeding to Kerama Retto anchorage. Steering from after steering station; all compasses battle casualty." Signed: C.A. SMYLE, Lt.USN. We reached Kerama Retto at 1700. The USS RIDDLE, DE 185 came alongside for assistance. She had received minor damage aft. Thus, we were able to have evening "chow" aboard her.

Our dead shipmates were taken to Zamami Island at Kerama Retto for temporary burial. Our wounded were taken aboard the USS GOSPER, APA170, for medical attention. The search for our dead continued.

The night of April 12, 1945, LT. (jg) K. BIRD, who was our division officer, came down to our aft compartment. He had a bottle of whiskey in his hand. Everybody in the compartment took a "good swig." Unfortunately, there were some newly created empty bunks. Eight shipmates from our compartment were killed in action that afternoon.

On April 13, we had meals on the USS RIDDLE. Searched for more dead. Additional dead shipmates were taken away for island burial. Pljans were being made for repairing our ship so we could go to the rear area. On April 14 more dead were taken off. They had been located in the forward diesel area. Forty-one of our shipmates were killed and thirty-eight injured. I still remember the small LST coming alongside to pick up bodies and body parts. Not a pleasant sight.

The period from April 14 to April 22, crew members cleared wreckage and repaired what damage they could. On April 22 we pulled alongside the repair ship USS ENDIYMION ARL9. Repairs started in earnest. Repairs were completed on April 30. We were underway at 0730 and went alongside the A04, USS BRAZOS to fuel. Anchored at Kerama Retto. During the repair period we saw thirty-eight Jap soldiers come down to the beach from the hills to surrender. They waved white flags, hands up in the air, stripped of all clothing. Sailors in landing barges went ashore and captured them. Must have been starving. It had been thirty days since our troops had captured the island. During the evening attack of April 28, the hospital ship USS COMFORT was hit by a Kamikaze. Hospital ships, of course, were painted white, and had a large red cross painted on them for humanitarian purposes. It meant nothing to one Jap pilot. On May 1 the USS TERROR CM5 was hit by a bomb in Kerama Retto.

At 1400 on May 4, 1945, the ZELLARS went into a floating dry dock to have our sound gear removed. It was number ARB 13. Saw the USS AARON WARD come into Kerama Retto, the graveyard of so many ships. The AARON WARD had been hit by six Kamikazes. Approximately one-hundred-fifty sailors were either killed or missing. I have never seen a ship so terribly damaged. It appeared that all of the superstructure had been blown up or damaged. After completing boot camp, I was assigned to the destroyer pool at Treasure Island, San Francisco Harbor. Five of us from the Northwest area had been assigned to the USS AARON WARD, which was nearing completion in Long Beach, California. One of our boot camp friends from Tacoma was assigned to work in the office at the destroyer pool. Through his efforts he got us all reassigned to the USS ZELLARS, which had just been completed. This gave all of us a chance to be close to home for another sixty days. I feel extremely fortunate that I was spared on April 12. There was nothing remaining of my same gun position (Mount 44) on the AARON WARD. DAVE CRAIG was not that fortunate. He perished.

During our repair period we had several air attacks in the Kerama Retto area. The night we were in dry dock a Jap plane sneaked into the harbor and dropped a bomb. To this day, I remember my thoughts of a bomb hitting us while in dry dock. With the air attacks came dangerous falling shrapnel. Every ship in the harbor that could fire did, of course. If the Jap plane, or planes, were near you, you would be engulfed with dangerous falling shrapnel.

On May 8, at 0830 we left Okinawa for the rear area. Our destination was Saipan. We were a part of a convoy of twenty-six ships, mostly Navy cargo ships. Distance 1240 miles. Coincidentally, this was VE Day in Europe. The Nazi monster had been defeated. We arrived Saipan at 1130 on May 12, 1945. On May 15, we left Saipan with the USS TERROR, CM5 for Eniwetok in the Marshall Islands, enroute to Pearl Harbor. After spending a few short days in Honolulu we left for home and extensive repairs to the 777 at the Harbor Island Shipyards in Long Beach, California.

We arrived in Long Beach on May 31, 1945. As we came alongside the dock we were all standing at attention. It appeared that those awaiting us on the dock were also at attention. The proud ship and crew were home. Our welcoming was tremendous. I can to this day feel the "excitement" of that moment, and the thankfulness I felt. The next day, June 1, I left for home on my thirty-day survivor's leave. The repairs were completed to the ZELLARS the middle of August, 1945, at which time the war ended. A very happy VJ night was spent in Long Beach. Prior to the announcement of war's end it was in all of our minds that we would be returning to the Pacific again to fight in the invasion of Japan. Fortunately it was not necessary. 148 destroyers of all classes participated in the Okinawa campaign. Of those, 122, over 80%, were either hit or sunk by Kamikazes.

I am extremely proud that I was able to serve my country, especially as a crewman of a destroyer. THE BEST — THE USS ZELLARS.

Bless the dear souls of our eternal shipmates. They have not been, and never will be, forgotten.

HOWARD B. WALTERS, S1c, plank owner.

USS ZELLARS (DD777)

RICHARD L. CORBIT

ENTERED NAVY: APRIL 1944

BOOT CAMP: FARRAGUT, IDAHO
CAMP WALDREN

ASSIGNED TO ZELLARS: OCTOBER 1944

LENGTH OF SERVICE ON ZELLARS: 2 YEARS.

RATING: S1c.

PLACES VISITED: Wherever the ZELLARS went, I went

During the bombardment at Okinawa, my brother was on the heavy Cruiser WITCHITA and they were firing over us. I did get to see him and visit while we were in Kerama Retta harbor.

EXCERPTS OF PERSONAL DIARY OF RICHARD CORBIT

April 10, 1945

We were firing at beach all last night. We went to GQ about 04:30 this AM. Nothing happened. Two of our scout planes were shot down this AM about 10:30. At 14:30 the Exec officer told us we had been complimented on our good firing in support of the Army on the beach. They said we knocked out guns that the TENNESSEE had been firing at for two days. At about 19:00 we were called to GQ. We fired a lot at a plane but it was dark so secured at 02:00. At about 8:05 we were called back to GQ. Fired and hit that plane and it went down in flames. When we hit it, it was aiming for us at about 165 knots, weaving back and forth about 50 feet above the water

April 11, 1945.

A fairly quiet day. Had two GQ's, rained all day.

April 12, 1945

Had GQ at 4:00 and saw a dog fight in the air. Our planes knocked down 2 Jap planes. The Exec told us to expect air attacks all day. At about 13:30 we were called back to GQ, and secured at 13:50. We were called right back and as soon as our guns were manned they were firing. Four planes were coming in on our port side, close to the water. Three of the planes were knocked down before reaching our ship. One scraped the fan tail and one hit the port side. I watched it come in all the way and hit with a huge explosion with his bomb or torpedo. It was a JILL torpedo bomber. It hit the aft part of mount two gun and the ward room. Flames all over the ship. The 20MM mount gun that was hit was where I was supposed to be standing. I was about 2 feet aft lying on the deck. The Jap plane knocked out sound, radio, radar, mess hall, galley, mount 2, plot, CIC, forward diesel room, gyro compasses, 37 gun directors, 2 20MM guns blown off, scullery, navigation room, Captains cabin, ward room, sick bay and laundry.

Our ship's doctor and a PhM 3c were killed and only portions of their bodies were found. Lt Kinkaid and Ensley PHM 3c were their names. We only had a Chief and 2nd class Pharmacist Mate to care for the wounded. We later had another doctor from another destroyer come on board.

I was on a quad 40MM gun on the starboard side as a #1 loader. When the plane hit, the flames were flying on the side where I generally stood. A large piece of shrapnel hit just behind my battle station. I thought it was part of a forward 20MM gun. Most of my friends and buddies were killed. There were 10 from our deck, 8 killed and 2 wounded severely. They were all in mount 2 handling room. It was about 2 feet forward of where the plane hit. The handling room burst into flames and burned H.A. JERCEK, BEEBER, POTTER, KEDFERLE. Also killed were MURPHY, KEANE, MOORE, DANKERT, LISTON, KRAMER, who were all in our division. Immediately after the hit I looked aft and saw a Torpedoman 2c torn in half. I immediately ran forward to assist with fires and wounded.

We worked all night and pulled into a harbor close to Okinawa.

OKINAWA,

We worked all day cleaning and throwing Jap plane parts overboard. I found a Jap coin. One mate found a wallet of one of the pilots. There were 3 Japanese in the plane. I had the watch from 8:00 to 12:00 to watch for Japanese swimmers. They recently had boarded a cruiser in the fleet and killed 13 men.

April 14, 1945

We are still cleaning up debris and finding bodies. Had a GQ at 20:00, laid smoke screen but nothing appeared. Numbers came in today and were told we had 35 dead and 20 wounded. There are about 20 or 30 ships in the harbor which have all been hit by Jap suicide planes and PT boats. We received mail today, first time since we left Ulithi.

April 15, 1945

Still cleaning. Can't get steel to patch up the holes, so many. May have to return to the states. Also trying to repair mess hall and galley as we're eating on other ships. If we do get steel, we have to trade damaged radio gear for it.

April 18, 1945

We are told now we will be leaving the harbor in about 7 days. Still having GQ every night. Some men over from the tender fixing up the ship so we can leave. Some men returning from the hospital ship, remainder of wounded being sent to Guam.

April 22, 1945

Still repairing and near completion so we can leave. Still having GQ. Other ships firing at planes but none came close enough to us. One Battleship took 15 Jap suicide planes. Beached the ship before it sank.

April 23, 1945

After quarters today, skipper called all down to fantail, everyone represented: remanded for stealing food and liquor. "No more beer parties," he said, but he did say that he had a letter complimenting us on our firing at Okinawa and that it was outstanding. Our mess hall will be ready tomorrow, supposedly.

April 26-29, 1945

Still working on ship. GQ some nights with lots of firing. No damage.

April 30, 1945

Got underway today but to a dry dock.

May 2-4, 1945

Still in dry dock. Last night ARRON WARD got hit with 5 suicide planes. Much damage.

May 8, 1945

Left Okinawa this AM with a convoy of 30 ships.

May 12, 1945

Arrived Saipan today and left May 15 for Eniwetok, Marshall Island. Refueled and left for Pearl Harbor, arriving May 24th. Left Pearl Harbor May 25 for San Pedro California.

I had 30 days leave while the ZELLARS was being repaired at San Pedro. ZELLARS along with USS COMFORT, hospital ship was put on display in San Pedro with 250,000 people touring them. After repair we went through Panama Canal to New York. ZELLARS was with the USS FRANKLIN D. ROOSEVELT on a shakedown cruise to Rio De Janeiro for a presidential inauguration there. Returning to Jacksonville, Florida, I left the ship for Minneapolis, Minn. and was discharged there in March, 1946.

RICHARD L. CORBIT. S1c plank owner.

USS ZELLARS (DD777)

DAROLD J. JORGENSEN

ENTERED NAVY

**BOOT CAMP: FARRAGUT, IDAHO.
COMPANY, 633-44**

ASSIGNED TO ZELLARS: OCT. 1944

RATING: S1C

PLACES VISITED: Treasure Island, San Francisco, CA; Seattle, WA; Pearl Harbor; Ulithi; Okinawa; Long Beach, CA; San Diego, CA; Panama Canal; New York; Guantanimo Bay, Cuba; Rio De Janeiro, Brazil; Pensacola, FL; and several ports in between.

GENERAL QUARTERS

0300: planes approaching

0500: secure from general quarters

0900: made official mail run

At that time I had gone to work with Coxswain PITTS, on the motor whale boat. We were coxcombing the aft rails and the tiller on the motor whaleboat. I had taken my skivvy T-shirt off to get a sun tan and put it in my back pocket. PITTS was killed that day (April 12, 1945).

1300: General Quarters: aircraft spotted.

At **13:30** left the whaleboat and went to mount 44 Quad 40MM gun, port side, where I was first loader. I put on my chambray shirt, life jacket and helmet

Planes were coming in on the port side, the crew splashed two planes. One Jill got through. There was one hell of an explosion. Fire was all over us. It opened a 38-foot hole on the starboard side. Our gun crew went to the fantail. We thought we were going to sink.

We then went forward to help with the wounded. I worked with Ensign BIRD. The sight of seeing the carnage is as clear to me today as it was that day. (April 12, 1945) seeing shipmates, some had been Boot Camp buddies, gone or badly burned, is still clear in my mind. "You Never Forget."

That evening when I took off my life jacket, my skivvy shirt that was in my back pants' pocket, was burned off to the pocket. It was very hot; I was lucky.

My General Quarters Station was Mount 44, Quad 40MM port side; I was first loader. My watch station at sea was, Helmsman. In Port I was on the motor whaleboat crew.

After temporary repairs in Kerama Retto we went to Saipan, then to Pearl harbor, and on to the States. We were in Long Beach for repairs when VJ day was announced. WOW. Thank God. We then went through the Panama Canal on to New York City, For NAVY DAY. Then on to Brazil for the Inauguration of their president.

While following the Carrier USS RANGER, picking up pilots that ditched their planes on flight training operations, I got my leg injured. B. J. SMITH, my bow hook and I, the coxswain on the whaleboat, were swinging the boat out to the ready position while underway. The hook on the bow of the boat broke letting the bow hit the water and left BJ. SMITH hanging on the davit. The ship being underway caught my leg in the boat falls and impaled the aft rail in the calf of my leg. After stopping the ship, they got my leg out and later sent me to the hospital in Pensacola.

I left the ZELLARS in April of 1946. Returned home and married Dorothy, my high school sweetheart, in April of 1947.

DAROLD JORGENSEN, S1c plank owner

USS ZELLARS (DD777)

CARL E. CROSBY

ENLISTED: FARRAGUT, IDAHO

BOOT CAMP: FARRAGUT IDAHO.
COMPANY 644-44

ASSIGNED ZELLARS: OCTOBER 1944

RATING: SF 3c

PLACES VISITED: Seattle, WA; San Diego, CA; Pearl Harbor, Hawaii; Ulithi; Okinawa; New York City; Guantanimo Bay, Cuba; Rio De Janeiro, Brazil; and many other ports in between.

I got my welding training at Bethlehem Steel at San Francisco, CA. I worked on the cruiser RENO and the destroyer SULLIVAN. Then we moved to Martinez, CA. and went to work at Richmond, CA. Kaiser Shipyard #2. That was where I received my ABS certification. (American Bureau of Ships).

BOOT CAMP

My boot training was for nine weeks at the Naval Training Center, Farragut, Idaho, named after Admiral D. Farragut of Civil War fame.

I was eager to learn all I could and they threw a lot of classes at us such as Seamanship, Swimming, Physical Ed, Karate, Marching and Drilling, Gunnery with small caliber rifles (22 and 30:06) etc. Most of these classes came easy to the recruits. Being young and in pretty good shape we didn't have much of a problem.

Growing up in Nebraska during the 1930 depression, I became a fair shot shooting rabbits and squirrels that supplemented our food source. I believe that's why I was picked as a gunner on the 20MMs.

I also thought I was pretty good at fighting/boxer, so I went out for boxing. One evening they called for the men who wanted to box to report to the gym. When I reported to the gym I was matched up with a red head from another company who was about the same weight and height as myself. We fought three rounds; they called the match a draw. Right then and there, I knew boxing wasn't my game. All in all, boot camp training wasn't that bad, the chow was pretty good, (better than the ZELLARS). I believe most of the recruits were volunteers like myself, and they just wanted to get that part of their lives over with.

I owned an Indian motorcycle and after boot camp, I was sent to Treasure Island CA. DAROLD JORGENSEN (JORGY) and I rode around Martinez, CA. on the Indian when we could get a liberty. The time was when we were stationed at Treasure Island where the NAVY was making up the crew for the USS ZELLARS.

ON BOARD THE ZELLARS

I was first assigned to the C.I.C. (combat information center) division, then to the first division, second deck division, third deck division, and after we got hit, to the shipfitters' gang and that is where I stayed until my discharge.

When I was assigned to the first division, I and another guy from Nebraska had to bunk in the forecastle. We had to sleep in our hammocks. I think his name was MEDINA. When we left for overseas, I don't remember seeing him again.

After we were hit and went to KERAMA RETTO for repairs, I spent this time helping make the ZELLARS seaworthy to return to the States.

I did have a hair-raising moment. I was over the side welding on the hull and raised my welding hood and looked up to see a steel plate that was being transferred over to the ZELLARS. They almost dropped it; it was oscillating right over my head.

After most of the damage repairs were completed, SF 3/C CLIFF POTTER, LEONARD GROTHOUSE and myself had to patch up the shrapnel hole damage to the bridge. Most of the damage was on the starboard side where the explosion took place. I believe we lost six of the crew that were manning the two 20MM guns at that level. In the photo enclosed you can see some of the holes we had to plug and one of the 20MM ready boxes.

Over the years patching those holes has bothered me more than anything. The starboard side of the bridge had minute particles of human flesh, bone, hair etc imbedded in and around each hole.

My battle station was gunner on a 20MM gun, port side of the number #2 stack. I attended a lot of gunnery firing classes with those men.

The time I served aboard the ZELLARS and during boot camp, I met and made good friends with a lot of shipmates, so many, I'll only note about one who was MAT HARTIGAN. RED and I made a lot of liberties together such as Los Angeles, New York and Rio de Janeiro. On one of these liberties we were hungry for chocolate ice cream. We wandered around till we found a 5 and 10 cent store. We went in and it was filled with women shoppers. We looked around and saw where they served ice cream, then we had a problem. We couldn't speak Spanish or Portuguese. It took about half-an-hour to get our ice cream cones. We had a lot of shoppers standing around us laughing with us as we tried to get our cones.

RED and I took in the famous beach called Copacabana. There were a lot of very pretty girls on the beach.

Not too many of the crew knew that RED'S father was a judge in Chicago, Ill., and the family were personal friends with then secretary of the NAVY, JAMES FORRESTAL.

When I was on my way home for discharge the troop train we were on had a layover in Chicago. Some of us contacted RED (he was discharged earlier) and met his family. They invited us to dinner and a white socks game.

Captain KINTBERGER was commander of the USS HOEL, DD 533 which was sunk October 25 1944 during the battle of LEYTE GULF. October 25,1944 was the same day the USS ZELLARS was put into commission in Seattle, WA..

I worked a period of time for CAPTAIN GRABROWSKI at NWS. Concord, CA. CAPTAIN GRABOWSKI was the skipper of the destroyer that pulled alongside of the ZELLARS after we were hit and helped us with our emergency. (NWS= Naval Weapons Station).

CARL E. CROSBY, SF3c, plank owner

USS ZELLARS (DD777)

VINCENT P. MURO

ENLISTED: MAY, 1943.

BOOT CAMP: FARRAGUT, IDAHO.

ASSIGNED TO ZELLARS: OCTOBER 1944

LENGTH ON ZELLARS: 14 MONTHS.

RATING: GM 1/C

PLACES VISITED: San Francisco, CA; Seattle, WA; San Diego, CA; Pearl Harbor, Hawaii; Ulithi; Okinawa; Guam; Eniwetok.

April 12, 1945, a day that will live forever in my memory.

From the time the U.S.S. ZELLARS was commissioned, I was assigned "Gun Captain" of mount 52. There were two sets of 20MM machine guns on the port side of the ships bridge. I shared the guns with a buddy that I knew only as "Pollock" his nick name. I've been told lately that it was JOSEPH KUZMICH, GM 1/c.

On April 12th, GQ sounded and we were on our gun mounts for the first time that day. GQ was cancelled and we went to the chow line. We had just received our fried chicken when GQ sounded again. I rushed back to mount 52 and was just getting my phones on when the Kamikaze was bearing down on us and main battery mount #2. We had barely had time to get to the side and jump to the lower deck. I slipped and fell, with "Polock" picking me up and throwing me ahead.

He very possibly saved my life. I cannot remember ever seeing him after that. I do think he was hit by shrapnel and was probably taken away for treatment.

I made it thru the first passageway aft and a Lt. was treating one of the crew who was badley burned. He gave me ointment to apply and soon we had exhausted the medication. He sent me to sick bay to see if I could find more. I ran down the passageway. The sick bay area had been blown out. As

I entered the devastated area medical supplies were scattered all over, but with God's help, I found the ointment immediately and we continued trying to help our wounded shipmates.

With the attack over, the attempt to carry on began with the officers requesting volunteers I volunteered to be the cook for the Chiefs. The main meals were prepared elsewhere, but one day a bunch of green bell peppers in my area tempted me and I made an Italian dish my mother used to fix, green peppers sautéed and eggs scrambled together. This was completely foreign to the Chiefs, but they soon acquired a taste for it and enjoyed pepper and egg sandwiches.

When we were in San Diego, a replacement by the name of FURR from New York City became a good buddy. When we were docked in New York City for Navy Day 1945, his parents invited me to their home for the Jewish Holidays. With the dinner over, FURR'S uncle gave him the keys to the car and money to take us out on the town. We went to the Stork Club only to be turned away because we were single sailors, so we took in Times Square, Radio City and all the sights. I will always remember their kindness and it was one great liberty.

Now I look back on a more humorous time, out in the Pacific Ocean. I was assigned the midnight watch on mount #52. There was a beautiful full moon; all was quiet when suddenly through binoculars I spotted a wake on the port side. It looked like a torpedo speeding straight for the ship. I called an alert and braced myself for the explosion. It didn't happen because the "torpedo" turned out to be a porpoise. I thought for sure a court martial would be ordered but the Captain gracefully said, "That's all right, always report anything suspicious!"

VINCENT MURO, GM1c, plank owner

USS ZELLARS (DD777)

LESTER O. ERICKSON

ENTERED NAVY: OCT. 6, 1941

RATING: BM1/C

PLACES VISITED: Seattle, Washington; San Diego, CA; Pearl Harbor, Hawaii; Ulithi; Okinawa; Long Beach, CA.

On April 12, 1945, as I remember, we had just finished passing mail to other ships in the area. USS ZELLARS swung around to get in position. We heard a loud explosion. It really jarred the ship and I knew we had been hit. Mount #2 hatch (my hatch) blew open, flames were all around from fuel from the suicide plane. My back was burned, but not seriously. The ship went dead.

I climbed out of the hatch and went to the starboard side where flames were roaring all over. The side behind us was blown out. Mount #2 handling crew were on fire; all were killed. Two crews on 20MM guns, starboard side, just disappeared and were never located..

There was no water available until someone from mount one went down and started an auxiliary pump. The gunners mate from mount #2 came out with one leg badly injured from shrapnel and powder coming up the powder chute. One week earlier he had asked me to change places with him. He was the gun captain and that was his cleaning station. The thoughts I had were that I would have been in that spot if we had not made the change.

I picked up a billfold belonging to the Jap pilot. It contained a picture of his children (most likely) and some Japanese money. The billfold was sent up to the bridge. I kept the picture, some money, and a piece of metal from the plane.

A ship came alongside. The wounded transferred to that ship. The doctor and all but one pharmacist on the ZELLARS were killed. So medical aid was about gone on the ZELLARS.

Power to the engine room was restored. The ZELLARS went to an Island for emergency repair. We tied to another ship that had been damaged. We used their galley as ours was blown up and they used the washroom on the ZELLARS. Nothing too exciting happened but the chance of being hit by the enemy was still there.

The USS ZELLARS set sail for the USA when emergency repairs were finished. Morale was so-so, sadness with the thought of the shipmates left behind in the cemetery on Okinawa, some that were never located, and the wounded on a ship, in the hospital, or maybe not even alive.

Underway, controlled by one engine. I was on the wheel (helm) 2 hours on, eight hours off.

Went into Saipan harbor for refueling. I asked the signalman about sending a message to the 148th general hospital on Saipan, to inquire about an Army nurse, Shirley Ueland, being there; a message came back that she was. I was given a pass and a ride to go ashore on a whaleboat I had about a two-hour visit, a noon meal at the officers' mess, and a warm beer, with Shirely, found a ride back to the ship, and we were on our way. Docked at Pearl Harbor.

Docked at Roosevelt Naval Operating Base. I had a physical, went home to North Dakota for 30-day leave. After ZELLARS was repaired at San Diego, (actually Long Beach). I was transferred off waiting for discharge orders. On October 5th I was discharged from the Navy at Great Lakes, 111. I went home to North Dakota and bought a farm, having grown up on a farm. I guess that was what I wanted to do. Shirley, the Army nurse on Saipan came back to the states in January 1946. We were married in September, 1946.

We have three daughters, Ingred, married to Ken Whipple; Sylvia, married to Robert Gonzales with two almost grown children, Kristina and Michael; Polly married to Lt. Col. Darrell Roll, with two children, David age 19, and Lisa, age 13.

We have lived near Cooperstown, North Dakota for 47 years now. I retired in 1985 but we still live on the farm.

LESTER O. ERICKSON, BM1c plank owner

LESTER PASSED AWAY APRIL 9, 1995.

USS ZELLARS (DD777)

HAROLD C. BUCK

ENTERED NAVY: MAY 5, 1942

BOOT CAMP: SAN DIEGO, CA.
COMPANY, 42-262

ASSIGNED TO ZELLARS, SEPT 1944

LENGTH OF SERVICE ON ZELLARS: 11 MONTHS.

RATING: TM1c

PLACES VISITED: Seattle, WA; San Diego, CA; Norfolk, VA; Panama Canal; Curaea, New Hebrides; Australia; New Guinea; New Brittain; Ulithi, Okinawa, Saipan, Eniwetok.

April 12, 1945, off Okinawa

We had been at GQ off and on for several hours and under attack from Japanese suicide planes. As I remember, we were making mail runs when this attack was mounted. I was on the bridge on torpedo firecontrol director with phones direct to firecontrol when the planes singled us out and started their approach.

As I remember, they were coming in from port stern at an almost parallel course low to the water. Our guns and other ships took them under fire. One down, The third plane turned and came straight into the port 20MM.

Our guns were tearing him up but he kept coming. At the last second, I ran to the starboard side of the bridge, hit the deck in front of the hatch to the Captain's bridge cabin when the plane hit.

A very loud explosion, the deck heaved and when I opened my eyes, the polaris on the starboard side was gone. Smoke and flames bellowed up the side of the bridge and I was aware that the man beside me was hit and moaning. Someone helped me put him in the bunk of the Captain's cabin and gave him morphine and then we left to go below to assist where needed. I remember dropping off the torpedo deck to the main deck, starboard side, amidships and being handed a charged fire hose and moving forward, dousing fire. I moved forward to the ready room of mount #2, reaching the hatch. 5-inch powder canisters were popping off but all I could see were some 5-inch projectiles in the racks starting to smoke. Thank GOD for water spray. We had the fire under control. I remember the skipper leaning over the bridge and hollering. "Get that ------ fire out." When the fire was secured, I remember seeing Chief Torpedoman on deck by the torpedo shack and went back. I made him as comfortable as I could. He was conscious but in pain from burns.

I remember several of us hauling VON HINKEN FC 3/c up from the lower deck thru the hole in the deck and our concern that we did not tear skin on the sharp metal edges where the deck had been blown up.

Also, about this time, I wondered how I could see the Captain from this part of the ship and then saw that the 20MM gun structure starboard side was blown completely off the side of the ship. Also, strange that I could see into the galley as the entire starboard main deck super structure was blown out. The officers' ward room was no more. The galley ovens were there, the doors were sprung and trays of chicken that had been baking for evening dinner were all over the deck.

It was a long and painful day, and a long, long time ago.

HAROLD BUCK, TM1c, plank owner

USS ZELLARS (DD777)

SHELDON E. BERNSTEIN

ENLISTED: JANUARY 13, 1944

OFFICER TRAINING: PRINCETON UNIV.

ASSIGNED ZELLARS: OCT. 25 1944

RANK: LT.

PLACES VISITED: Seattle, WA; San Diego, CA; Pearl Harbor, Hawaii; Ulithi; Okinawa; Guam; Eniwetok; Long Beach, CA; Panama Canal; Guantanamo Bay, Cuba; Norfolk, VA. New York City.

Before enlisting, I was an assistant to the Attorney General of the United States, heading a section whose functions included representing the military service in litigations involving personnel.

I was married and had one child with another on the way. I chose the Navy because I had extensive small boat experienced, as I still do, believe that our revolution gave birth to this great nation and it's magnificent philosophy of freedom so too would the outcome of WWII determine whether all of us would be slaves of tyrants or free men.

In spite of the rigors and risks we all came to know, I would do it all over again, particularly if I could serve in a crew like we of the U.S.S. ZELLARS knew.

After my introduction into the Navy my first assignment was in the North Atlantic on an old four piper. I had not served aboard the old ship long before I received orders to report to Norfolk VA, which resulted in CIC training. The school was on the top floor of a motel in Hollywood Beach, FL. As a new Ensign I was the most junior officer at that time, but qualified number two in the class and was given a choice of duty. Of course, I chose destroyer duty. After completing the CIC training, I had a succession of very quick exposure in radar, sonar, ship handling, flying, amphibious activities, engineering, torpedos, gunnery, etc. All in three months.

My next orders were to Treasure Island in the bay at San Francisco, CA. The orders read, „to assist in the training and help form up a new crew for the destroyer ZELLARS soon to be commissioned in Seattle WA.“ There was a lot to be done in training a new crew, mostly seamen just out of boot camp, in the ways of sea duty. There was a constant class going on in seamanship, fire fighting, rescue, life saving, and gunnery. The live gunnery training was conducted some miles south of the bay at a remote place called Point Montara. The new crewmembers trained on 20MM, 40MM and 5" 38 guns. The fire fighting training was at the Mare Island shipyard, Richmond CA, just across the bay from San Francisco.

As October 1944 came, the major portion of the crew boarded a train in Oakland and slowly made their way up thru the mid section of Oregon and on to Seattle, WA. We were met by a string of busses and transported to the shipyard where the ZELLARS had been built. Crewmembers were immediately assigned the different duties of final cleaning of the ship and making preparations for commissioning, her first sea trials and shakedown.

On October 25, 1944, with a slight mist, 345 officers and enlisted men stood at attention as Captain Wallin and Commander Van Mater shared the orders putting the ZELLARS DD 777 into commission and part of the U.S. Naval fleet. After a very short period of final calibration and testing the ship and her men set sail for San Diego and shakedown.

Much of what the crew had been learning became real — standing watches, drills of all kinds, war related procedures such as ASW, torpedo, depth charge, and most of all gunnery. All of the regular requirements for normal motor whaleboat use were carried out daily.

An interesting event happened during one of the many gunnery practices. We were firing shore bombardment exercises at the southern end of the gunnery range on San Demente Island, some 40 miles off the cost of Southern CA. The point of aim was to the west on the island at large white painted targets. Due to an electrical/mechanical failure in the firecontrol system, the round went east instead of west. The four salvos from our 5" main battery guns caused the cows and horses to run for their lives. (The problem later was found to be a faulty fuse in the training system.)

By early December, the ship was back at the Bremerton Ship Yard for final tests and preparations for deployment to the Pacific.

The ship docked in Seattle for a few days and one sailor took his girlfriend out to a special dinner in one of the local restaurants. When the bill came, it was twice the amount that it was supposed to be. Too embarrassed to complain, he paid the bill and upon returning to the ship, told his story to his shipmates. A sizable party visited the restaurant and took it apart piece by piece, laying each piece out on the floor.

The next morning the police and city officials raised hell with the Captain and threatened prosecution. Captain Van Mater called me and reminded me that I was still a lawyer and ordered me to clear the mess up. I met with the unhappy group and listened to their yapping. My suggestion was to drop the whole matter and if it was not done, the news media would get the details of how the restaurant was cheating and gouging sailors and that liberty would be denied to all participants. The city dropped the matter.

Pearl Harbor was an eye opener. I am sure that all hands on board, like me, were confirmed in the necessity of striking back to get even for the awesome wreckage we saw. We did get some shore leave in Honolulu and most of it I spent looking for presents for my wife and two children with marks, "made in Hawaii." I found almost everything labeled "made in Brooklyn, Chicago or Los Angeles."

During a final inspection, I had the com and the Captain and Commodore, in dress whites, occupied the forward bridge chairs. My limited education was in evidence when a junior officer of the deck said, "Sir, the engine room requests authority to blow tubes." (An item that I had not learned in engineering.) Assuming that RITTER, the chief engineer, would not make such a request unless it was appropriate, I replied, "Permission granted." Our ship was moving at about five knots with a ten-knot following wind. I woke up a few moments later as thick black smoke and dirty ash drifted over the bridge and the CO's dress white uniform. "Bernstein, get your relief to the bridge."

"Yes, sir."

And a few minutes later, the captain called me forward and asked, "Do you know what you did?"

Again, "Yes, sir."

"Well, a little more education might help, you will stand engineering watches after every bridge watch for the next month."

January, February and the first part of March was training and more training. We got a new Captain in February, Commander Leon KINTBERGER, who had lost his destroyer the same day our ship was placed in commission. He made things more friendly on the ship.

As we left Pearl Harbor and headed west, for two days we accompanied the first Queen Elizabeth who constantly cruised at 30-32 knots, inevitably causing groaning and weariness for both the ship and crew.

Our next stop was an island group called Ulithi, part of the Caroline group, and some 30 miles from the still Jap-held Island of Yap. Upon arriving at Ulithi, I though the string of islands looked as though they had mountains. As we closed the islands, we realized that the mountains were "mountains" of supplies, 20MM, 40MM and 5" ammunitions along with many oil tanks stacked 200 to 300 feet high. I was told that the stuff was our supplies for the upcoming invasion of Iwo Jima and Okinawa.

The ZELLARS was assigned security patrol several times during our stay at Ulithi. During one occasion at night, a radar pip lit up on the scope showing a target at some 21,000 yards. It looked the size of a battleship and did not respond to IFF. It soon broke into two blips, one large and one small. I recommended a star shell salvo which disclosed a large fat freighter and a patrol craft of the Coast Guard.

On March 21, we quietly slipped out of Ulithi and continued west for the last bastion of the Japanese empire, another place that we had never heard of called Okinawa. It took all day to form the massive Task Force. Men of war were joined in one massive fleet covering from one, horizon to the other and beyond. It was reported that over 1000 ships all headed for one place, Okinawa.

As we steamed toward our meeting with the Japanese, we refueled from the Carrier FRANKLIN and the battleship TENNESSEE. It was always a pleasant visit as the gigantic ships and small destroyers crossed the open sea welded together with fuel and mail lines. There was always a lot of shouting from ship to ship between the crews.

As we made our way west, we were in constant misery from the high winds and massive seas which caused the ship to roll some 35 degrees from center line most of the way. On the bridge the conning officer and his phone talker generally were lashed to the forward rail of the open bridge.

Upon reaching Okinawa, one of our first assignments, along with four other destroyers, was to map the area for we had no charts due to the Japanese excluding all countries from the area. For a number of days, the destroyers under the command of our commodore, ran courses north, south, east and west, undertaking soundings. All the data was transmitted to a cruiser which had the proper printing facilities and the experts to create the needed charts. After the charts were completed, the ZELLARS and one other DD became the agents of the U.S. Post office, delivering the mail (charts) to the arriving fleet.

Two facts stand out in my mind: The innate ability and skill of the CIC crew, many of whom had little or no formal education, to grasp and apply the multitude of physical, mathematical and scientific aspects of the problems that had to be dealt with; and speedily and accurately provide the results which saved any of our fleet from going aground.

The remarkable discipline of the crew who worked without sleep and little food for the three or four days that it took to complete the chart making task under the very guns of the Japanese held island. God bless America for a creed that produces such men!

I know that the Okinawa campaign is well documented and I will relate only a few bits.

Our resupply and safe anchorage was a group of small hilly islands about 30 miles north east of Okinawa called Kerama Retto. One of our assignments was to support the Marines as their heavy cannon fire power. Due to the hilly terrain, the Marines could not use their heavy guns so the ZELLARS was called in. In the course of our bombardment, we shelled a factory. When the Captain and I attended a conference, we learned that the factory was making porcelain dishes. We must have done a great job for all that was left was crumbs. There was not one satisfactory souvenir.

As the Captain and Commodore attended the meeting, Art Lindh and I traipsed thru several Jap caves and found an abandoned Jap torpedo boat. It was set up for two torpedos, but was one big torpedo in itself. We took the boat back to the ZELLARS and the engineers fixed it so that it ran. Two at a time would take off in the darned machine and we found that it was fast, real fast. At full throttle, it would do close to 55 MPH. I rode in it one time. It was frightening for me.

On about April 8th or 9th, a few days before we were hit, we received orders to go to the east side of Okinawa to a bay and navigate for a few miles to a low mountain. Our assignment was to fire over the mountain and wipe out a number of Japanese machine gun nests. (The mountain was some 200-300 ft high.) The machine guns had prevented the Marines from crossing a wooden bridge and gain the top of the mountain, which was badly needed in order for the Marines to fire down on the airfield at Naha. We had several problems in order to carry out the task. The final conclusion was to navigate from the bridge, while approaching on a fixed path, firing regular barrages, adjusting the distance as we moved. Our observer was a Marine Col. whose excessive use of the "F" word almost confounded the job that we successfully achieved. We, the ship, marched the shell pattern down from the top of the mountain to the Japanese machine gun placements, and the Marines landed.

A lesser item that I recall, we frequently came close inshore to bombard the Naha airfield so as to preclude reconstruction of the airfield and use by the Japanese planes. On such an occasion, the captain ordered me to the bridge, pointing to a cemetery and said, "Watch." I did, to discover that artillery was firing from the cemetery. Visual direction of their main battery quickly assured that only the dead occupied the cemetery.

The ZELLARS finally came-to the day when we were added to the vast list of destroyers that had paid the price, April 12, 1945 — a day that will not be forgotten. About an hour after we were put out of action, we lost one of our greatest presidents, FRANKLIN D. ROOSEVELT.

I will never forget standing behind the SG radar screen with my eyes glued to the "pips" that reflected our successful attacker as they bored down to the center line of the radar until the crash and explosion terminated so much and so many on the ZELLARS.

I was in deep shock as everything tumbled and shattered around us. I found the same was true of many others but the discipline cultivated by many practices paid off and, from what I observed that day, a battered defenseless ship, with great character and will, did what had to be done.

The crew managed to regain steering control as engineering sweated out the rudder moves on voice command from the bridge. All communications had been knocked out. Limited communications were restored because two radiomen responded and told me that they might be able to build a transmitter from the rubble that had once been the radio room. They did it in about three hours.

With CIC in a shambles and completely out of commission, I went to the bridge for orders. I started toward the captain who was followed by his telephone talker, Y2c SEXTON, holding one of the Captain's shoes in his hand. The shoe had been blown off by the blast. The Captain, with one shoe on and one off, was carrying on his duty as though nothing was wrong.

Having lost Dr. KINKAID and one other of our medical staff we were in great difficulty. The fleet order was to stay away from cripples. Another destroyer came alongside and by megaphone inquired, "Is there anything we can do?"

The Captain replied, "We need a doctor." A few minutes later, reducing speed, but not stopping, the destroyer bumped us on the port side and its ship's doctor jumped on board the ZELLARS. Not long after the aiding destroyer left us, it was also hit by a Kamikaze, but I did not learn the details and her damage. I will never forget this memorial to the brotherhood of the destroyer and her crew.

With our mangled ship and crew, we made our way back to Kerama Retto, the refuge for all crippled ships.

On the 13th, the crew began the task of cleaning up. An LST rigged out as a repair ship came alongside and it's crew were marvels. The entire lower deck was equipped with a machine shop and the crew could build anything.

We didn't look very pretty from our bow to near midships, from the bridge to the water line on the starboard side. The repair crew, with the help of many of our crew, covered the massive hole on the starboard side and created a temporary ward room. We would, and could, get by.

A few days before we left Okinawa and headed for home, the Captain told me that I would be the navigator, because our navigator had been wounded. I locked myself in an available space and boned up on navigation. Fortunately our Chief Quartermaster knew the stars as well as any ancient mariner and so luckily, we had a navigation team to lead five or six other cripples on the long trip home. Because all of our navigation equipment was gone, I gained some empathy for Columbus.

Our first stop was the Island of Guam and on to Eniwetok. That brings to mind that everyone was writing home in hopes that the mail leaving Eniwetok would arrive before we did. As officers, we were required to censor all mail leaving the ship. I never minded the duty, for example, one of the shipmates managed to maintain three different romances at the same time, who, without any other content or expression, could daily write eight to ten pages with the ending, "I love you." More significantly, my own writings to my wife were enhanced by my borrowing suggestions that she take a long look at her floor because when I got back, all she would see would be the ceiling.

Pearl Harbor to Long Beach was uneventful except to live with five to seven knots and the groans and squeaks of a wounded ship temporarily tied together, Arriving in Long Beach, the dock was loaded with families, friends, a band and a line of milk trucks

The ship's reconstruction was completed and as we began our retraining and second shakedown, the war came to an end with the Japanese surrendering. A brief shakedown was conducted off San Diego and the ZELLARS joined some 50-75 warships reassigned to the Atlantic Fleet. There was a great adventure passing thru the Panama Canal and to New York City for the first post-war Navy Day celebration.

I could never get away from being "the lawyer." The Captain called me to his cabin and advised me that one of the crew was in the hands of the Panama police and that I should go over and work some of my legal charm on them. The police gave me a torrent of talk (or shouting), describing how my shipmate had beat up on a person at a whore house and three Panamanian police, when he had demanded a second round without funds to pay for it. I informed the police officer that a couple hundred of his shipmates would look very unkindly at the mate being kept in jail and might pay him a visit. As hoped, the police officer relented and said that he would be pleased to turn the sailor over to me if the Navy would keep the sailor on board until the ship sailed.

Arriving in New York, we anchored just south of the George Washington Bridge for the Navy Day events and President Truman's parade. When our turn came, we tied up at one of the shipping piers where for two days more than one million visitors came aboard. We had three gangways and the biggest job was to keep people from falling and shielding the ladies from embarrassment when they used the vertical ladders. We soon set sail for the great Naval base at Norfolk.

After several days, we refueled and replenished our stores. We sailed with the new carrier FRANKLIN D. ROOSEVELT for her shakedown cruise to Guantanamo Bay, Cuba. During our tour with the carrier FRANKLIN, we were specialists in carrier escort and plane guard detail. Our duty as service destroyer generally was to ride 500 yards astern of the carrier on her starboard side and turn to take station as the carrier signals ordered. I had the com and the carrier flags and TBS (talk between ships) ordered a turn which could have sent me to a court martial, but for a very strong statement from the Commodore and Captain.

We were steaming at standard speed with the Commodore and Captain sitting in their forward bridge chairs. The whole bridge staff, signalmen, etc., as well as yours truly, read the signal from the carrier that said, "I would execute a ninety-degree left turn upon "execute." It required an immediate turn to form some 500 yards astern on the carrier's starboard side. They signaled, "execute." The maneuver was grossly jeopardized by the carrier as it turned right instead of the command to turn left. The ZELLARS and I were on a serious collision course, with the Captain and Commodore both yelling at me. At best, I clipped off a series of commands, „port engine full astern- starboard engine full forward, rudder hard aport," then waited for what would come. The ship barely cleared the carrier.

From the Captain, "Go to your quarters and get your relief up on deck." About one-half hour later, I was called to the bridge and I learned that I had been cleared. The Captain said, "Why did you ignore the Commodore and me when we were offering help?"

"Captain, did I give the right commands?"

"Yes, but why didn't you listen?"

"Because, sir, there was not enough time. If the command had not been given instantly, we probably would have collided. What's more, had you seen fit under the articles, you could have said, 'I relieve you sir' and taken command." Other than cussing me out as 'that darned lawyer,' there was no further word from the Commodore or the Captain.

After completing this duty, we sailed back to Norfolk, VA, where we learned we were to take the FDR down to Rio de Janeiro Brazil. Since I had only a few more days to satisfy discharge on the point system, I asked the Captain if I could stay over at Norfolk. He had my orders prepared, along with the Commodore's OK and I departed for the Naval District Headquarters with the transfer orders.

On March 9, 1946 at 9 PM, I was discharged from active duty. I last saw the ZELLARS about one year later after the Captain sent me already executed orders. I was going aboard for a two-week cruise to help train new Academy graduates in CIC operation.

SHELDON BERNSTEIN, Lt., plank owner

USS ZELLARS (DD777)

BERNARD T. GOLDATE

ENTERED NAVY: OCTOBER 28, 1942

BOOT CAMP: SAN DIEGO, CA.
COMPANY 672-42

ASSIGNED TO ZELLARS: AUG. 1944

LENGTH OF SERVICE ON ZELLARS: OCT. 44 - DEC. 45

RATING: SM3c

PLACES VISITED: Seattle, Washington: San Diego, CA;. Pearl Harbor, Hawaii; Ulithi; Okinawa; Guam; Eniwetok; Panama Canal; New York City; Guantanamo Bay, Cuba.

April 12, 1945, around 14:00, the General alarm sounded.

After a short time at our battle station, the watch was secured. It seemed that the radar room didn't want to secure the General Quarters watch. By the time we returned to our regular duties, the alarm sounded again. To the best of my knowledge, BOB EATON, DAVE CONNAUGHTON and myself, with other signal crew, were up on the bridge when we spotted planes coming from all directions on the port side. We had to rush like hell to get back to our regular battle stations.

I was a loader next to DAROLD JORGENSEN. I couldn't find my life jacket. The sky was full of dark smoke from exploding ammunition as every ship had their work cut out for them.

I was on a 40MM quad gun mount, port side when one plane passed overhead and went on to attack the battleship TENNESSEE. About the same time the other planes got to us. The plane hit mount two in the upper handling room. The base of a 20MM gun from the starboard side, landed on the deck just behind our station. It knocked a big hole in the deck. I think a shipmate was slightly injured. Mount

44 was turning forward to fire on a second plane. The turning of the mount may have saved Darold and myself. It was getting pretty damn hot from the flames where the plane hit our ship.

TOM BREWSTER, a hometown friend who I grew up with, was on the Tennessee. He said the flames were higher than our mast and the fire and smoke looked very bad to him. He thought I was never going to make it out alive. Tom and I still talk about the event to this day.

It was not pleasing to see all of my shipmates dead and wounded but everyone did their best. I can't recall his name, but a shipmate on the aft torpedo tube was cut in half by flying shrapnel.

Because all power was lost, we had to operate the guns manually. Later that afternoon we went into Kerma Retto where we dropped anchor and began to repair the damage.

Every night we had to stand guard around the ship to make sure no Japs would try to swim to the ship, sneak on and throw grenades into the compartments. We were armed with rifles with bayonets at the end and had to keep a close eye on our station. I was one who had to stand guard one night, and believe me, that will make your ass bite buttonholes.

We were put in drydock to get our sound system off and do some repairing on the bottom of the ship. After dark we were raided again by airplanes. Under smoke screen, the Japs dropped a bomb close to the drydock that shook the ship. That was another scary night.

It was sure great to depart for the good old US of A. The war ended just about the time we were to go back and join with other ships overseas.

We left San Diego to meet with other ships and were transferred to the Atlantic Fleet and went thru the Panama Canal to New York for Navy Day.

In December of 1945, I left the ship in New York and went to New Orleans where I was discharged on the point system. In 1953, at the age of 29, Mary and I married. I have a son, Bennie and a step-son, Iggie. We have three granddaughters and one grandson. I retired at the age of 62. I worked at a shipyard as a ship fitter foreman. Whenever we worked on grab rails around the super structure, I always told the men to make sure they fit the grab rails real good and to be sure they were welded right. One day the General Alarm went off. When I was running to mount 44, the ship made a swift turn to port. The water came over the deck and I had to grab onto the hand rails to save myself from going overboard. I got a wet ass but I'm still here to talk about it. In closing, it was great to be a sailor aboard the ZELLARS and the reunions are the greatest — to be with and talk with, a whole bunch of shipmates who served aboard the ZELLARS.

If I remember correctly, there was a shipmate who had enough time in the Navy to retire after 20 years or more. He had the choice to be stationed anywhere he wanted until the war ended. When the ZELLARS arrived at Pearl Harbor, he liked the looks of the ship and wanted to serve on a Navy destroyer. He was killed on April 12, 1945.

BERNARD T. GOLDATE. Sm3c, plank owner

USS ZELLARS (DD777)

GLENN E. WILLIG

ENLISTED: DECEMBER 27, 1941

BOOT CAMP: GREAT LAKES, ILL.

FIRST ASSIGNED TO ZELLARS: AUGUST 1944

LENGTH ON ZELLARS: 3 YEARS, 2 MONTHS

RATING: WT1c.

PLACES VISITED: Alaska; Aleutian Islands; many Islands in the South Pacific.

August of 1941, three of my friends were pretty sure we would be caught in the Army draft. We decided to go to Chicago to see a big league baseball game. It rained for three days. We never got to see any ball games. I came home.

I was at work on December 7th when the Japs struck Pearl Harbor. The 14th of December I got my draft notice to come to Iowa Falls for my physical. The 20th of December I passed and they asked me if I would like to be deferred and I asked if there was something wrong. They said NO, but could get me a deferment and I said if there is nothing wrong, I would like to stay home for Christmas. They indicated that if I would not take the deferment, I was in the Army and I would be sent out in two days.

I told them I was going to Waterloo and join the Navy. They said I was too late and that I was in the Army. I told them that I was going to see about that and drove to Waterloo and joined the Navy. I asked if I could stay home for Christmas. They told me I could stay home for New Year's also.

The Navy put us all on a bus for Des Moines. We were put up in a hotel that night. The next morning we were sworn in. We then took another physical and shipped off to Great Lakes.

We stayed in a barracks overnight, then the next morning we got our uniforms, bedding, hammocks, and were sent to Navy Pier. After getting our shots, we did some marching and finished boot camp.

Next we were shipped in three train loads to the West Coast. The second day we stopped in the desert and had to do some walking for 45 minutes, then back on the train again, to Goat Island, in Oakland, California.

We stayed there for the night and the next day we were sent to Treasure Island for a couple of days. Then 29 of us were sent by tug to Mare Island where we were assigned to the U.S.S. Sands DD 249. She was being outfitted for escort duty, so a month from the time I left home, I was aboard a ship. We escorted oil tankers from San Pedro to Seattle and took troop ships about 500 miles out and escorted some freighters back.

On one of our trips to Seattle we encountered a two-man submarine off the coast of Oregon. We dropped some depth charges. It came up and turned over and disappeared. We never saw it again.

We then escorted some troops to Dutch Harbor, Alaska. We had word that the Japs were coming so we were assigned to shoot our torpedos at the battleship of the Japs and then go to the most secure port which we were going to, Seattle. But it never materialized. Our Air Force turned them around. We then patrolled Unimac Island, the Bearing Sea and the Pribilof Islands. We saw all the seals, then on up to Nome and back to Anchorage. The ship worked the Alaskan Islands from May to November 1942, then back to the states. The ship was then refitted, taking out both boilers and #1 fire room and was converted to an APD high speed troop transport. We could carry 200 Marines or Soldiers. Then it was off to the South Pacific.

At Guadalcanal, the cruiser Chicago had been hit. We went alongside but the sea was very rough. We had to pull away. The Chicago was put in tow, we were alongside her. The Japs came back and dropped some more bombs on the Chicago and sank her. We picked up the survivors. I don't remember where we took them. I remember that I was cleaning one of the guys up and was going to cut off his T-shirt, which was full of oil. Just as I brought the knife up to cut the T-shirt, he let out one of the most blood-curdling yells that I have ever heard. I jumped back and then came back and told him I was just going to clean him up so that the doctor could look at him.

We escorted some troops to Port Morsby, New Guinea, then further up the coast, and then some to New Britton. We had come back to Port Morsby to pick up 200 soldiers and a big plane came in and landed. It came pretty close to the shore and some people got out and walked ashore, then another plane came in and also landed; another group waded ashore. Those on shore were taking pictures of them. The next Life Magazine came out showing McArthur leading his men in battle. We secured in October 1943. There was a call for a Chief and a 2nd class Water Tender to go to school in Philadelphia so a Chief and I took the challenge and came back to the states to go to Philadelphia

Navy Yard for 9 weeks, then to Norfolk, Virginia for 8 weeks. In August 1944 I was sent to Seattle Washington and Todd Shipyard as a member of the new construction crew of the U.S.S. ZELLARS DD 777. 30 some men made up the early training crew. It was our responsibility to train the new men who would serve in the different departments. I was assigned to the number 1 fire room along with an officer and a Chief.

In early October, the rest of the crew came up from Treasure Island, California, making a total of 350 officers and men. On October 25, the ZELLARS was placed in commission.

We took our shakedown and headed back to the South Pacific. We did some practicing and simulating of different situations, and then went on to Ulithi. I never saw so many ships as there were at Ulithi. We had some recreation and relaxation, then headed for Okinawa. To pass the time of day and some nights, we played Poker, Pinochle, Acy Ducy, Cribbage and shot a little "bull" with the other guys. We did some singing also and had a good time.

The morning of April 12, 1945, a beautiful day, we all started to lay a barrage on the shore. After an hour there was so much flack it was like a cloudy day. We had a few GQs in the morning and several more just after noon.

The ship had been at General Quarters about 1400 and had secured from that GQ. From the first day of shore bombardment in late March, the crew were walking zombies. We did two things, standing our regular sea detail watch and GQ. No one moved too far from their GQ station and sleep was just a dream. It was only moments after the 1400 GQ all clear had been sounded when the alarm went off again.

Some planes were coming in. We followed them with radar to within 20 miles. They were coming in high but turned around and went back. We had secured from GQ and I had gone back to our quarters since I was not on watch. I had just gotten back to my bunk when word came over the PA system to get back to the GQ station. The Jap planes were coming in at us, just skimming the water.

The section that had the gun watch began to fire immediately and I knew Jap planes were very close. The 40MM and almost at the same time, the 20MM began to fire. Of the four Jap planes in the attack, we shot down two, and the third one struck us forward with P.K. WATSON, GM1c downing the 4th from the 20MM on the port side of the aft stack. The 4th plane was headed straight for the aft section of the ship and had P.K. not been such a great gunner, many more of the crew would have been killed. It exploded about 100 yards from the ship.

I had just secured the living quarters hatch when some one said the ship was hit and was on fire from the midship passageway forward. I pulled the fire hose out on the port side amidships and fought the fire going forward. There were tubes about the size of caulking tubes burning. I could swing, grasp and throw them one at a time overboard. They went under the water and came back up burning.

I picked up a life jacket. It had a body in it; no arms, legs or head. I gasped, someone said to just lay it up by the bulkhead, and I kept on fighting the fire.

I moved over to the starboard side. The deck was blown out down below the scullery to the auxiliary power generator room. Someone was calling for help and he would go under water. Another shipmate and I — I don't know who he was — went down, lifted the generator and motor off him and brought him up. I don't know who he was but when we got him out someone took him from us to be taken for treatment. I went on cleaning up.

I had fuel oil all over my clothes. The fire was out. I got myself cleaned up in the aft fire room. DAN CHOVAN handed me a cup of coffee. I shook so bad I almost burned my hand.

CHOVAN then handed me a cigarette, I could not light it; I shook so bad. I couldn't talk; I just stuttered. Just a while ago, I had the strength of a bull and was well under control and now I was so weak I stuttered and shook. Just to show you, when you need it you have it, but when it leaves you, you are weak and tired. It sounds like I did it all myself but there was always someone there to help.

My General Quarters station was the aft repair party, repairing the ship if hit, and securing the aft quarters of the living and sleeping space. My secondary responsibility was to carry 40MM ammunition to gun mounts when needed.

After we got back to the states, got repaired and another shake down cruise, the war was over. I had enough points and a Water Tender 1 class but they offered me Chief if I would go with the ship to the East Coast and help keep the ship on an even keel. I had enough points, so I got out and was married on March 27, 1947. .

GLENN E. WILLIG, WT1c plank Owner.

USS ZELLARS (DD777)

LEONARD ALLEN BELL

ENTERED NAVY: NOV. 3, 1943

BOOT CAMP, GREAT LAKES, ILL.
COMPANY 1712, CAMP PERRY

ASSIGNED TO ZELLARS: AUGUST 1944

LENGTH OF SERVICE ON ZELLARS: OCT. 1944 TO
MAY 6, 1946

RATING: F1C

PLACES VISITED: Seattle, WA; San Diego, CA; Long
Beach, CA; Pearl Harbor, Hawaii; Ulithi: Panama
Canal; Guantonamo Bay, Cuba; Pensacola, FL;
Brooklyn Navy Yard; Norfolk, VA.

After boot camp, I was sent to a gunnery training base called Point Montara, Calif. There I was on ship's company for four of my most hated months. That's when I wanted to be a boiler repairman. The gunnery base was for transits to train for 5" guns, 40MM, 20MM guns. There was no liberty for the base was 18 miles from San Francisco. This is where I had my first "short arm inspection." Montara is where I met my shipmate who was killed, CHESTER MORMAN. CHESTER and I had a chance to learn about 20MM guns. Later, I think that is why I was assigned to 20MM gun battle stations.

At Montara, I learned the hard way that you do not tell an ensign he's a "chicken shit." He walked across the deck that I was swabbing and ordered me to stop mopping as he tracked thru the freshly cleaned deck. The officer made tracks to the administration office to put me on report. It cost me ten days in the brig on bread and water. The Captain's mast was the worst day of my Navy life.

Montara was just being built when myself and some fifty other sailors were sent there. I chose to work with the engineers, building the boiler room space, learning the trade that I would need in the future. Sometimes on my own, I would go to the gunnery firing range and get to shoot the 20MM machine guns. I learned to be pretty good at hitting the target.

After I was assigned to the ZELLARS, P.K. WATSON, GM1c tried to get me to become a gunners mate.

Something extra I remember. Most of the boiler room crew had personal things that they worked on. (Personally I worked on making a knife out of a piece of stainless steel.) When I was wounded on April 12, 1945, my pants were cut off me and my pants and knife went over the side.

RED PETERSON, another boiler room shipmate, was working on his project one day. He had his project in the vise at the work table in the boiler room. Engrossed in doing the work, he didn't see or hear the Captain coming down the ladder for a visit. Standing behind PETERSON, Commander KINTBERGER asked PETERSON what it was he was making. Without looking around or up, he casually stated, "I am making an asshole for a hobby horse."

The Captain responded, "Whatever it is, you are doing a good job," and the Captain retreated back up the ladder.

It was not uncommon for the Captain to wander down to the different spaces and visit with the crew. He frequently stopped by the boiler room for a great cup of coffee and told about being an engineering officer on board his first destroyer.

April 12, 1945, while supporting a task group that included the battleship TENNESSEE, we were hit by a Jap suicide plane that caused a great deal of damage and killed 44 of my shipmates. My gun station was on a 20MM gun, starboard side, just aft of mount 43. A piece of one of the 20MM gun mounts that was on the starboard side forward was blown over the ship and cut the TM2c in half. He was just in front of his battle station which was the aft torpedo tubes. A piece of the metal flew off as it hit the deck and severely damaged my leg. When I came to my senses, I was lying on the top of my ammunition locker just behind my gun. P.K. WATSON, DAROLD JORGENSEN and, I think, WARNER MACKAY, were working on my wounds. One of the three cut off my pants. P.K. applied a bandage to my leg and gave me a shot of morphine.

With the ship dead in the water, explosions and fires, another destroyer, the BENNION, DD 724 came alongside to help put out the fires and pass over their Doctor. Our Doctor had been killed outright in the explosion.

I remember that my shipmates from the after boiler room came up to where I was lying to see and talk to me. As we were talking, I remember another DD came alongside to help remove our wounded. I was carried off on a stretcher and put on a top bunk. I could look down on several of my also-wounded shipmates. I saw EUGENE LEVITS with burns on his arms, face and shoulders. I saw HAROLD WYCKOFF with badly injured legs. I did not know that he had lost both of his legs just below his knees.

As I lay in the bunk, one of the PhMs from the ship came up to me and said, "I'm going to give you a shot." I did not know that it was another morphine shot. That's two morphine shots in less than two hours. That was the last thing that I remembered for three days. (From Okinawa to Guam)

I was put on a hospital ship that I think was the HSS HAVEN. I didn't wake up from my long sleep until I was being loaded into a basket stretcher, with two men carrying me up a ladder and out to an open deck. I truly remember how beautiful fresh air smells.

I was put on a truck along with nine other shipmates and taken to hospital 102 on Guam. For the first three days, I was one of the walking wounded until it was my time for an operation on my right leg. In the meantime I carried cold water and ice for the men in the same ward. I also made cigarette holders for some of the men that were badly burned. If a man can't feel the presence of God in his life it's times like this that make a good man know His presence. God was truly watching over me. The burn ward at this hospital was crammed full of men, some completely covered with their eyes and mouth exposed. Did you ever smell burnt flesh? If you have, you will never forget it.

One morning we were told that Admiral CHESTER NIMITZ was coming to see us. Sure enough he came into our ward, talked with each man, and even talked to me. One of his aids took my home address and my PURPLE HEART so that he could send it to my home. The next day, I was taken into the operating room where two pieces of shrapnel were removed from my leg. For the next four days I stayed in bed and received 36 penicillin shots.

After three more days working around the ward, I was sent to a OGU barracks. I was there for six days doing various things such as standing watch in a building. I was also sent on a working party to dig a trench for a platform and I still remember one of the men was working near me with a pick. He struck an unexploded shell which exploded, sending the sailor's body parts in many different directions. He never knew what he had hit but we did. In war death comes so easily.

Orders were posted and all the men on the "shipping out list" were directed to get their gear, and were taken to the waterfront to be loaded on a merchant ship with the name of "Seaflasher." The scroungiest ship that I had ever seen. How it remained afloat only the Captain knew. Being a true sailor, I felt that I was going to be used on the ship in an never-ending work party. They did not know that I was a master at "gold bricking."

I'll tell this true. I spent five days from Guam to San Francisco. I found some great hiding places that the crew didn't know about. I came up for chow and fire drills and talked with other Sailors and Marines. I remember one of the ship's crew came up to me several times and asked if I knew the sailor called BELL. Without cracking a smile, I told him he is always down in the boiler room. This avoiding work didn't last. I got caught and had to go before the leading officer in charge of transits. I was given a reprimand and a letter to be given to my ZELLARS Captain, Commander KINTBERGER.

It was May 20th when I got to Treasure Island Navy Base. For the next two weeks I stood watches and was assigned to work parties. I also had liberty that allowed for hunting girls in town, and I did. One gal taught me all about sex. (This in itself would be a book.) Catching up with the ZELLARS, I was sent by train to Long Beach where the ship was being repaired. It was on the morning of June 2, 1945. All of the crew that had returned with the ship were housed in some temporary buildings. As I walked into the building something happened that I will never forget. I got the warmest and most gratifying greeting a young sailor could ever have. P.K. WATSON, JORGENSEN and all my boiler room shipmates, PETERSON, BROKOP, MENSEN, Mr. MARLOW, Chief POOL, and a lot more. After a greeting like this I was indeed very proud to be on the ZELLARS and living and sailing with such good men.

I found myself a locker and a bunk. BROKOP and I walked down the main road of the shipyard, talking about our ship and I learned how many of my shipmates had been killed. As we got to the dry dock where the ZELLARS was, tears came to my eyes, looking at the massive hole in her starboard side and the wound to her port side. There were four other ships in the same drydock but I could only see the ZELLARS .

The next day at muster, Lt. BIRD came up to me and said, "glad to see you, welcome back to the crew." Mr. MARLOW was there also. I had to see Commander KINTBERGER to have him give me a requisition to replace all my clothes that were lost after the ship was hit. At the same time I gave the Captain the letter that the Seaflasher transfer officer ordered me to give to him some three weeks earlier. Would you believe, KINTBERGER looked at me after reading the letter, flashed a broad smile and stated that I should be given some kind of medal for being the best goldbricker in the Navy.

After our brief tour at Okinawa and being hit by a Jill suicide plane, we returned to the states and Long Beach, CA. for repairs and that is where we were when the war came to an end.

After the ZELLARS was repaired, the ship went to San Diego for training. It was not too long after that the ship was sent around, thru the Panama Canal to the Atlantic. We first stopped in Panama City. What a liberty town that was — sex, sex, and more sex. Cheap at that, two dollars. After four days, we set sail for Colon, the Atlantic side of the canal.

Our next stop was New York City, getting there in November. The ZELLARS anchored in the Hudson River just below the George Washington Bridge. There were about 50 different ships assembled to render a salute to President Truman. There were Battleships, Cruisers, Carriers, and about 20 destroyers all strung out up and down the Hudson River. Later The «Z» tied up to a dock near Greenwich Village. The ship held open house and many of the area people came aboard to visit. Some of the ZELLARS crew marched down 5th Avenue as part of the parade. The city of New York changed the street of Park Avenue to the Avenue of Americas and during the celebration the ZELLARS crew was right in front of the podium.

From January through most of February we spent escorting our new carrier, the FRANKLIN D ROOSEVELT, on her shakedown cruise, stopping at Jamaica, then on down to Rio de Janeiro, Brazil.

On January 29th the ZELLARS crossed the Equator and all those who had not crossed before, called Polywogs, went thru the traditional ceremony of hazing and great comradeship by those who had been across before. We were all now proud Shell Backs, and forever part of Neptunus Rex's domain, *Ruler of the Raging Main.*

The ZELLARS was one of three destroyers to escort the ROOSEVELT to Rio. Along with the mighty „Z" were the U.S.S. FOX DD 778 and the U.S.S. Storm DD 779. We spent 10 days in Rio de Janeiro. The Carrier and destroyers set sail back to Guantanamo Bay, Cuba. In late February, underway again for a high speed run to New York. The three destroyers left port hours before the carrier. The ZELLARS had all four boilers and super heaters on line with a great strain on all engines. We were really moving. 34 knots was the best we could do. When the Carrier left port, she had six double boilers and six screws on line. I remember that the Carrier passed us and got into New York about six hours ahead of us and the other two destroyers. We tied up at a pier at the Brooklyn Navy Yard, secured the boilers and after such a strain, the boilers were pulsating, panting like dogs. We spent the next three weeks in the Navy Yard.

I left the ZELLARS May 6th 1946, but stayed in the reserves. I was called back in November, 1950. I sailed on another destroyer named the U.S.S.ROGERS DDR 876. In 1954, I got my final discharge from the Navy.

LEONARD BELL. F1c plank owner

USS ZELLARS (DD777)

VERLYN H. PETERSON

ENLISTED: MARCH 8, 1944

BOOT CAMP: GREAT LAKES, ILL.

ASSIGNED ZELLARS: SEPT. 1944

RATING: WT/3c

PLACES VISITED: Great lakes, ILL; Philadelphia Navy Yard, Treasure Island, CA; Seattle, WA: San Diego, CA; Pearl Harbor, Hawaii; Ulithi: Okinawa: Panama Canal; Recife, Brazil; Trinidad; Guantanamo Bay, Cuba; Pensacola, FL; Norfolk, VA; New York City.

Our boot camp was cut short because of heavy losses in the Pacific. It lasted only four weeks.

I went to basic engineering school and it was a sixteen-week course. I was one of eight that went to school from boot camp. The rest went to camp Shoemaker for amphibious training. I left Great Lakes and went to Philadelphia Naval Ship Yard for Water Tender training arriving 6/28/44. I spent the 4th of July there. I was a Fireman 1st class then. We went on a clam bake with some families from church that we went to on Sunday. It was really a blast.

Then we went to Pier 25 in New York to be assigned, then to Treasure Island. We made the long trip from New York to California in July. In Iowa City they hooked a carload of Waves behind us. We were behind the diner car, so we locked the door. It seemed like the right thing to do.

I was in charge of the draft so I had the compartment. I also celebrated my birthday. We were met by a group of ladies from several churches in the area, it was awful hot. I remember that it was in Nebraska.

We arrived in Oakland, California, then the ferry ride to Treasure Island where we were to become part of the ZELLARS crew. More training shipboard on the U.S.S. LITTLE (2100 class DD) out for day cruises. Rough to ride on the outside of the Golden gate. We then went to fire fighting school which was really rough, then to Gunnery school at Point Montara CA.

I then worked at a Master at Arms station. Had KP for 5 days so we didn't have to stand in line, also got to eat early. I boxed in the smokers on weekend nights as money was real short.

Then came the train ride to Seattle to meet our ship. It was a slow ride as we were not cargo, just sailors headed for a ship that wasn't even in commission. The cars were like cattle cars, bunks four high. I grabbed the top bunk which was not folded up during the day. I always had a place to rest.

We moved into some barracks to wait to move onto the ship. I think that we were kept busy. I don't remember much about that.

Four of us got together to buy a bottle which cost $20.00. The promoter then dropped it in the curb. It ran into the sewer. He cried and is lucky that we did not kill him.

On the 25th of October, the ship was placed into commission and things really began to happen. First some preliminary engine trials in the Puget Sound, then back to the shipyard docks for tune-up.

On an overcast morning, the ship slipped out of the inland waters and tasted her first deep salt-water home. Shakedown was down to San Diego where everything on the ship was tested and retested: gunnery, ship handling, rescue at sea anti-submarine drills and so on. Then back to Bremerton Naval Shipyard for any repairs or deficiencies noted during our shakedown. By then we had the fire room pretty well set. My watch was with WILLIG in charge. Battle station was on the checks.

The last night in Bremerton we were short of time so we went to a beer joint just off the base. The bar maid was well endowed. The action of a couple of our fearless petty officers (Hutch and Johnson) just about got us all in the brig. The ZELLARS spent Christmas 1944 at the Seattle Shipyard.

In mid-January I knew that a change was about to happen. Special stores came on board. Ammo was stored to the limits and fuel oil to the maximum. On Jan. 25, muster as usual, then all hands to sea details was sounded by the Bos'n mate. We slowly backed out of our dock and pointed the bow toward the West and Pearl Harbor. The ship was in serious training all the way. General Quarters drills at all times of the night, especially around 2 AM.

We made our way into the destroyer anchorage on the North side of Ford Island. It sure made us realize that there was a war on, and it was real horrible. First there was an inspection by the Commander of Destroyers Pacific. Then loaded more supplies. No rest. Immediately, we began very serious training with the Aircraft Carrier FRANKLIN. We were her plane guard for pilots that might miss their landings on the carrier. It was our responsibility to try to rescue the pilots if possible. Sometimes we would go out to sea for just a day, other times we would be out for the week.

Our Pearl Harbor training was more of the same but greatly intensified. A lot of attention was paid to ASW and shore bombardment with special emphasis on air attacks. A plane would meet us out to sea towing a long colored sleeve. As it passed down one side of the ship all guns would open fire with hopes of knocking it down on the first rounds. Sometimes we did and sometimes we didn't. Each time we got better.

One of the more exciting training events was the firing of practice torpedos. We would fire at a target ship with the torpedos set to run deep under the target ship should our aim be true. At the end of the torpedo run, air in the center tank would blast the water out of the warhead and most of the time, it would float to the surface for recovery.

On February 28th, we got a new Captain. Commander Kintberger who had lost a destroyer (U.S.S. HOEL DD 533) at the battle of Leyte on the same day our ship was placed into commission, October 25, became our new skipper. With the new Captain, things really began to pick up. He was very experienced in combat and had real drills to offer. Our routine was pretty much the same. Out to escort the FRANKLIN then as we returned to port, we would be met by a target towing plane and the guns would open up.

March 1, 1945 was a full day of loading all stores to the maximum: fuel, ammo, food stuff and such. The supply officer even piled extra sacks of potatoes just aft of the number two stack. The third of March, early in the morning, along with three carriers, one battle cruiser and seven other destroyers, we headed due West for an unheard of Island in the Carolinas called ULITHI.

Sea detail watches were four on and eight off. GQ all hours of the day and night. Refueling from the carriers, target practice, getting us ready for what was to come.

There were several beer parties on the Island of MOG MOG, part of the Islands of Ulithi. We had several nights of patrol out of the anchorage, mainly to do anti-submarine patrols.

March 21 was the departure date for the whole task force. There were over 1000 ships scattered all over the sea, from horizon to horizon, nothing but warships of all kinds.

On March 25, 1944, we arrived at our target destination, OKINAWA, sailed around the island and dumped shells on everything that looked useful. The routine was to fire all our ammo, return to our anchorage and refuel, load ammo and supplies, then off again to bombard the island. We got very little sleep. Then came the landing on April 1st (Easter) and April Fools' Day. I don't think we fooled anyone on Okinawa. We went into AHA harbor after a big gun, I didn't volunteer, but I was there. I couldn't see anything but it was sure noisy and then came the all astern bell and it was time to get the hell out of there.

Tokyo Rose told us the DIVINE WIND would take care of us. A couple of days later she said she was sorry that the weather was bad but they would be down the next day.

APRIL 12, 1945

It was General Quarters. I was on watch till 13.00 hours on the 12th. Shortly after 13.00 the alarm went off with the „Old Man" doing the yelling on the P.A. The watch guns were already firing. I had been trying to get some rest and was in my bunk which was under the mess deck. I ran from my bunk to the forward fire room by way of the inside passageway. By the time I was on my station, all hell was going on. Of course I couldn't see any of it. It was all noise. I was on the checks, which was on the upper level of the fire room. The rest of the fire room crew was down in the lower level which gave them some protection. They were all able to get out of there; of course, I did not know anything about that.

The next thing I knew, I found myself lying over the fresh water tanks. The fire room was dark and full of steam, smoke and fire. I made my exit into the blower room which was still running so I had plenty of fresh air. The ship was dead in the water. I could hear a lot of the noise from topside but it didn't seem to be too alarming. I went up to the louver to get out, but decided not to. I then went to the hatch in the blower room. I heard noises so I opened the hatch and there stood FLEMING and MAXWELL. Now I wish I'd had a camera, I guess the look on their faces probably was matched by mine. We went topside by the outboard hatch. When we hit the deck they said, "get the 40MM cans overboard." The next few minutes were spent unloading 40 MM cans. I then went to the port side where WILLIG and CUSHING were trying to get a fire pump in operation. CUSHING headed aft with the wire and WILLIG and I went forward to get the pump going. We finally got power, thanks to CUSHING. We were in the hatch of mount #2 while the „old man" was telling the BENNION to get out of there because #2 was going to blow up any minute. I guess that we would have had a ringside seat. We got the fire out, then went to see what happened to BELL. He was on the aft stack 20MM machine gun. He was on the ready box and had been hit in the leg and butt. I talked to him and told him that we were not going to sink. I couldn't swim and still can't.

I then went to the after fire room for further orders. RITTER tagged me for a runner. Shortly, I was sent to the bridge to tell the Captain that the #1 fire room was out but we could proceed with two boilers and both engines, with no engine room compartments being flooded. The Chief torpedoman and a Steward were lying on the deck with bad burns from which they both died later.

We finished shutting down the forward fire room as all the lines forward had been broken. The galley, officers ward room, the Captain's quarters, scullery, CIC, plotting room, forward emergency power generator room and the forward bulkhead of the forward engine room were gone, along with a lot of good shipmates.

A doctor and corpsman from one of the "tincans" came aboard to patch up the walking wounded and the guys that needed more help to make it to the hospital ships. I think that there were around 70 wounded. We were busy, as you can imagine. Later we rescued a couple bottles that had been rolling around the deck. It seemed that it was the only "right" thing to do. We checked it to make sure it was "OK". Eight cases of beer somehow appeared along with a five gallon can of clear grain. Nothing was wrong with that either. Things were a little foggy till the next day, but we came close to losing a couple of shipmates that night. JOHNSON and HUTCH were going to sleep in the forward Chiefs quarters as the bunks were gone under the mess deck. They were on their hands and knees as they had gotten on the drunk side. There had been a warning about Japs slipping aboard ships and the deck force was on guard, and a little trigger-happy. One of the watch said something to them and they got a drunk sailor's reply which calmed everyone down. I have no idea where I was at that time.

Under the ship's own power we made it into the anchorage of Kerama Retto for removal of our dead and wounded. We stayed in this harbor of wounded ships doing as much repair work as we could with a lot of help from the repair ships and floating drydock. It was time to get everything ready for going home. STEWARD was a welder so he worked with the repair crew to help where he could. The repair party tacked plates on the port side and deck so the ship's crew could work at night. The repair crew quit at suppertime. The repair work was nearing completion. They were going to remove one of the ship's screws and the Sonar stack. That meant we were going to be lifted in a floating dry dock. That same night, we were bombed by Japanese planes but they missed us. That was a little hairy.

On May 7th 1945, the ship joined several other ships that also had been Kamikazed. It was about 10:00AM when all ships slipped out of the Okinawa anchorage and formed into a convoy line headed for the Island of Saipan, our first refueling stop.

In Saipan we lost all power somehow and shut down the boilers. It was hotter than hell, 126 degrees on the deck plates. The rescue crew had to get the boiler room crew out. GLEN WILLIG and I went down and lit the boilers off. We got a bunch of men that needed transportation to the States. Most had been released from the hospital. We had all types of servicemen. Most were not good at poker so, of course, sailors never play poker for real money.

The ZELLARS arrived back at Pearl Harbor on May 25, after a fuel stop at the island of Eniwetok. COMDESPAC gave a beer party upon our arrival but I had lost all my clothes. All I had was some dungarees, socks, Tee shirts, and underwear, and missed the party.

I think it was May 30th when we arrived at the Roosevelt Naval Shipyard. They really had a welcome home for us. We got all the attention along with front page stories in the L.A. papers. My mother saved them for me and I still have them in a gold frame.

The ship's crew was broken up into two leave parties. I was in the second leave party so I had the watch in the forward fire room. The shipyard brought some prisoners onboard to work cleaning up and pulling out the brick work out of the #1 boiler. Then they cleaned firesides and all that good stuff.

My father came down from Oregon to spend a few days with me. He really didn't think much of our living quarters or where we spent our time. Everyone treated him real fine. Later, I went home on leave to Wisconsin. I got home on the third, "party time". All the guys that I went to school with were in the service. The gals all worked in the defense plants. I got sick the last day of my leave before I was to return back to the ship. They had a Naval ward at the University of Wisconsin hospital. I spent 10 days there and they decided that I had to have my tonsils out. I still have them.

After I returned to the ship, I found out that I was the new "oil king," just the job I wanted. It cost me an extra six months in December when I was supposed to get out.

We were just getting ready to take on fuel when President Truman came on the air to let us know that the war had ended. The guys on the oil barge told us we had two choices, "give us the hoses or we will drag them back." Being of sound mind we wrapped them up to avoid any mess and returned them to the barge. Then liberty.

We went to San Diego for shakedown and retraining and to test everything out. We were scheduled to return to the invasion fleet but the Navy changed plans and we were sent to join the Atlantic Fleet. We went thru the Panama Canal and again liberty was divided into two sections, One for the Pacific side, Panama City; the other for the Atlantic side, Colon. I went ashore on the Pacific side. It was the rottenest place that I have ever been.

I met the "grand old lady" when we got to New York. I had hit three anchor pools so I had spending money. We tied up at Pier 42, then moved into the north part of the Hudson River for Truman's review. I stood out in the cold wind until 18.00 when "HARRY" went by. I grabbed the first liberty boat, landing at 125th street pier, which was at the edge of Harlem. It was 20.30 when I was walking up 125th street. I spied a sign that said the "Half Moon" in drinks and eats and a good time had by all. It was an all white bar. They were having a Navy Day party and I was the only sailor that stopped on the way to the EL.

During our short stay at Pier 42, in the village, it was open house aboard ship. I think that we stayed in New York until January the 8th, then we went to Norfolk, Virginia. We then played with the big new carrier "MIDWAY" down to Guantanamo Bay Cuba. After taking the MIDWAY for part of her shakedown cruise, we had the honor to escort the also new carrier ROOSEVELT down to Rio de Janeiro. The U.S.S. FOX was with us. Had a great time in Rio.

On the way home from Rio, the officers somehow had gotten a bunch of "Old Granddad" with the wire caps. They were in wooden boxes and were put in mount 43 40MM handling room by the whaleboat. They spent a couple days trying to find some of it that was missing. They finally gave up.

Our next stop was Pensacola Florida to escort the carrier RANGER to pick up the pilots that missed the deck while trying to land. We were there until April 22 1946.

We then proceeded to Earle, New Jersey to unload ammo and fuel. Our next stop was the Navy Yard in Brooklyn, New York. There was a list of important things that needed to be fixed. June 1st was the end of my six-month extension that I mentioned earlier. They spent a lot of time trying to get me to re-up. I had wanted to leave to go home at Christmas but they said I couldn't. If it hadn't been for that I may have stayed in.

I spent one night on Pier 25 in New York, and then two nights on a train to Great Lakes. I got there at 01.00 PM and was put in a line. They didn't even give us a bunk. The 8th of June 1946 at 12.30 my Naval time was done. I got the Northwestern to Waukegan and on to North Shore so I could get the bus to Madison.

I worked in Madison, then to Washington and Oregon working in the saw mills and logging camps, then back to Wisconsin. I then went to work in the building trades and became a master plumber and I am still trying to fool them.

VERLYN H. PETERSON WT3c, plank owner

USS ZELLARS (DD777)

WILLIAM L. GOGAN

ENLISTED, DECEMBER 14, 1942

BOOT CAMP, GREAT LAKES, ILL.

ASSIGNED TO ZELLARS, SPRING 1944

RATING, PhM1c (T).

PLACES VISITED: Hastings, Neb; Ammunitions Depot, Corpus Christi, TX; Norfolk Naval Station (Medical Training); Seattle, Wa; San Diego, CA; Pearl Harbor, Hawaii; Ulithi; Okinawa; Panama Canal; New York City; Guantanamo Bay, Cuba.

U.S. NAVY AMBULANCE

I was assigned to the U.S.S. ZELLARS DD 777 while the ship was being built in Seattle Washington, I arrived in Seattle in the fall and the ship was launched July 19, 1944. The ship was commissioned October 25, 1944. I was the first medical corpsman assigned to the ship.

The U.S.S. ZELLARS had been assigned to the fleet that was to assist in the invasion of Okinawa. On the day of the invasion, about one-half of the fleet was assigned to bombard and support the invasion site on one side of the island and the remainder of the fleet was to bombard and simulate an invasion on the other side of the island so as to add confusion for the Japanese leaders.

We had many General Quarters situations on our ship due to anticipated air raids and actual raids during the days leading up to the date the ZELLARS was hit (April 12,1945) by a Kamikaze plane. We had so many General Quarters situations that had been uneventful that some of us had become somewhat complacent about them. Up until the day the ship was hit most attacks on us were rather exciting as we were able to shoot down the planes and record such on the stack of our ship. We had many Japanese flags painted on the stack (mast) due to our gunners shooting down planes.

In some instances, our gunners started firing at planes as far away as twenty miles and eventually we would see a light in the sky that looked like a falling star — which indicated the plane was hit. The crew then would applaud. We were proud of our gunnery crew for their skills and marksmanship. Even on the day the ship was hit the crew was super because four planes attacked the ship simultaneously and the gunners were able to shoot down three — all were coming in close to the water which made it difficult for the 5-inch guns in trying to fire close to the water.

Our complement of medical personnel on the ship of 345 shipmates was one medical doctor and three medical corpsmen (one Chief, one PhM2c, and one PhM2c). Our assignment for General Quarters was as follows: The Doctor and PhM3c were assigned to the fore or bow area and they were usually camped in the officers' quarters in that part of the ship. The PhM2c was assigned to the middle part of the ship and usually camped out near the passage way leading from one side of the ship to the other. PhM2c was yours truly on the port side of the ship near the passageway. The Chief Pharmacist was assigned to the aft area (stern) of the ship and I am not sure where he camped out. This separation was designed so that if a hit was made on the ship it would be unlikely that all medical personnel would be lost at one time. The Japanese plane (classified as a Betty, a larger Kamikaze plane which carried a pilot and two gunners and a 1,100-pound bomb) hit the forward part of the ship on the port side just behind the five-inch guns and resulted in the death of Doctor KINKAID and PhM3c ENSLEY of the medical corps.

It was reported on April 12, 1945 that 500 Japanese suicide planes had left the islands of Japan in a rather last ditch effort to strike a telling blow to the fleet that was supporting the invasion of Okinawa.

Another fleet located between Japan and Okinawa, and commanded by Admiral NIMITZ, shot down all but 125 of the planes as they attempted to reach Okinawa.

The Japanese had realized that their plan of coming out of the sky high in the air and diving on ships made them easy prey for our ships and guns and they were not very successful in making many hits on ships. Their strategy changed when they had the aid of mountains and land. They came up over the mountains and stayed low to the water as they attacked and headed for the ships.

On the day of April 12th, we had several General Quarters which were called off as the alert passed. We had just been called off an alert and very quickly General Quarters sounded again, so we quickly assumed our positions. This difficulty was likely caused by the planes coming along the other side of the mountains low to the water which made it difficult for radar to pick up. We were in our General Quarters position only a short while and I was sitting on the port side of the central part of the ship and was looking out over the waters bordering the island when all of a sudden I noticed planes coming at our ship with guns firing. Four planes were headed for the ship — two headed for the bow part of the ship, one headed for the middle and one headed for the aft. I could see the propellers hitting the water as the planes approached — also some gunfire. It didn't take me long to come to my senses that I had better be on the move to the other side of the ship. Along with the others assigned to this area of the ship, I quickly ran through the passage way to the starboard side of the ship to escape the gun fire and whatever.

There was smoke from the guns of the ship and quite a bit of confusion and fear as to where to go. There were probably about 14 of us in this position.

It just happened when we arrived on the starboard side of the ship about one-half of us turned right for protection (almost like cattle in a storm on the plains of Nebraska) and the other half turned left. It just so happened tragically that all of our shipmates that turned left for protection were killed outright or were seriously burned and died later aboard a hospital ship. Not knowing what would happen and all of us seeking protection, they ran almost right into the impact of the bomb explosion. All of us that turned right were okay and not injured except one received a slight shrapnel wound in the arm. There was so much smoke and everything after the bomb exploded that it was difficult to realize what had happened and what would be the next move. I knew my responsibility was to attend to the injured once a person could see where to go. Whatever possessed some of us to turn right or left no one will ever know. Perhaps it just wasn't our time to go if we turned right.

Leading up to the incident of running to the starboard side of the ship, there was a constant barrage of gun fire from the ZELLARS intended for the Kamikaze planes attacking the ship. The gunners on our ship did an excellent job of hitting and knocking out three of the four planes that were headed toward the ship on a suicide mission.

One of the planes hit the ship on the port side about three fourths of the way toward the bow of the ship. The plane hit just behind the 5 inch gun on the port side. The plane just splattered on the side of the ship and on the deck. A 1,100 pound torpedo was launched from a height of no more than 15 feet shortly before the plane crashed into the side of the ship. The "deadly fish" was launched before the suicide plane crashed into the side of the ship. The plane crashed into the "rat race" (ammunition handling room) for gun mount No 2. The torpedo slid across the deck and exploded on the starboard side.

The blast tore a 31-foot hole in the starboard side of the ZELLARS from the water line to the main deck and did miscellaneous fire and explosion damage throughout the ship. The plotting room took the main force of the blast.

The plane carried a pilot and two gunners. The three bodies of the Japanese were lying on the main deck after the hit with very little clothing on their bodies. The hand of the Japanese pilot was still clutching the plane's controls. The Doctor and PhM3c were killed instantly with very little trace of their bodies. The plane and bomb killed 44 shipmates and wounded 36. Several of our shipmates were killed outright by concussion and were lying on the deck without any visible injuries to their bodies. The impact of the plane which caused a large hole on the starboard side of the ship, and other damages, took about thirty days for temporary repair so the ship could return to San Diego. Our ship was repaired in a few months and was headed back to the Pacific area when the war was declared over.

As one of the two surviving corpsman, it was my duty to move to the area of the ship where there were injuries and casualties. I was one of the first people to reach the area to assist the injured. The Chief Pharmacist from the aft area joined us shortly. In moving to the area to assist amid all the smoke, fire and confusion, I had to leap over a couple of the bodies of the Japanese who had been in the plane. After I had done this, I noticed a rather large Japanese flag on the deck which evidently was carried on the plane. As soon as I realized this I retraced my steps to retrieve it as a souvenir but in the meantime another shipmate had picked it up.

For several hours we attended the injured. We first attended and administered life saving techniques to the critically injured and critically burned shipmates. After a period of time, a medical doctor from another ship came aboard to work with the critically injured and to handle some of the things that needed to be done that we, as corpsman, were not qualified or licensed to do, e.g. such as amputate a very mangled leg so life saving methods could be administered. Several shipmates were so severely burned due to portions of the ship falling on them, that it was difficult to find veins that could handle intravenous life support — sometimes we could only find a vein in the big toe.

Our ship was hit at about 2 PM, and by late afternoon, before darkness prevailed, all the wounded and dead had been removed to other ships, which had all the needed medical facilities.

Heroism was shown by many shipmates during the crisis. The most heroic was that of Seaman Second Class WILLIAM BIEBER of Center, South Dakota, who was burned to death when he entered the flaming bombed area to rescue some of his shipmates who were trapped in the inferno. Chief Electrician's mate FRANK CUSHING of Los Angeles was commended for his single handed fight against flames which threatened the ship's main powder magazine — an action which, officers said, saved the ship from destruction.

The Japanese were not very successful that day, because out of 500 planes that left Japan that morning and the 125 planes that reached Okinawa, I believe that they were only able to damage four ships in our fleet and I believe that the ZELLARS may have been the only direct hit.

At sundown and after the removal of the injured and dead from the ship, everyone continued to clean up the debris and eventually we were able to settle down into living quarters. This was a time for remorse, sadness, tears and fear due to the loss of so many of our shipmates. Constantly being at sea caused a closeness of most of the crew because we were living and working together twenty-four hours every day and a lot of friendships are developed. We all lost friends and some of us lost our buddies and best friends — friends that one had worked with, laughed with, played cards with, visited with about families and locations, drank with on shore leave — we were a closely knit group and the loss of our friends and shipmates cut deeply into our hearts. I had lost my co-worker PhM3c and medical Doctor, the people that I had daily worked with since boarding the ship in Seattle. We had been together leading up to two years.

The reality of the situation began to set in and emotions began to take over. There had not been time before, due to the emergency work of the situation and the valiant efforts of so many of our shipmates during the crisis. Some of the shipmates were in shock by the event and the loss of shipmates — some laid in their bunks (sacks) some had their heads in their hands not wanting to believe that it all had really happened and there were many tears — some comforted each other with friendly comforting arm around the shoulder of a shipmate. Some fear also accompanied all of this as to what might be ahead for all of us. We needed each other to get through this and to have a close binding to get through the days ahead.

As the ZELLARS was no longer capable of remaining with the fleet, we were pulled and assigned to a cove which was called TIN CAN HOSPITAL. It was an area where damaged ships were placed so temporary repairs could be made so they could return to the United States harbors for permanent repair. It was called Tin Can Hospital as many of the ships damaged were destroyers which were always on the outskirts of a fleet as a first line of protection.

Destroyers were referred to as Tin Cans in the Navy. We were in this location for about 30 days. This was a very frightening and stressful time for our crew because when there was General Quarters alert all we could do was lay a smoke screen over the ships hoping the Japanese planes could not see where we were located. We could hear the firing of guns from the other ships and all we could do was sit around in the smoke screen fearful that bombs could be dropped and /or Japanese Kamikaze planes could dive into the area of the smoke screen. As these ships were out of commission, this did not seem likely but the Japanese were unpredictable. At any rate it was a very stressful time of 30 days being in a position of not being able to defend ourselves.

The ZELLARS docked in Los Angeles Harbor as we had docked there as a new ship on our shakedown cruise before being commissioned. Battered but unbeaten, the destroyer ZELLARS, victim of a mass Japanese air raid off Okinawa, steamed proudly into Los Angeles Harbor to dock for a few days before going to Long Beach for repairs, and, eventually back to the Pacific to rejoin her fleet.

While docked in Los Angeles, we were allowed shore leave to visit the city and any relatives and friends that we might have in the area. I had a sister, Bernadette DesNoyer, living in the Los Angeles area so my buddy, GM3c HAROLD BAKER, and I hopped in a cab and paid a visit.

The arrival of the ZELLARS in Los Angeles area created quite a stir, because it was sort of a celebrity occasion. This ship had been in battle during the invasion of Okinawa and had been hit by a Japanese Kamikaze. Many people were interested in viewing the ship and came to the harbor to see it. The only people allowed aboard the ship for guided tours of the sleeping quarters, chow hall, bridge, etc., were relatives of the ship's crew. My sister, Bernadette, felt very privileged that she could come aboard for the tour and she thoroughly enjoyed it.

While in Long Beach during ship repair, we were allowed shore leave about every other night. As we knew we would return to combat after the ship was repaired, a lot of the crew felt we would live it up as we might not be so lucky next time. It was sort of a silly philosophy as one looks at it now, nevertheless, it was there — perhaps typical of young people. The result was that many of us went out and indulged in a lot of drinking, evidently trying to douse our experiences and fears. Singapore Slings seemed to be this individual's favorite drink during this period although one had much opportunity to try others. Beer never was a favorite of mine even though shipmates said to keep drinking it and you will learn to like it. To this day, this has never happened.

Orders later took our ship to the East coast and in the process we had the chance to view the Panama Canal as we passed through. That was exciting for many of us. As our group of ships was moving toward the canal off the coast of Mexico we encountered a bad storm. One of the ships lost a mate overboard and a couple of ships turned back to try and locate him but he was never found. We spent much of our time on the East Coast in the New York City area during which time we enjoyed the many sites of the city.

It was at New York City that I left the ship, being honorably discharged from the Navy one month short of three years. I had given some thought of signing on for another stint. If I had, I would have had the opportunity of sailing around the world as that is what the ZELLARS did. That would have been an experience of a life time with all the shore leaves in various ports and cities around the world. If I had known this is what the ZELLARS would be doing in the next several months, I probably would have signed on as I had enjoyed the Navy experience other than the tragic happening with the Kamikaze plane and the loss of shipmates. I have occasionally thought about how my life and family might be so different if this would have happened. I probably would not have the wonderful family that I now have and cherish and love so much.

I decided to enter the education field as a teacher, coach and public school administrator. I obtained a Doctor's Degree in Educational Administration and eventually became a Superintendent of Schools and part-time University Professor. I spent a total of 43 years in education in Phoenix, Arizona; Denver, Colorado, and central Nebraska.

WILLIAM L. GOGAN PhM1c, plank owner

USS ZELLARS (DD777)

ARTHUR H. BARNES

ENTERED NAVY: MARCH 1944

BOOT CAMP: FARRAGUT IDAHO
COMPANY 569-44

ASSIGNED TO ZELLARS: SEPT. 1944

LENGTH OF SERVICE ON ZELLARS: 2 YEARS AND 2 MONTHS

RATING: FC 3/C

PLACES VISITED: San Francisco, Calif; Seattle, WA; San Diego, Calif; Pearl Harbor, Hawaii; Ulithi, Caroline Island; Okinawa; Guam; Eniwetok; Long Beach, CA; Panama Canal; New York City; Guantanamo Bay, Cuba; Norfolk, VA; Reciefe, Brazil; Rio de Janeiro; Pensacola, FL; Annapolis, MD.(Naval Academy.)

I was visiting an aunt in San Francisco in late 1943 and was working at the Pacific Shipyard as a welder. The shipyard was building Kaiser cargo type ships. For several days, a destroyer would steam pass the shipyard dock, turn around and under full steam, return to the northern part of the bay.

After several days of this exhibition, I could not take it any longer. I knew that my father would not sign my enlistment papers. My aunt's husband was a machinist in San Francisco. About 0900, I dropped my welding unit and headed for his shop.

After some fast talking with my uncle, I convinced him to play my father for about 30 minutes. Somewhere near 11:00, he signed my father's name to some papers. Thus began the greatest and most rewarding time of my young life. By 2:30, I was on a train, along with many other equally young men, heading for a place called FARRAGUT NAVAL RECRUIT TRAINING STATION, IDAHO.

Boot Camp in the middle of some of the most beautiful parts of our country was not what I had envisioned. No ships, no big guns and none of the other stuff one would think a major Naval center would have. A bunch of shave- headed recruits just above kids stage, were being herded through the many different drills and marches that were required in order to give some semblance of a military presence.

There were life-saving drills where all of the company was required to pass a minimum swimming achievement, boat rowing on lake Pend Oreille with the company commander (BM 3/c) yelling "stroke, stroke." Only once did they march us through a building for poison gas indoctrination. We had several classes on seamanship (knot tying and general rope handling) and on and on. There were a number of different camps surrounding a very large field called a «grinder,» the marching and review place.

The uniform during the day was full dress dungarees with leggings (heavy canvas gadgets that were laced about one's shoe and up to just below the knee) with the dungaree pant legs folded inside. There were many other training routines also. Small bore rifle firing, and a long march to the big bore (30:06) rifle range. I did not realize that a sailor needed to know about small caliber fire arms. Remembering guns, we stood watches at night with a most formidable weapon, a wooden facsimile of a 30:06 rifle and no wooden bullets.

Company 569 became aware that our time at Farragut was becoming short. The number of shots in arms and buttocks increased and we were aware that companies just ahead of us were being shipped out. During a final physical exam, it was noted that I had some kind of crazy rupture in my right testicle called a hydrocele. It required some minor surgery so just before our company graduation, off to the base hospital.

I had spent the past 13 weeks with some of the best new friends that I was ever to make and all of a sudden they were going one way and I alone was going to the hospital. "We" did not have a very good attitude at that time. After about 11 days I joined another company that was about to graduate, company 633-44. I really felt cheated cast among a lot of new faces. I did not feel like I was among friends like the ones of my first company. (Later as we were formed into a destroyer pool at Treasure Island, many of company 633 became very important to all of the rest of my life.)

As the last days at Farragut closed in on the company, we were tested and asked, "In what part of the Navy would you like to serve?" Many of us were herded onto a train and headed out to Treasure Island, in San Francisco Bay. The train ride was one of the longest that I can remember.

It started all over again — training and more training. This time it was somewhat different. In small groups, we were bussed to Mare Island for fire-fighting training. Another time we went down the coast to a somewhat remote place called Point Montara, a cold and damp finger of land jutting out into the Pacific Ocean. The Navy had built a live firing gunnery range where real live firing of everything from 5" 38 medium bore guns to 30 and 50 caliber machine guns had been placed. They fired out to sea at towed targets, some by boat and most by airplane.

One morning, to my great surprise, a small group of seamen were called out at muster and told to pack seabags, that we were going on a destroyer for a two week training cruise. The destroyer was the

U.S.S. FOOTE DD 511. The cruise was to San Diego, with a lot of day and night drills that soon let us in on what we would be experiencing when we got aboard an assigned ship. Along the way South, at different places, a plane would fly out to meet the FOOTE and anti-aircraft firing training would begin. The Foote had been at Guadalcanal and struck by a Jap long lance torpedo, doing a great deal of damage to the aft part of the ship. Many of her crew was as green as we were.

Each morning a list was posted assigning sailors to different duty and ships. Most of the men were in what they called the destroyer pool as I was, and each morning it was a rush to see if your name, or a shipmate's name, was on the board. In late August my name came up on a list for a new destroyer mine layer, the ARRON WARD. (DM-34) We were to be shipped out in about two weeks. Some of my boot camp shipmate's names were also on the order. Within a few days, a new list with my name was posted and I was reassigned to a new destroyer that was nearing commissioning in Seattle Washington. I was real pleased to see most of the friends that I'd had the pleasure of making were on the same list. So in early September about 90% of what would be the "CREW" were put on a train and began another slow ride up through some of the prettiest parts of our country.

Seattle's welcome was one of cold and overcast dew. Our accommodations were tar-paper-type barracks with very little heat. A pre-commissioning crew had been at the shipyard for several months preparing for the balance of the crew to arrive. As we became acquainted with each other, a feeling of great pride and patriotism began to bond all of us together.

The first view of the U.S.S. ZELLARS DD 777 was a little disappointing to me. I had visualized a sparkling new ship ready to go charging off to defeat our enemy and she sat manacled to the docks, cluttered with cables and equipment, looking very unclean. Workmen were crawling all over her and making her look like anything but a fighting ship. (Youth's imagination at work.) As all members of the crew received their assignments and were put to work finalizing last details, the ZELLARS began to look as she should (sleek, sharp and ready to begin her shakedown period) before becoming part of the active fleet. But all of us were anxious and raring to get on with our purpose. „Swabbies" swabbed the ship from bow to stern, and from the bridge to bilges. As the ship's commissioning day neared, the ZELLARS looked every bit a fighting ship in her shining armor. All that she needed was to pass her shakedown cruise and be sent on her way.

The shakedown cruise was to San Diego with drills of every sort that would be the welding of a first class crew: gunnery at shore targets, antisubmarine training, anti-aircraft firing at towed targets, emergency drills and, of course, watches — always watches. The crew had been divided into three sections and functioned as such except for the most important watch of all, General Quarters, the position for major action. When this alarm went off the entire ship was manned and ready for whatever might be coming our way. The last item before we were released for final inspection was to move thru the "degaussing range." It was located up one of the more unpopulated areas of Pudget Sound and we would cruise slowly as the ship was bombarded with a magnetic underwater field to hopefully remove some of the sensitivity to enemy mines. This operation took several days and we would anchor just off of the range for the night. During one evening, while looking down into the clear waters, it was noticed that there were one heck of a lot of big fish swarming about the ship. I do not know where the fishing equipment came from but in seconds large silver Salmon were flopping about the deck. SK1c NAVA promised that if they were cleaned and cut into steaks, he would serve one great fish dinner. We did and he did, with the best and first Salmon dinner that I had ever had.

Everyone knew that the ship was about to change climates. During the week of January 20th, supplies of every kind began to be stored aboard: boxes of frozen meats, eggs by the crates, potatoes by the ton, flour, shortening, canned goods of every variety, etc. Ammunition loaded and fueled, the ZELLARS quietly slipped out of her dockside mooring and headed out thru the Straits of Juan de Fuca. Her course was due West, to Pearl Harbor, Hawaii. The ship arrived at Pearl Harbor on January 31 with beautiful clear skies and coral blue water. Some of the devastation that the Japs created on December 7th was still visible. As we passed the stilled hulk of the great Battleship Arizona, the ship's crew stood at attention. Our American flag, proudly flying from our main mast, was dipped and many tears slowly moistened our faces. Our shipmates, 1100 of whom were still at their stations, were lying forever in the Arizona's hull under many feet of sacred waters of Pearl Harbor; never to be forgotten, and forever honored.

On February 8th, we had a change of command. Commander Van Mater, who placed the ship in commission and was the ship's first Commanding Officer, was relieved and replaced by Commander Leon Kintberger. He had lost his last destroyer during what would be called the greatest sea battle of the war, and maybe US history. In command of the U.S.S. Hoel DD533, he found his task force being shelled by a very large and aggressive Japanese battle group, which included the YAMATO and the MUSASHI, two of the largest battleships ever built. The HOEL was just off Leyte in the sea of Samar, part of the Islands of the Philippines.

On the morning of October 25, 1944, Admiral C. A. SPRAGUE, the task force commander, found his whole task force under fire from the Jap task force. Per the battle report, Sprague simply ordered the destroyers/ escort destroyers "LITTLE BOYS, ATTACK," and all of them did. Kintberger was awarded the Navy Cross for his action in the battle. (Great reading "VALOR AT SAMAR, Zebra #26).

As our training became more aggressive, we had live torpedo firings and always anti-aircraft firing. Round after round of 5" 38, 40MM and 20MM ammunition went hurling out the barrels of our many guns. During antisubmarine training we dropped several real depth charges that shook the ship from stem to stern (old Navy saying). One of our main functions during our sea training time was to escort the Carrier FRANKLIN as her plane guard detail. The duty was kinda boring. We would either be some hundred yards in front of the carrier or off her stern as her planes practiced takeoffs and landings. At times one of her planes would not make it for one reason or another. It was the ZELLARS' responsibility to attempt to retrieve the plane crew if they had escaped the crash. Some did and some didn't. By this time the crew of the ZELLARS began to act and feel like „OLD SALTS" and some of the pilots looked much younger than any of us.

February 26 thru the first of March things suddenly changed. The log for those dates read:

LOADED AMMUNITION ALL DAY, TOOK ON MASSIVE AMOUNTS OF SUPPLIES AND FUEL.

March 3 was a great day. The weather around the Hawaiian Islands was slightly breezy with trade winds. Large banks of pure white clouds, thunder head type, stretched from horizon to horizon. The ZELLARS, along with other destroyers, began a column moving out of their anchorage and out to sea, on a westerly compass heading. No word of our destination had been announced but we now knew that all the training and long hours were about to be put to the test; we were bound for harms way.

On the morning of the fourth, we joined up with three aircraft carriers. One of them was our dear friend the FRANKLIN, plus a battle cruiser, and a screen of destroyers.

Now we learned of our destination. A place that none of us had ever heard of before. ULITHI, an anchorage in a group of Islands that was part of the greater Caroline's. Here we would become a part of a much larger task force, Task Force 58.

Not having had experience with cocoanut trees, and looking at the inviting large fruit in the top of the trees, I decided to try and climb up for a treat. It was fine going up the tree. The palm fronds grow up the tree and as the fronds fall, they leave a rather fine, sharp fiber all along the tree trunk. After my one and only climb and return to the sand, my chest was one big shaved, skinned mess. Fortunately I had no real hair on my chest so I did not have a feeling of a lost symbol of manhood. To this day (1998) I still have little hair on my chest and I feel that the palm tree is at fault.

Taking turns, different destroyers slipped out of the anchorage late in the evening and began night patrol. On March 15, two Jap planes slipped in and one did its Kamikaze thing, causing great damage on the flight deck of one the carriers. This shed some light on what we could expect in the coming days. On one occasion during our night security patrol, we picked up radar contact of approaching Jap airplanes. Ulithi was only some 50 miles from YAP Island and still in Japanese hands. YAP is where the enemy planes came from. At times the ZELLARS was only 15 miles from this Jap held Island.

My MK 14 gun director sight was having moisture problems and was taken to the DD tender YOSEMITE for exchange. We topped off our supplies, ammo and fuel on the 20th of March. This just happened to be my 18th birthday and I don't think that I even noticed it. There was so much going on all the time that one birthday was lost in the serious surroundings.

On March 21, we slipped anchor and soon left our almost secure anchorage as we moved out into the deep blue sea, going closer into harms way. The exec passed the word that we were bound for OKINAWA, the last major island before Japan homelands. The shit was about to hit the fan and we were going to make sure who's shit it was. As we looked from one horizon to the next, regardless of the direction - port, starboard, bow or stern — all one could see was ship, after ship — all men of war, and, what seemed like, endless fast moving escorts. The ZELLARS was right by her friend, the carrier FRANKLIN. In passing days she would be our refueling supply and it was great to steam at her side.

Some things do not remain the same. As we neared our objective, OKINAWA, the task force split up. The fast moving carriers and selected escorts of the newer battleships, cruisers and destroyers, departed to go very close to the mainland of Japan. The ZELLARS had been selected as part of the main invasion task force, now called Task Group 54.3, under Admiral GEYO's command. This task group was made up of older battleships, some of which had been at Pearl Harbor. Our new fuel supply was the Battleship TENNESSEE. It was the first time that I can remember, while having the ship's sea detail helm watch, that the refueling and going alongside was done without one of the quartermasters at the helm. I was asked to keep the helm, and let me express to all, it was one great thrill for me to be at the helm of a ship like the ZELLARS anytime. There I was responding to every slight change on the compass as the Captain moved the ship alongside that big piece of iron. After our refueling, the Captain turned to me and expressed that I had done a good job. I do not know what he expected from any of the crew other than a good job, for we were the greatest: every one of us.

Our first view of enemy territory was a group of small islands named KERAMA RETTO. As we made our way slowly into the area selected as our anchorage, we could see a group of Marines with a flame throwing tank moving up a hillside flushing out groups of Jap soldiers. All of a sudden, we knew the first taste of death, even if they were our country's enemy. Kerama Retto was some 30 miles from OKINAWA and provided a reasonable safe anchorage even in the heart of Japanese territory.

March 25, 1945 became the first time that the ZELLARS fired her 5" guns at a target that held human life. The thought of killing someone was not in our minds. We thought more about the 1100 plus shipmates still lying beneath the water in Pearl Harbor, the crew of the ARIZONA. What we were now doing was the whole purpose of long months of training and determination. The ZELLARS was hell bent on doing her part of bringing the war to a speedy end and OKINAWA was the center of action at that time.

We began firing in support of the planned landing. Standing just off shore, we could not see many significant targets but we fired our fire mission with the precision of a surgeon. Round after round screamed over the beach and onto the island.

The battleships Tennessee and Nevada stood farther from the beach and as they fired their 14 and 16 inch main batteries the shells passed over us.

We could see the base of them. I thought that such a shell would make a screaming shrill sound but it sounded more like a freight train going down hill out of control. They rumbled rather than screamed. As shells fell on the Island, huge mountains of soil leaped into the air and slowly fell back from where they came. This was a sight that most of us had only seen in the movies and now we were a part of making such things happen.

I had been assigned to the second division deck gang. Somewhere between Ulithi and Okinawa, the firecontrol officer, Ensign BROCKMAN, passed by my work station and asked me if I would like to be a firecontrolman. I did not really know just what a firecontrolman was so I told him I did not want anything to do with being in an engine room. I wanted to be topside where I could see what was going on. He laughed and said "follow me." Somewhere in the very stern was a training device called a range finder system. He began to explain firecontrol and at the same time began to set some dials on the machine. His next explanation was all the parts of the darned device and why. After adjusting the system so that he could range properly, he turned it over to me and asked if I could accurately make the range. I guess that I did OK for as we left the compartment, he told me that I would be transferred to his gang. I would be a Firecontrol striker, S1c. On March 3, 1945, it was on the plan of the day.

My General Quarters station was the secondary battery gun control director - mainly computer control of mount 43 and, if needed, mount 3 of the 5" gun. Mount 43 was just aft of the number two stack starboard side. It was a great place to see everything toward the stern and starboard side. Let any Jap come our way, mount 43 and I were ready.

The ZELLARS made pass after pass for the next several days, firing her main battery at many different targets. On March 17, we went to GQ at 0455 and stayed at our stations At 06:20 three Jap planes came over making their suicide runs. We opened fire as did every ship in the area I watched in total amazement as one plane that was flying rather high came in on a straight line, then nosed over and made a hit on the Battleship NEVADA. It was real weird. Two other ships were also hit, the old four piper destroyer DORSEY and the cruiser BILOXI. Later in the day, another destroyer made sonar contact with a sub, dropped a number of depth charges and sank the undersea devil.

There was not a moment throughout the days, without some action going on in one part of the task group or another. It was a real different kind of hell. And so it went. Into Kerama Retto for resupply, then out to the beaches of OKINAWA to dispense with the ammunition.

It was April Fool's Day, but we were not fooling anyone. The invasion of the Island of OKINAWA began in breathtaking shore bombardments. 16" and many other caliber guns blasted the beaches from above the town of NAHA, the main town of the Island. Our rounds at first were air bursts, fuses set to explode just above the beaches chopping up everything below They looked rather beautiful. Our troops went ashore and had little resistance, by the radio reports. The airfields of KADENA and YANTAN were taken in two hours.

On April 3rd we went to GQ at 02:30 AM. The Japs had aircraft flying around all night Around 03:20 we made radar contact with close flying planes and opened up with our main battery. The firing was to starboard and the night was black as ink. As our rounds found the plane, it burst into flames and curled into the darkened sea. This was the ZELLARS' first known real kill and a Jap flag graced our main battery gun director. It looked real nice against the light Navy gray paint.

Our routine began to change — bombardment during the day to support the troops on the Island and radar picket search all night. Sleep became a forgotten function. The crew walked about the ship with eyes sunken deep in their sockets and very little conversation. Most of us slept in or very near our battle station. There were times when sandwiches were served along with great hot coffee due to constant presence of enemy planes.

April 12, 1945 was a little different as a copy of the official ship log will note. Shortly after 08:00, the ZELLARS was designated as task force mail deliverer. The ship delivered task force mail, first to the U.S.S. IDAHO, and next to the U.S.S. NEW MEXICO. At 11:24, we sent mail to the U.S.S. NAVADA and on to the U.S.S. TUSCALOOSA. 12:35 - to the U.S.S. NEW YORK, the U.S.S. TEXAS, the U.S.S. SALT LAKE CITY, then the U.S.S. PORTLAND. Things began to change in one big hurry. Many Jap „bogies" were reported some 20 miles and closing. At 14:37, the U.S.S. TENNESSEE was designated as the disposition guide. As can be seen, we were in some real big gun company which made us feel proud.

The ZELLARS went to General Quarters at 14:44 with Jap suicide planes some 18,000 yards and closing. The ZELLARS opened fire just as soon as the guns were trained on target. First one, then two planes went down in flames. The third suicide plane, although shot full of holes, pressed on. It hit just below mount two on port side, into the upper handling room. The high explosive 1100-pound torpedo skidded across the deck passing through the forward officer quarters and the officers ward room. It exploded on the starboard side just above the ship's scullery. The blast was devastating.

At the time of the attack, I was at my GQ station, which was the starboard secondary gun director just aft of the second stack. One of the attacking planes passed just off of our stern as it pressed its attack on the forward part of the ship. All port side guns were firing but several of my shipmates stated later, that I had yelled, "those are Jap planes; you better start firing." Don't ask me why in the middle of a battle such dumb comments are made.

I knew that we were in real trouble when Chief Electrician CUSHING came running by my GQ station headed aft on the starboard side. I do remember looking forward expecting a Jap plane to come my way. My main control was for mount 43, a quad 40MM mean firing weapon. WARNER MACKAY was the gun's captain. As I looked forward, the torpedo must have exploded for it looked like someone had thrown a very large bunch of trash into the air. At the time I did not know about the starboard side explosion and the devastation that had just occurred and that many of my shipmates had been killed and wounded. (As I type the personal histories, I cannot hold back the tears.)

The ship lost all power instantly. My director was useless so I yelled to MACKAY to take over in manual control. I could not do anything at my GQ station and I do not remember thinking about offering any help. I just bailed out of my director station and was ghastly greeted by a body lying almost at the foot of the ladder that went to my director. It was cut completely in half yet the hands were opening and closing. God I still see that image as though it was a few moments ago. It was Torpedoman 2c JONES.

I hurriedly went forward on the port side and was met by a second class petty officer sitting down in the passageway with burns and skin sluffing off of his arms, yet he was mixing two bottles of plasma. I asked him if I could do that for him and he strongly replied/' this is my job, go get your own." Going farther forward just past the weather break, which was burned black, I met Gunners Mate KUZMICH trying to roll the engine of the Jap plane off the deck and into the water. It still had one of the suicide plane crew smashed over the engine parts. We tried to roll the damn thing off the side of the ship but it was still hot and heavy. I do not know who but another shipmate came from the bow and the three of us managed to dispose of the grotesque remains of the Jap and the engine.

My whole direction was to get to the two main battery gun mounts on the forward part of the ship. Several of my closest friends had GQ stations in those mounts and I was concerned beyond reason for their safety. WILLIAM BIEBER S2c, was one of the special friends. We had spent many hours talking about his family and his great North Dakota.

I found him standing outside of mount one with some of his shirt burned off, but alive. I remember taking his arm and expressing my relief that he was OK. Concerned about being away from my GQ station, I returned toward the midship area passing thru the now destroyed forward officer quarters and their ward room. For an unknown reason, I did not look out to the starboard side of the ship but passed through the ward room. I think that the distraction was a head the exact likeness of JOHN ENSLEY, PhM3c hanging up-side-down on the ward room port bulkhead. I am sure, if I could have seen my expression at that time, it would have been sheer horror and now some many years later, it is still deeply imbedded in my mind.

The ward room was the primary medical aid station for our doctor and his main staff. Also, it was the GQ station of the damage control personnel. All were gone.

Back on the port side, returning to my GQ station, I saw a number of shipmates rushing to give medical aid, and whatever assistance that was needed. During our very early shakedown period, the constant hard training was sometimes objectionable. The early 01:00, 02:30 and 04:35 GQ drills seemed to be a lousy time to be running to a dark place on the ship.

Today, April the 12, it more than paid off. Every shipmate that could, some wounded, did not hesitate to respond to the needs of their more seriously wounded shipmates.

Sometime shortly after we were hit, the U.S.S BENNION came along our port side and passed over their doctor and a PhM3c. The BENNION also assisted our own repair party in putting out the fierce fires.

I have had an advantage over most of the shipmates regarding the ZELLARS' movements during the March, April and May period. Reading the ship's logs has afforded me a review of all the daily entries to confirm many of the details and dates. So guys, my memory is no better than yours.

Per the ship's log of April 12, page 265-45:

> 15:15 all fires under control. Wounded removed form damaged area. 15:49, underway on port engine. Proceeding Kerama Retto Anchorage. Steering from Aft Steering station, all compasses battle casualty.
>
> signed, CA. SMILIE, Lieut. USN

After entering Kerama Retto, the wounded and those who were killed were removed immediately — the wounded to the hospital ship and the dead to a special temporary interment site on the Island of Kerama Retto.

The evening of April 12, 1945, was the strangest and most painful evening that all of the crew had ever known. Sure, those of us who were alive were very grateful, but the loss of so many of our shipmates and special friends created a hole in our lives that would never be filled.

I am going to try and express the bond that develops among most service persons that go in harms way and have a loss of buddies, shipmates and very special people in their lives. I have to express this issue from my own feelings and grief at the loss of shipmates.

In time of war or such stress, the gathering of men together in one place such as boot camp, plants a seed that begins to grow slowly. A person attaches himself to certain other members of the company and they share many personal parts of their life: home, family, girl friends, the state they are from, etc. Some even delve into their politics and religion. From this simple beginning a trust develops that becomes an unbreakable link between them. As they move on into further training and are assigned to ships, just knowing that special shipmates are near you as part of the "CREW," allows a certain value of security. In Other words, "hold my hand and I will hold your hand, regardless," or, our brothers' keeper.

There are still some that want to forget all that happened during their Navy duty and place no importance on such close relationships. That's life.

As darkness fell on the anchorage, most of the crew wandered about the stern half of the ship. "Lost" is not the right word. It is said that grown men do not cry. BULL! very few of those who remained did not weep simply for the loss of shipmates and special friends. Some would not go to their bunk to sleep, they just found a quiet place topside and curled up in their grief. Others sought out the needed closeness of friends and joined in a niche of security that the bond had given.

April 13, began the matter of muster to count the crew and to begin the massive clean up of the wounded ship. Torn metal was dangerously hanging from the blast. Heavy rib steel beams that were the mainstay of the ship's hull had been torn like paper and the sharp edges were still a danger.

It was interesting to see where some of the more important skills came from as we began to recover ourselves. CARL CROSBY (Bing) was a deck hand in the third division and did his job well. Deck hands are at the beck and "yell" of the Bos'n of each division. As the cleanup began, CROSBY went to the division officer and informed him that he was an ABS certified welder. I'm not sure that the front office was aware of his skills. He was immediately „shanghaied" into the damage control gang as shipfitter and was at the heart of the cutting off of the torn steel and the welding of replacement parts. (See CROSBY's personal history, pg. 166)

As the remaining days of April passed, new steel beams and cover plates were welded into place. The anchorage had many other problems. Almost every day and night, Jap planes would try to sneak into the anchorage and drop a few bombs. Nerves already bent to the breaking point were stretched a little further each time one of the planes came over. At times all ships in the "destroyer hospital" would start their smoke generators and fog the whole anchorage with heavy dense smoke.

The smoke was made from a special unit that burned diesel oil and it left that harsh oily smell through the anchorage. The smell was better than the Japs.

Other rumors had it that some Japs had swum out to the anchored destroyers and climbed on board killing some of the crew. Our Captain made sure that it would not happen on the ZELLARS. Watches with rifles were posted on the bow, midships, and the stern with orders to shoot at any swimming thing and questions might be asked later. I stood many of these watches (two men to a watch) and was nervous every time.

A crazy thing happened on April 26th. The ZELLARS was anchored fairly close to the beach and about 14:00, a group of Japs came down to the beach just off our starboard stern. I'm not sure, but I heard that some of our crew wanted to turn a 20MM gun loose on them. They wanted to surrender so several landing craft came and picked them up.

While we were tied up in the anchorage, we shared the time with a number of other ships, just a few: U.S.S. MULLANY (DD 528), U.S.S. STANLEY (DD 478), U.S.S. BROWN (DD 546), U.S.S. MORRIS (DD 417), U.S.S. RATHBURN (APD 25), ARD 13, (the floating dry dock), U.S.S. AGACIA (AG- 70), U.S.S.HUTCHINS, U.S.S ENDYMOIN (ARL-9), U.S.S. BARTON (DD722), and the U.S.S. BRAZOS (AO 4). I am sure that there were others, in fact, on May 4 or 5, the ARRON WARD (DM 34) came into the anchorage and for a brief time tied along our starboard side. She had been hit by no less than five Kamikazes. From her number one stack to her fantail, it was nothing but a junk yard. Her stern compartment had been breached and about half of her stern from the water line to about half-way-up her side was under water. Much of the hurt that we were feeling all of a sudden was amplified for the pain that all of us knew was taking place on the ARRON WARD.

As a matter of record, there were 13 destroyers and destroyer escorts sunk at Okinawa and another 88 seriously damaged. Over 7000 sailors lost their lives during the capture of the island, and many of them were "tin can" sailors, our fellow shipmates.

By May 12 our damage had been repaired to the point that we could make it back to the United States. On Tuesday, May 8th at 09:16, the ZELLARS along with several other ships, silently steamed out of Hagushi anchorage off Okinawa and pointed her bow towards Saipan in the Marinnas Islands.

We were leaving behind thoughts and great memories that would never die, of 44 shipmates. God Bless them all.

Our next and most important stop was the Navy repair shipyard at Long Beach, California, "HOME." Our reception at the Navy yard was something else. I don't think that the local, beautiful people had experienced a "WAR HERO SHIP" return to their shipyard and the community really turned out.

For two days after entering the shipyard, a somewhat happy, yet also saddened, stream of sailors made their way across the United States, going home to a most happy welcome. A 30-day leave was the order of the day. My home was only about 150 miles away, Bakersfield, California. I was single and really had no urgency to go home so I chose to take the second section leave.

For a reason I still don't believe, on the tenth day of my leave I got lonesome for the ZELLARS and reported back. As close as I was to home I felt that I could take a weekend to visit my family.

The ship was a total mess. Where the starboard hole was, the shipyard workers had cut an even bigger hole so that they could rejoin all the main steel beams and deck plates. It took the shipyard only two-and-one-half months to repair the ship to just like new. Of course, every one knows that WWII ended and the world went mad with peace.

October 8 found us moving through the Panama Canal on our way to New York City. The first event that the Navy entered us in was some kind of special day with President Truman showing off. (Navy Day) We anchored in the Hudson River just below the George Washington Bridge and enjoyed a good look at the famous New York City skyline. October 16 we entered the New York Naval Shipyard.

The ZELLARS first real peacetime job was to escort the big new Carrier MIDWAY on her shakedown cruise. Much of what we learned and did for the Carrier FRANKLIN was repeated as we charged down the Atlantic to the Caribbean and Guantanamo Bay, Cuba.

January and February 1946 was a great time. Our new responsibility was again to escort an aircraft carrier. This time it was the carrier FRANKLIN D ROOSEVELT (CVB-42) I think that the B in her designation stood for "BIG" she was big and could out run a gazelle

The course set was south, all the way down to Rio de Janeiro, Brazil. I am not sure, but Carnival or something, was just about to happen. The city was jammed full of very nice people. We were tied up to a dock with our sister ship, the U.S.S. FOX (DD 779). The two of us looked real sharp alongside that dock. Upon our return to the US, we were assigned to escort a carrier training pilots out of Pensacola, Florida. On April 22, 1946, there was a special trip to the Naval Academy to pick up cadets for a summer cruise that lasted until August.

Upon our return to New York City, I wanted to attend one of the two firecontrol schools and made an agreement with the exec. If I was in school with the next class, I would ship over and make the Navy my career. The next class was to begin in late September. October came and went so I decided to leave the Navy and be discharged.

THE ZELLARS!

Over the past 50 years I have tried to measure all that the Navy did for me and to me. Becoming a small part of the crew of the best destroyer that ever served her country was by far the most significant. Boot Camp was a foundation started. The ZELLARS became the cement in so many important aspects of my life. I had the opportunity to see and learn so many different things that they cannot be counted. I have never had any problems in getting along with almost anyone. The Navy gave me something that is not easy to learn, self discipline. If a person cannot manage himself, trouble is usually just around the corner. The respect and trust of people around you, becomes a, strength and belief in one's self.

One of our shipmates said it best about destroyer sailors:

"A 'tin can' sailor that has spent several years on a 'can' can go anywhere in other ships regardless of size, for on a destroyer you learn to do many jobs outside of your rate. You're a Jack of all Navy trades and master of many."

Arthur H. Barnes FC3c, plank owner

USS ZELLARS (DD777)

EUGENE F. EARP

ENLISTED: JANUARY, 1945

BOOT CAMP: GREAT LAKES, ILL.

ASSIGNED ZELLARS: JULY, 1945

RATING: S1c, TORPEDO GANG.

PLACES VISITED: San Diego, CA; Panama Canal; Guantanamo Bay, Cuba; Trinidad; Recife, Brazil; Rio De Janeiro; Brazil, New York City; Norfolk, VA.

My dedication:

"TO THE GALLANT CREW OF THE USS ZELLARS WHO FOUGHT AT OKINAWA, AND TO THE MEN WHO PREPARED THEMSELVES TO STAND IN FOR THE CREW'S FALLEN COMRADES-AT-ARMS. I also dedicate this work to my brother, TOM, who was himself a "Blue Water sailor."

My work place at age 17 was near Mobile, Alabama and Pensacola, Florida. For the first time in my young life, I saw ships and planes. Now the war did not seem so far away.

As I stood on the dock one Sunday morning in Pensacola, my course was set. I was inexorably pulled to the sea. I just had to find out what was going on beyond my life line of sight. What better way to find out than in the U.S. NAVY.

I was 17 years old and giving my parents a hard time about enlisting. My father was not to be trifled with, but I persisted." How about school?" asked Dad "I'll finish when I return." I said. Dad countered, "you may not return." Nonsense, I thought. I am 17 years old and indestructible. I must not miss any more of this great American adventure.

January 1945, I held up my right hand and became part of the U.S. Navy. After a short wait my orders came through. A large group of recruits boarded a train for a trip to Chicago and the Great Lakes Naval Training Center. My patriotism was at an all time high.

Boot camp was a stern awakening. Once inside, we were shouted at and humiliated by being called the worst looking, and probably the most stupid class of recruits ever to be forced upon the Navy. We were then aligned to company ranks and told to "knock it off. No talking."

Our Company Commander's first words were, "how many of you believe in God?" All hands went up. "Good," he said, "give your hearts to God because your ass belongs to the U.S. NAVY!" It now occurred to me that I might have made a mistake.

Boot Camp was an ordeal that all sailors must endure. There was nothing unique about Great Lakes unless it was the bone chilling cold. Mercifully, Boot Camp ended for me in early April, 1945.

The "Boots" were promoted from Apprentice Seamen to Seamen second class and given a 10 day leave and orders for me to report to the Out Going Unit in Chicago. Upon reporting to the OGU I learned that I was going to Treasure Island in San Francisco. More physical exams and dental check ups and placement exams, but in the end, I knew what my final destination would be. I had been assigned to the U.S.S. ZELLARS DD 777. Scuttlebutt had it she had already seen action in the Pacific and had sustained battle damage. I rationalized that it couldn't have been too serious; after all, she made it back to the United States. I was ill prepared for what I would see several days hence.

The ZELLARS was undergoing war repairs at the Long Beach Naval Shipyard in Long Beach, California.

The new replacements were marched down the dock to view the ship for the first time. The ZELLARS, with a gaping hole in her starboard side, starting somewhere under her number two 5" gun mount and the bridge, continuing down to what seemed like eternity. There was also collateral damage that included the ward room, galley and chow deck. We ate a lot of sandwiches during the repair period even though there was a chow hall on the base. Welcome aboard.

Half of the crew was on leave; some would be discharged or reassigned and those waiting for the next leave had little to do with us. As one replacement put it, "I feel like a bastard at a family reunion." We were perceived as outsiders and, as far as they were concerned, we would never take the place of their shipmates lost at Okinawa.

NOW HEAR THIS,

On the second day the new replacements were given a complete tour of the ship and then given work assignments, being turned over to a petty officer or leading seaman. We were to help in the clean up, especially where the ship had been hit. Whether real or imaginary, it smelled like death. As I worked, I thought, how in the name of heaven did this thing stay afloat? I also wondered how many brave men had died where I was working. Suddenly I was filled with rage. Those no good Jap S.O.B.s would get theirs. Little did I know how soon and how much they would get.

By mid-June of 1945 work on the ZELLARS was nearing completion. Most of the crew had returned and we, 'recruits' were beginning to learn our way around the ship.

The ZELLARS was once again becoming a whole ship. The original crew was beginning to communicate with the replacements. Plank owners like Darold Jorgenson S1c, Leroy Brim S1c, or Ernie Lynch S1c made sure that we did our jobs in seamen like fashion. At certain times we would be assigned to men like GM2c Jimmie Bilyue or Barney Schuh FC2c for special details.

It was time to get underway for the shakedown cruise. Captain Kintberger could be seen on the deck and many other parts of the ship more often. He would personally check the progress of the ongoing work. Few doubted that the skipper wanted to shove off as soon as possible.

All kinds of stores were loaded aboard. At last we were going to sea. It seemed to me that no sooner out of sight of land when General Quarters sounded. I had been assigned to the forward 5" gun magazine. The faster the guns were fired, the faster we had to work. FIRE, FIRE, keep them coming.

Finally the main battery was secured for lunch and all of us scurried topside for fresh air. Some of the "new" crew had become sea sick and the older crew members recognizing the symptoms, asked if we were ready for some greasy pork chops being served at chow. It was chuck-up time. As soon as lunch was completed, the main battery began to fire again and back down into the magazine we went. Have mercy! So much for our first day at sea.

During shakedown, every aspect of the ship and crew was tested and retested. The ZELLARS still had an outstanding gunnery crew. They could place antiaircraft fire in a precise line at various altitudes giving the appearance that one could almost walk along on it. By the same token, they were equally good at surface fire. The gunners were quite serious about their work.

On a leisure day, I found myself wandering about the ship. In the midship passageway, was the ship's daily bulletin board. As I scanned the board, I noted a plan of the day. It had been there a long time for it had turned yellow with age and at the bottom of the page in large letters was printed:

KILL JAPS, KILL, JAPS, KILL JAPS.

I asked the Yeoman how long had the plan of the day been up? "I don't know," he growled. I pressed on, "When will we change it?" "When the war is over, dummy."

A sailor's place is at sea. The Navy certainly felt that way with regard to destroyers. Shakedown drills continued to be carried out even at night. Night operations were done under war time Conditions — no lights of any kind on deck.

Tests of all kinds continued to be carried out, including those having to do with the ship's engines, boilers, evaporators, ventilators and other important spaces below decks. The men who toiled below decks kept the ship moving and they were good at what they did. An Officer like Lt. (jg) MARLOW, Petty officers WTs Red PETERSON and Chalmer MAXWELL, brought along new men like Bob DANKO and Ed EUWELE, to assure that the ZELLARS would pass her shakedown with flying colors. I admired these men, but jeeze, how could anyone spend their Navy life in the bowels of a ship? It crossed my mind that they must be a couple degrees to the right of center.

V.E. Day came and the Nippon Rising Sun was slowly sinking. In spite of the obvious progress, many of the ship's older crewmen would not accept the idea that the ZELLARS would not be committed to do battle again. Their attitude permeated the environment and the new men were pumped up. I wondered, how would I react in the face of an enemy? Would I even get used to the main battery going off around me. My answer was yes, I did get used to the violent blast and shudder of the guns. I could only hope that I would not let my shipmates down. One thing I did know, I would be in the company of sailors who knew how to fight at sea.

THE WAR'S END

With the Atomic bombing of Hiroshima on August 6th, and Nagasaki August 9th, the war came to an abrupt end. I remember thanking God that it was over and I wondered if he thought "well done."

On October 8, 1945, the ZELLARS slipped anchor and headed south for the Panama Canal. We had been in and out of San Diego for our shakedown training and it felt good to be in deep water headed for the great city of New York. With our sister destroyer the U.S.S. FOX, we transited the big ditch and made our way thru the Caribbean Sea and on to New York. The Battleship WASHINGTON was our group command ship and the destroyers refueled by coming alongside, passing heavy fuel lines replenishing the bunker oil.

Somewhere between the canal and New York I joined the torpedo gang and soon after received the new rating S1c, I was moving up in the Navy.

Upon entering the Hudson River, the Zellars along with many of the other fleet ships, anchored in the Hudson and prepared for NAVY Day with President Truman to view the fleet. The ZELLARS was the first ship south of the Washington Bridge and had a great view of the city. Broadway, Oklahoma, Follow the Girls, The Empire State building and the Rockettes. The city was opened to the fleet. Navy Day, October 27th, was a bright sunny day. Every shipmate on the ZELLARS was decked out in Navy blues, white hats and did we look sharp. The veterans, with campaign ribbons on their chest were to be at their best. It was a handsome crew.

With the partying over, it was back to sea. Our first short stop was to Newport News, Virginia for minor repairs and routine service. Soon, we departed for the Navy base at Guantanamo Bay, Cuba. It was back to the basics. Gunnery practice was an ongoing drill Lt. FREEMAN was the gunnery officer at the time. He was a mustang (former enlisted man) and well liked by the crew. He had to start from scratch forming and training new men.

Most of the plank owner gun crews had left the ship for discharge and it left a void in trained gunners.

The ZELLARS had a short trip back to New York for a stay in the Brooklyn Navy yard then back down to Guantanamo Bay. The first of a new line of super aircraft carriers were entering the fleet and the ZELLARS and FOX had the duty of escort and plane guard detail. First it was the U.S.S. MIDWAY for her shakedown cruise, then we received a real great treat. The ZELLARS and the FOX would take the U.S.S. ROOSEVELT down to Rio de Janeiro, Brazil.

On the way to Guantanamo Bay, the fleet hit a very bad storm, or rather the storm hit us. The ship turned to, lashing down anything that might move. As the storm hit there was not a man on deck. It was far too dangerous. Sailors have been swept over the side in such weather.

The cold biting wind was screaming through the signal flag halyards. The ever-darkening sky and sea was giving me great concern as I am sure it did to other men who had never experienced such weather before. The skipper, as he paced the bridge, calmly lit his pipe and attempted to drink a cup of coffee.

Before the ROOSEVELT arrived at "Gitmo," the ZELLARS and the FOX conducted routine gunnery and seamanship drills in the area. I was beginning to feel like a real "blue water sailor."

As we steamed into the South Atlantic, training exercises for the carrier commenced. Aircraft were launched most every day. As the great ship turned into the wind, plane after plane would take off, complete it's flight and return. Some days it seemed to be nonstop. It was the responsibility of the ZELLARS to stay just astern of the carrier and act as plane guard detail. Should a plane miss a landing, and crash into the sea, The "Z" would dash to the site and hoped to rescue the pilot and crew. Most times we did but on one occasion, the pilot was never found.

On the way south, we stopped for fuel and some minor stores at Recife, Brazil, just on the Equator and were bathed in hot bright sun. Not a fun place.

Many of the crew, including officers, had crossed the imaginary line of the equator and endured the initiation that invariably goes with the crossing. They were shellbacks and we were pollywogs. As the ship got closer to the equator, the shellbacks began to huddle in small groups, whispering to each other, pointing and laughing at us as if to say, "just wait, have we got something for you." A number of us pollywogs gathered in the chow hall one evening to discuss our fate. I recall one seaman comparing it to a maiden losing her virginity. "It probably hurts like hell, but it only happens once. Let's just get it over with." We all knew that we were going to be initiated regardless of how any of us felt.

The initiation was very ritualistic. The morning of the great day we were awakened about dawn and made to go to breakfast through the passageways. After chow we returned to our compartments the same way. We were not allowed on deck.

At last we were told to strip down to our skivvies (under shorts). Next we were led down the passageway out on to the deck and sprayed down with salt water. What we saw then was a long line of shellbacks with straps made of canvas that had been soaked in brine. "OK, pollywogs, hall ass!" One by one we ran the gauntlet. After the painful gauntlet run, we were directed to various stations for further humiliation. Next was the Royal Doctor, Royal Barber, Royal Baby, Royal Cook and others who continued to demoralize us. The biggest moment was with the Royal of all Royals, King NEPTUNE REX, Ruler of the Raging Main, who declared in a deep voice, "all pollywogs are lower than whale dung!"

Somewhat disoriented, we wondered what more could they possibly do to us? We didn't have long to wait. Promptly, we were blindfolded and told, "You are now going to walk the plank!" We were hoisted up and placed on what felt like a diving board, and as we cautiously walked toward the end of the board. We were struck once again on the rear, this time with such force that we were knocked off the plank and into a pool of sea water that had been constructed for our personal misery. The blindfolds were removed and what we saw were the shellbacks, officers and enlisted men alike, taking pictures of us and our indignation. Great fun, after all I was now a treasured shellback.

At last we were in sight of land, and the long days and nights at sea would soon give way to liberty for all hands. We eagerly waited to go ashore and check out Rio. It was truly an exotic city. Famous Sugarloaf Mountain seemed to spring up from the very blue water of the bay, and beyond that the mountain range ended with the statue of Christ erected at its highest peak. The ZELLARS docked with the FOX alongside.

The famous Copacabana Beach was not far from town and was populated by some very healthy looking women. While somewhat prim and well guarded by older women when in town, on the beach, they were much less inhibited. There were many different stories from the crew about the great times had in Rio.

"Now hear this! Prepare to get underway. Single up all lines." It was time to leave the beautiful city of Rio de Janeiro. The ZELLARS slowly made her way from the dock and into the harbor. We looked back at Rio and bid her a very fond farewell. We were aware that we'd had an experience most Americans would never have, and it was very satisfying.

Upon returning to the States the ZELLARS was ordered to operate as escort to the training carrier RANGER out of Pensacola. The RANGER was used only for pilot training of student Naval aviators. During our operations with the RANGER an incident occurred that could have resulted in the death of two shipmates.

The mission of the ZELLARS was to rescue any aviator in the event of a crash in the water during flight operations. One of the motorwhale boats was always swung out over the side so as to effect the rescue in the least possible time. The whaleboat was held in place by a bow and stern davit. S1c Darold JORGENSON was the coxswain in charge of the boat and SMITH S1c was bow hook. As the davits swung around, the davit hook holding the bow of the boat came loose. As a result, the bow swung down into the sea, hanging the whaleboat vertically, suspending only the rear. JORGENSON was caught between the rear davit hook and it's attached suspending line in front of him and the boat railing behind him. Since the ship was moving slowly through the water, the hanging bow of the boat was battered by the water repeatedly sending shocks through the boat and Jorgenson's leg. The ship stopped and JORGENSON was freed from the position in which he was trapped. Later the same day, he was transferred from the ship to Naval medical facilities ashore. Jorgie's knee was seriously damaged and he was in considerable pain. He was going to be in drydock for some time.

My time was getting short. Oh, boy, going home! At last it was discharge time. As I opened my locker and began to take out my clothes and a few belongings to place in my seabag, an unexpected melancholy came over me. While I, like other shipmates, couldn't wait for discharge, it had never occurred to me that I would feel ambivalent about leaving. After saying goodbye to the few original crew members and replacements left aboard, I signed out at the quarter deck and requested permission from the OOD to leave the ship. I saluted the jack for the last time as I made my way across the gangway. As I walked down the dock to the waiting bus, I looked back one last time at the sleek lines of the ZELLARS. I knew this was probably the last time I would see her. Leaving home was not easy.

Several days later I arrived in Memphis, then boarded a bus for Birmingham, then a city bus for Fairfield. I got off the bus, sea bag in tow, walked three blocks to my other home and through the door. "Mom, I'm home. What's for dinner."

I have had no greater honor than to serve with the men of the U.S.S. ZELLARS. I thank Almighty God and the United States of America for allowing me the privilege.

EUGENE EARP S1c

USS ZELLARS (DD777)

MARION A. KRAWCZYK

ENLISTED: APRIL 24, 1944

BOOT CAMP: BAINBRIDGE MD.
COMPANY, 3274

ASSIGNED ZELLARS: FEBUARY 25, 1946

LENGTH OF SERVICE: 19 MONTHS

RATING: S1c

PLACES VISITED: Guantanamo Bay, Cuba; Pensacola, FL; New York, Newport, Casco Bay, Plymouth, England; Torquay, South End on Sea, London; Gibralter & Suda Bay, Crete; Cowes on the Island of Wight.

As a (QM) quartermaster striker on my watch, I took care of the ship's rough log. Eventually I was lead helmsman on special sea detail and General Quarters. The reason I can come up with dates and times is I have the ship's logs when I was on the ZELLARS.

Tuesday, 1/21/47, while on the 20:00 to 24:00 Quartermaster watch, I was on the port wing of the bridge when I saw a destroyer heading for us on a collision course. I yelled to the OOD (Officer of the Deck) Ensign H.E. Lyons, who immediately turned to starboard to avoid the U.S.S. HYMAN DD732.

The Hyman had lost power in her steering control. It was pretty close and The HYMAN had lost power in her steering control. It was pretty close and darned scary. What gets me, the HYMAN never blew her whistle to alert the ZELLARS. She had to see us. If I had not been on the port wing, she would have hit us amid ship.

On October 2nd, 1946, we were in Casco Bay, Maine moored to a pier, when a thirty-foot Hampton fishing boat, piloted by R.H. MacVane of Long Island, making a speed of about fifteen knots, collided head on with the ZELLARS. It hit on the port quarter just aft of the propeller guard. It dented the hull of the ship just above the water line. The fishing boat got underway at once and pulled alongside the pier directly ahead of the ZELLARS where it sank. Ensign JANDRELL was the OOD.

On 2/3/47, the ship got underway for Commander, Logistic Supply Force, for fleet maneuvers with Task Force 29 to conduct 2nd Task Fleet tactical exercises. While on these maneuvers, on Wednesday 2/12/47, I was on the 18:00 to 20:00 Quartermaster watch. It was a real dark night but warm. I was standing on the starboard wing of the bridge, near the adelaide when the ship got a call from the hospital ship, the U.S.S CONSOLATION AH-15 that she felt an "unusual bump." I looked over to where the hospital ship was steaming and saw three red flares go up. This happened at 19:12 hours. I took a bearing. It so happened that the U.S.S. TUSK SS 426 came up under the hospital ship. The ZELLARS stood by and sent a whaleboat over with our doctor to assist with the injuries to personnel on the submarine. I don't know how many of the sub's crew were injured. She lost her periscope and her conning tower was crumpled. We stayed with her awaiting instructions from CTG-29 in regards to escorting the disabled submarine to port.

The U.S.S. MASSEY DD 778 was detailed to escort the TUSK to port. Oddly enough this happened in the Caribbean in a place called "BRONSON's Deep." If I recall correctly, it is 8000 to 24000 fathoms deep in that area. The TUSK was lucky she did not go down. She came up but could not submerge.

Monday, 2/17/47 I transferred to the U.S.S. ALDEBRON AF-10 for temporary duty. I went over in a Bos'n chair. When you are between two ships you get awful close to the water. I returned to the ZELLARS on Wednesday 2/26/47 the same way. There were 10 of us that went over to handle cargo. The big ships such as a Carriers and Battleships would come along the port side of the ALDEBRON. Destroyers and such would come along the starboard side. We would send over potatoes, eggs and other food stuffs in a cargo net and hand pull them over to the other ships. It was quite an experience.

Friday, 7/18/47, Commander J.M. ALEXANDER relieved Commander L.S. KINTBERGER as the ZELLARS' Commanding Officer. Commander KINTBERGER had been CO since February 1945.

Monday 7/21/47, underway for Plymouth, England. Arrived Thursday 7/31/47. I received my first weekend pass with special permission from Lt. ZUMWALT to visit Salcombe, England. I was stationed there during the war and knew a lot of the people.

I went on liberty in Portland, Maine. The fog rolled in very thick. The Naval Base sent a whaleboat in with an Ensign as the navigator to get back to Casco Bay. After traveling for what seemed like hours, they thought they saw a ship's truck lights and headed for them. The lights turned out to be on telephone poles on an island. We ran aground near midnight and couldn't back off, so we sat there. The tide went out tilting the boat over on its starboard side. We finally yelled loud enough for a woman to hear us. She called the Naval base. We walked ashore and down a road to a pier where another boat picked us up. It was daylight by the time we got back to the ZELLARS and just in time to get underway. I got off the ZELLARS 9/21/47 in Soda Bay, Crete. I then went on the U.S.S. CHIPOLA AO-63 for transportation home and discharge. From Soda Bay we went thru the Suez Canal to Bahrain then back thru the Suez Canal, stopping in Oran and finally to Norfolk, Virginia,

I enjoyed sailing in Newport, Rhode Island with Bob and Frances Baumgardner. I wish that I could find them. He was from California. I was discharged Friday October 13, 1947.

As for my liberties, they were uneventful.

An EX "Tin Can Sailor" — Marion A. Krawczyk S1c

USS ZELLARS (DD777)

ROBERT G. CHASE

ENLISTED: FEBRUARY 9, 1943

BOOT CAMP: BAINBRIDGE, MD.

ASSIGNED TO ZELLARS: JANUARY 1950

RATE: BM 3c

PLACES VISITED: Guantanamo Bay, Cuba; Panama Canal, San Diego, CA; Pearl Harbor, Hawaii; Midway, Japan, Korea.

BOOT CAMP, Bainbridge, MD.

Bainbridge opened to receive recruits only a month or two before I arrived. The 1st regiment was complete. I was assigned to the 2nd regiment which was incomplete. We had to march to the 1st regiment for almost everything, issuing of clothes, shots, haircuts etc At three weeks I still did not have my boot haircut, since we were showering and had no hair dressing (Vitalis) my hair was always in my eyes.

The drill field was frozen when we arrived but by the end of February, it began to thaw. It did not have asphalt yet. On the march to the mess hall we were marched right out of our rubbers. On the return we would pick up a pair from the mud.

Most of the company suffered quarantine and our company took over their duties. Needless to say, my training consisted mostly of Regimental Guard My 16 weeks became just 8 weeks.

In early 1950 while undergoing operational readiness training at Guantanamo Bay, Cuba, we were allowed liberty on a visit to Santiago, Cuba. We were the first U.S. Navy ship to visit that port since a previous visit by a U.S. Naval ship had been there. One of their sailors was observed urinating on a statue of national significance. This almost caused an international incident between Cuba and the U.S. We were told to be on our best behavior or no other U.S. Naval vessel would be allowed to visit.

I remember patrolling outside a Japanese harbor and the ZELLARS sliced through and sank a Japanese cargo vessel that tried to cross our bow to cut evil spirits trailing their wake. I also remember in October 1950, in company of the U.S.S. MASSEY DD 778, while escorting a cruiser refueling 17 miles out of Vladivostok, Siberia, challenging a sub contact, with the MASSEY, dropping in excess of 35 depth charges. Results??? We were told not to reveal the information or all censorship could occur to all Armed Forces in Korea.

I also remember Army Engineers blowing up Hungnam harbor. Two cruisers and seven destroyers, including the ZELLARS, and three rocket firing vessels standing several hundred yards off shore were unleashing a hellish barrage at the abandoned town. Nearly 34,000 shells and 12,800 rockets, this was a heavier rain of fire than that preceding the Inchon invasion. The parting roar and detonation by the Army Engineers of 400 tons of frozen dynamite and 500, 1000-pound bombs made the entire Hungnam waterfront seem to be blown in one volcanic eruption of flame.

In 1950, while anchored in Wanson Harbor, Korea, which was known to have 5,000 mines in the harbor, there were many mine sweepers trying to clear lanes for shipping and five of them blew up and sank. The ZELLARS was assigned for a while as harbor control vessel. We had to stop ships arriving and transfer information of the mines and show cleared lanes. This meant putting our starboard whaleboat in the water. It was done so many times each day as many ships were supplying our forces ashore that we referred to the starboard whaleboat as the starboard "Yo-Yo." It really kept the mates busy.

ROBERT G. CHASE, BM 3c

USS ZELLARS (DD777)

J. F. GUSTAFERRO

COMMISSIONED: STATE UNIV. COLUMBUS OHIO.

ASSIGNED TO ZELLARS: JUNE 1950

RANK: CAPTAIN

PLACES VISITED: Too many to be listed over total career.

I spent my first 17 years in Conneaut, Ohio, a Great Lakes seaport between Erie, PA, and Ashtabula, Ohio. I then went off to college at the Ohio State University in Columbus, Ohio. I spent my college summers sailing the ore boats on the Great Lakes. These boats went from Conneaut to Duluth. Before graduation I was offered a few jobs but the only realistic ones were to be drafted in the Army as a foot soldier, or to accept a direct commission in the Navy as an Ensign O-vs-USNR. (Ordnance Volunteer Specialist.)

I graduated in Electrical Engineering in May of 1941, and reported to the Naval Gun Factory (The old and current Navy Yard) in Washington D.C. on July 1 1941. Skipping much narrative, I was in Pearl Harbor on December 7, 1941. Shortly thereafter I was the assistant Gunnery Officer on the USS GANSEVOORT (DD 608), and then Gunnery Officer on the USS MERTZ (DD 691) and then finished the war as the Executive Officer of the USS TAYLOR (DD 468).

We were alongside the Battleship Missouri (BB 63) when General MacArthur did his thing. So I saw the whole blessed war!

Immediately after the war, I was ordered to take command of the USS BOGGS (AG 19). She was a converted four-stack destroyer, being used to tow targets in Pearl Harbor and she was to be decommissioned in Philadelphia.

This was followed with a tour of duty at the Naval Amphibious Command, Pacific Training Command as an instructor in Gunfire support. Then I was ordered to Newport, RI, to General Line School as a LCDR to get educated and have officers "BOOT CAMP" except it was all classroom stuff. We finished this in about June of 1950 and we (my wife of 2 years and two babies) headed for Norfolk, VA, to report aboard the USS ZELLARS (DD 777) as Executive Officer. I reported aboard on 23 June 1949. The Officer whom I relieved was LCDR RICHARD TIBBETS and I relieved him on July 1, 1949. As I recall he had relieved LCDR ELMO ZUMWALT a year before this.

The commanding Officer was FRED MICHAEL. He was one of the finest officers that I have ever met in the Navy. I cannot think of enough adjectives to describe him. We got along beautifully and our wives were fond of each other. In short order (after scanning my official orders) I found that I became the Executive Officer, the Navigator, the senior member of the Training Board, the head of the Survey Board and head of the Recreation Council.

I do not remember how much time that I spent on each of these assignments. I do know that Dr. ROBERT STEINBERG of the DesDiv Staff (16, and 161/162) who was aboard taught me how to play bridge. Games usually started just before or just after supper and we played until midnight. Bob and I were partners since he was a master bridge player and I was a trainee. We played against the Captain and LCDR WALTER (Bud) BOYLE, the DesDiv 162 Operations Officer. As I recall we started playing enroute to the Panama Canal and we played all the way to Korea, and we quit on the day that I was detached to go to the PG School in Annapolis.

We had a very friendly wardroom, we all got along very nicely and we underwent a lot of training exercises out of Norfolk. The relationship between the Officers and crew was excellent. Yet the discipline on the ship was of the highest order. The thought uppermost in the mind of each member of the crew was to find out what his boss wanted and then give it to him. Loyalty worked both ways. The chain of command was always used. As Executive Officer I always backed up my direct subordinates.

A case in point. One day in port one of the seamen knocked at my door and asked me if he could talk to me. I told him of course. I recognized him as one of the men who was not too enthusiastic about working. He told me that the Chief Master at Arms (CMA) had struck him. I saw no bruises on him and asked him where he had been struck. He responded by rubbing his lower backside. So, I sent for the CMA. I asked for his side of the story. His story was that he had ordered the seaman to go up to the fo'c's'le to chip paint. The seaman was a little slow in carrying out the order, and slowly went up the ladder. It appeared to the CMA that the seaman was about to fall backwards, so the CMA, who was sitting down, steadied the seaman with his foot. I asked the seaman if this was probably true. He concurred that it was probably true, and I suggested that he thank the CMA for breaking his fall. He did. Henceforth his work improved and he was rated with the CMA's blessing.

The war in Korea was a long way away and we were concentrating on going on a Mediterranean Cruise. I had never served in the Atlantic and the idea of going to Italy, where I have relatives, sounded great to me. We went to Cuba at least once on training exercises. How well I remember (some) of Guantanamo Bay (GITMO). The O Club served triple martinis for two bits and they gave you a second one for a penny. I walked off with one of their glasses. We still have it. I put it inside my coat jacket and slept with it all night. I can not recall whether I spent 52 cents or 78 cents. That was an incident of which I have no recollection. Someday I plan on returning to GITMO and give the club its glass back. Since neither the CO nor the Commodore was ever on my back, I had a very happy tour of duty. I believe we always got the "Es" in the squadron so it was not a high pressure job. We were in GITMO from July I, to August 5, 1950. In my files, I have a letter of commendation to our ship and the USS MASSEY (DD 778) for our coordinated attacks against a submarine (s), we got a score of 23.9 out of 25. Which I presume was pretty good.

As I recall at GITMO we were training to go on a Med. Cruise, but on our return to Norfolk we got an ominous dispatch from the Navigator (me!) to report to the operations office of one of the Senior Staffs (Cinclant?). I went there and found out that they had a bunch of charts for us. I was only permitted to study the charts that took us to Balboa, on the Pacific side of the Panama Canal. It did not take a genius to figure out where we were going. When I got back to the ship I found that Captain MICHAEL had already been summoned to visit our boss and he knew that we would not be going to Napoli. Sometime in August or early September of 1950 at the break of dawn we sailed for an "extended cruise." Very few members of the crew were told of our destination. Most had guessed it. A few of the wives were on the dock to see us off. My wife was one of them. I was on shore duty when we were married, and she knew that I would be going to sea, but she did not really fully realize what it meant to be a Navy wife.

My records do not have the dates that we transited the Canal, but by October 25, 1950 I had applied for a correspondence course and my return address was FPO San Francisco. I believe we went to Korea in a squadron of DD s and that one was missing because of repairs but would catch up with us later. The recollection might be of another ship at another time. Our squadron had been "lent" from Commander Cruiser/Destroyer, Atlantic to Commander Cruiser/Destroyer Pacific. We were the orphan squadron. All the Pacific ships had definite schedules of when their tour of duty would be over. Our squadron had no such luxury. We were scheduled to return to Norfolk whenever the Atlantic Fleet was willing to send another squadron of destroyers to replace us. The squadron seldom if ever, operated as a squadron.

Winter weather closed in and the Chinese came down in masses and pushed our troops back to Hungnam.

This became the Dunkirk of the Korean War. The troops came down in full retreat and were loaded on many transports in the harbor. The USS ZELLARS was sent to Hungnam and was used as a messenger ship, a shore bombardment ship, and an ASW screen ship. We kept track of our troops as they were retreating. Tons of supplies were left on the beach and much of it was burned.

Because of an over-supply of officers I shared my small cabin with my good friend Dr. STEINBERG. We slept just aft of the laundry. STEINBERG was a physician, a pianist, pitcher on our soft ball team, and a master bridge player. He also spoke fluent Spanish. When we went to a Cocktail party in Guantanamo he got to speaking in Spanish with a couple of mid-aged (to us) women in Spanish. Somehow he and I did not realize that the ladies also spoke English. Bob turned to me and in English said, "let's get rid of these old broads and see if we can find some good looking chicks." Bob was a bachelor. One of the ladies turned to him and in perfect English said something to him that was not flattering. Bob turned beet red and there were many evenings, in Korea when I reminded him of his misdeed. As Hungnam was being evacuated Dr. STEINBERG, who was on either the Squadron or Division Staff, found some reason to go ashore. There he found a storeroom, which was rapidly becoming the front line, which contained two grand pianos. He returned immediately to the ship and asked me for a working party so that he could get one of the pianos before it was torched. The storeroom was several miles from the beach and was about to be engulfed in gunfire. With great reluctance I turned down his request for several reasons. Where would we store a piano? In the ward room because of lack of space we were already eating in shifts, would we eat off the piano?

For the rest of the war in Korea, Wonsan was our "home port." We were told to fire intermittent fire at the beach and stop the traffic that was passing on Kalma Gap Peninsula. We were told to fire about 100 rounds of 5" 38 ammo, every day but not in one burst. So under my leadership we set up a Gunfire Support Plan (I told you that in 1947-48 I had been an instructor at the Gunfire Support School, now I had to put into practice what I had been teaching). This assignment earned me a Bronze Star with a combat V. *(The award document is on the wall in front of me as I type this letter.)*

As I said before, I left the ship in April and when I left they were still using my Gunfire Support plan. All day long and all night the five inch kept firing intermittent gunfire. We got so used to the noise of gunfire that we never heard it. I remember one of the officers asking me why we had quit firing, when about ten minutes before that question we had fired two rounds! Some days we were taking on ammo, or fuel, or supplies on the port side and firing randomly to starboard.

Christmas Eve of 1950 was the coldest day of my life. I was born and raised in Conneaut, Ohio which gets the raw weather and tames it before it goes to Buffalo, NY. (which has a countrywide reputation for miserable weather). Conneaut was cold but it was nothing like the bridge of the USS ZELLARS DD 777 on that Christmas eve night. It was a moonless night. That was the reason why we picked this night for this particular mission. As soon as it had become dark, we lowered the motorwhale boat and loaded it with Col. Coe of the Korean army, two Korean agents and the sculler.

The motorwhale boat was to tow a small punt. When the whaleboat inched into the beach as close as Col. Coe dared to go, then all the passengers got into the punt and the sculler rowed them ashore with a single oar, a method of rowing which he had used all his life. The motorwhale boat was to lie to, about 300 yards from the beach and wait until Col. Coe and the sculler returned. The two agents were to run with their radios and other supplies and make their way into North Korea and to report periodically to Col. Coe of the whereabouts of the enemy. The boat had left the ship about 1900 hours and was due back about 2130 hours.

On the bridge of the ZELLARS we were trying to get some heat out of the two bridge heaters. I had two pairs of everything and foul weather gear on top of that and a parka covering my body. We were navigating by radar sonar and fathometer. We were trying to keep the ship in one spot without dropping the anchor. We kept going outside in the bitter cold to see if we could spot the motor whale boat. The moon was due to rise about 2330 and we had to be out of there before it came up — and no sign of the MWB. Finally about 2300 we broke radio silence and ordered the MWB to return to the ship. After much biting of fingernails, (figuratively) the whale boat showed up a few minutes before the moon came up. The crew reported that Col. Coe and the sculler never returned to the MWB and we assumed that they had been captured or killed. Their business was very hazardous. We also had two young American agents aboard ship. They were grim and morose on hearing the sad news. We had all grown very fond of Col. Coe. The two Korean agents that had gone ashore were strangers to us. We had simply picked them up and they stayed close to the American agents in the short time that they were aboard ship. A few of the crew members had gotten to know the sculler although he could not speak English, and the crew did not speak a word of Korean. They knew that he was a fisherman, a family man with several minor children, and that he had not volunteered for this duty. As a matter of fact the MWB crew had seen him get conscripted for the duty.

Before this mission, the American agents kept reminding Col. Coe that they would need a sculler for this particular mission and for the next several missions. Col. Coe would simply tell them to quit worrying, that he would take care of everything in due time. So as we were leaving Pusan with the two agents that were going ashore far north of Hungnam, Col. Coe asked for the MWB. He would give the crew its orders. The crew was told to head for a certain fishing spot. There was the sculler with his boat happily sculling along. Col. Coe ordered the MWB to throw him a line and after a bit of conversation the sculler and his punt were taken in tow and ended up aboard the ZELLARS. We never knew if Col. Coe and the sculler had known each other prior to this casual encounter. But for a month they were entwined to each other.

I cannot recall exactly when and where the two American agents and Col. Coe came aboard. Our orders were to give them whatever logistic support they needed to carry out their mission. We were not even told for whom they worked. Sometimes they were in civilian clothes and then other times in Army uniforms and their rank or rating seemed to be quite flexible. They were nice young men who had graduated from one of the Ivy League schools. I do not remember how we addressed them. One of them had a "shoe box" filled with American money of various denominations. The rest of us used "script," which was an American Forces money supply invented to discourage military men from using American currency on the "Black Market." The American agents did a lot of kidding between themselves and Col. Coe. Apparently they were delayed in leaving Seoul as the enemy approached the city. We gathered from their conversation that they had a busy time debriefing a couple of young Korean damsels to ensure that their memories of Americans left them longing to come to America, perhaps with their new offspring. The two Americans kept pretty much to themselves although periodically they dined with the Commodore (ComDesDiv 162) Captain JAMES WHITFIELD.

Col. Coe liked to talk and fraternize with the crew. He spoke Korean, Japanese, Chinese, Russian, French and English. We never measured his IQ but it must have been in the highest 1% bracket. One of the ZELLARS crew played the accordion which he had brought on board with him. Col. Coe was fascinated by it and in short, order borrowed it and learned to play American songs on it. It was a matter of hours in which he accomplished this feat.

For some reason one afternoon we put into Pusan quite unexpectedly. Perhaps we were picking up agents. Col. Coe announced that he would be giving a party at one of the big hotels and that all officers off duty were invited to attend. We were tied up to some dock and on the other side of the dock was one of the hospital ships, perhaps the USS SOLACE. As the Executive Officer I had some business on the hospital ship. If my memory serves me correctly, Dr STEINBERG knew someone on board her and had decided to skip Col. Coe's party, or perhaps the entire staff took the occasion to go aboard one of the other ships in the division and render assistance if it was needed. In the course of my business on the hospital ship I met a very nice female physician who was also a Lieutenant Commander. I invited her to join us at Col. Coe's party and she accepted the invitation. Col. Coe had a beautiful wife at this party. We must have had about forty people at the party. Lots of beer, Saki and other beverages were served.

The food was good Chinese type food. There were even a small dance floor and a small oriental dance band which played American songs. Some of the officers were dancing with various ladies and with some of the nurses from the hospital ship. I even thought it might be nice to dance with Col. Coe's wife. He also thought it would be nice. So we took to the dance floor as a slow waltz was being played. I had visions of getting a bit cozy on the dance floor. As soon as we started to dance, I realized she had been eating Kimchi, a Korean delicacy made of cabbage stuffed with garlic and allowed to ferment in horse manure. The smell of Kimchi was enough to fell a grown American. We waltzed at arm's length.

In a short while I decided to go to the men's room. I mentioned this to my physician guest and she said that she would join me and would go to the ladies room. Together we went and found the appropriate signs of female and male silhouettes on two adjacent doors. We both said in unison, "I will meet you out here in a few minutes!" It was a common rest room for both sexes. I did not think that it would bother her since she was a physician. She immediately stepped outside and tugged on my sleeve, so I went with her. She asked me to clear out the rest room and then stand guard outside while she used the facilities! Since I was in uniform, I had no trouble clearing out the rest room and standing guard to accommodate her. She asked me if she could do the same for me. All of the above events are shared so that one can understand how we had become attached to our American and Korean passengers.

Just before midnight on Christmas evening 1950, we put out to sea without Col. Coe or the sculler and the two American agents assumed that the entire mission was a failure and worse yet that all the gear might be captured. Sadness hung over the entire ship. On Christmas day the cooks managed to put out their version of a Christmas feast and it did little to cheer up the crew. But the mood changed shortly. Early in the afternoon we received a radio message telling us that one of our Cruisers had picked up two Koreans riding on an overturned punt. One claimed that he was Col. Coe and that he belonged on the USS ZELLARS. Could we verify the story? Happily we did and we made arrangements to rendezvous with the Cruiser and transfer the hapless pair back to the ship. By high line we transferred both men aboard and then somehow brought the punt aboard.

They successfully had gotten the two trained agents, with gear off and into the bush. However, as soon as they tried to get the punt back out to sea it had overturned. Col. Coe and the sculler were not able to right the boat and it started to drift with the tide out to sea. Eventually they cleared the beach and it appeared to Col. Coe that the sea would take them to Japan in about a week. He did not consider this a major calamity. In his life this was a routine happening. He apparently knew enough about navigation that he was not concerned. After all he thought that he had a waterproof watch which would be of tremendous use in navigating. But, alas, the watch had failed to run when soaked.

The mood changed aboard ship when the American agents reported that they had made contact with the Korean agents ashore and that all was going according to schedule. I believe that we made one or two additional missions with Col. Coe and the sculler before we were ordered to disembark the two Americans and Col. Coe. No mention was made of the sculler. In fact, I do not believe that anyone knew that he was aboard. He was returned in the same manner in which he was obtained. The Americans reminded Col. Coe that it was his responsibility to take positive steps to ensure that the sculler told no one of his whereabouts for the past several weeks. Col. Coe was positive that he would be able to convince the sculler to keep his mouth shut. As we approached the same port Col. Coe asked for the use of the motor whaleboat. He and the sculler were brought to a deserted beach. Col. Coe ordered the MWB to wait for him. He and the sculler walked behind a sand dune and disappeared for a short period of time. Col. Coe returned alone. No one ever was able to find out what had happened to the hapless sculler. One of the MWB crewmen said he had heard a single gunshot. The other crewman had heard nothing. Col. Coe told me that he had warned the sculler to keep quiet about the duty that he had performed and that he had done a great deed for South Korea in the past few weeks. I have always had my suspicion about the fate of the sculler, but wars make military people take some rather drastic measures in order to win.

I am not sure of the chronology of events that transpired in Korea. I believe after that episode we returned to Wonsan and continued our gunfire. January, February and possible March were spent "on the line." Much of the time we were alone in an enemy port. We became so brazen that we anchored "at short stay" (with a few fathoms out). We could quickly retrieve the anchor and get underway if need be.

By early March the crew was becoming restless and people were increasingly irritable. For over sixty days no one had been off the ship. Supplies, ammo and fuel were delivered to us as we continued our shore bombardment. As I mentioned above, one of my collateral duties was recreation officer. I decided to do something about the title. We did carry beer aboard in a sealed compartment; it was time to have a beer party.

We were not allowed to drink aboard ship. So why not go ashore to one of the nearby islands and have a beach party? The nearest and most accessible island had about one hundred inhabitants and they were flying the North Korean flag. I was sure that they could easily be persuaded to allow us the use of part of the beach for a party. We loaded up the motor whale boat with two 100-pound bags of rice and four or five husky well armed sailors. Each wore helmets and carried a handgun of some sort. I decided to lead the party. I strapped on my trusty .45, and armed with a Korean dictionary, went ashore to negotiate a deal with the natives. We also had a few cigarettes and some candy for the children. As we approached the island the North Korean flag was replaced with an American flag. We landed on the beach and none of the grownups approached us. In a short while a few of the children came to investigate. The candy worked fine. Gradually a few of the adults came down to the site. The cigarettes encouraged a few more to join us. Finally with the aid of the dictionary I let it be known that I wanted to speak with the "head" man. At first no one was willing to admit that he was the head man. They were under the impression that as soon as we located him that we would obliterate him. Finally I made one understand that I had brought him two bags of rice. The head man saw that I was about to give the rice to one who was not the boss and he admitted that he was number one.

By this time the entire village had gathered to see what was going on. They kept getting closer to me. Soon I was in the midst of curious children and a number of young women, and talking to the head man with the aid of the dictionary.

One woman was right next to me. I was at least a head taller than any of the villagers. This woman was staring intently at me. Laboriously the head man and I "talked." I was trying to make him understand that I wanted a space on the beach to have a party. I assured him that we would not interfere with their activities and that we wanted no intrusion from them. As they understood the atmosphere became more relaxed. Suddenly I was aware that the woman standing next to me had been getting shorter and shorter. No one noticed her but me. I looked down at her and she was still intently watching my facial expressions, and at the same time she had squatted and had decided to relieve her bladder. She almost peed on my shoes. The negotiations continued without a hitch.

In batches, we allowed every member of the crew to go ashore for a few hours and drink a couple of beers. Some of the irritation wore off. Even the Captain went ashore.

Daily the bridge game continued. We now played for an hour or two before supper. One early evening as we were playing bridge the Officer of The deck called down on the "squawk box" and reported to the Captain that someone on the beach was firing a mortar at us and that they were short of us but coming closer with their gunfire. The Captain answered saying, "Take in the anchor, warn the engine room that we will be underway in a minute or two and I will be on the bridge in a minute." He released the button on the "squawk box" and said to the other three players, "right after this hand." Captain MICHAEL'S had bid a little slam and proceeded to make the slam before rushing to the bridge. In truth there was little he could do until the anchor was up. We then got under way and increased our distance from the beach. We did have a good idea of the location of the mortar that had fired at us, but increased our rate of fire to let the enemy know that we were irritated. The firing kept on day after day, week after week, and month after month.

Then out of the blue in late April we got a radio message telling the Captain to detach me and send me to the Naval Postgraduate School at Annapolis. We were enroute to Sasebo, Japan when the message arrived. When we arrived I was hurriedly detached as I had a quick arrival date. But before I was detached the enlisted men of the ship took up a collection and quickly went ashore and bought me a gift. It was a silver tray. I flew from Sasebo, Japan to Norfolk Virginia in propeller airplanes with air speeds of about 200 miles per hour for four days carrying this precious reminder of my service on the U.S.S. ZELLARS.

This is my story of the GOOD SHIP U.S.S. ZELLARS (DD 777). As I mentioned I had not given the ship much thought for almost a half a century. Undoubtedly I could have remembered more if I had notes or someone from the ship to talk to who had been on at the same time I was. In this period the only person that I have met from the ship was WALTER (Bud) BOTLE. He was the ops Officer on the staff. Fran and I spent a lovely day with him and his wife, Bonnie, in Florida.

I hope that this fulfills the request for my story of my service on board the ZELLARS.

GUS GUSTSFERRO. Captain.

USS ZELLARS (DD777)

RALPH C. PATTERSON

ENLISTED: AUGUST 17, 1950

BOOT CAMP: SAN DIEGO, CA.

FIRST ASSIGNED TO ZELLARS: NOVEMBER, 1950

RATING: EM3c

PLACES VISITED: Korea: Chongin, Songen, Hungnam, Wonsan, Pusan. Japan: Yokosuka, Yokohama, Sasebo, Tokyo. Midway Island, Pearl Harbor. Labrador: Hamilton Inlet, Gooseneck Bay, Cape Porcupine, South Strand Beach. Cuba: Santiago, Guantanamo Bay. Nova Scotia: Halifax. Carribean Sea: Cadad, Triyilla. Kingston, Jamaica. Argentia, New Foundland; Reykjavic, Iceland; Plymouth, England; Flushing, Holland; Bremerhaven, Germany; Penzance, England; Southend, England; Aberystythe, Wales; Dunkirque, France; Hastings, England; Gibralter, Pireaus, Greece; Toranto, Italy; Naples, Italy; Cartagena, Spain; Marcia, Spain; Cannes, France; Mock invasion of Kavalla, Greece; Cagliari, Sardinia.

When I first came aboard the ZELLARS in November 1950, all three gun mounts were firing on North Korean enemy troops. I was told to leave my sea bag on the main deck aft and report to the lower handling room of 5" 38 gun mount 3.

There I was told to load the elevator with powder casings for the upper gun mount. Only after we had ceased firing did I know where my "E" division and bunk was located. I slept in the same bunk until June 1954 when I received my honorable discharge.

The number 3 gun mount was my battle station as the first loader (powder case) port gun for the rest of our stay in Korea.

On Christmas day 1950 I was standing in the chow line on the port side forward just ready to go below. About seventy-five yards forward and to the left, I saw a large water spout. I thought boy it sure is cold here in Korea for whales. At this time battle stations was sounded and I realized the water spout I had seen was from enemy fire. I got my second wind going back to mount 3 and I think I made it in three or four steps. We ate Christmas dinner late that day.

While in Korea we had been shelling the beach for several hours. My back was sore and the smoke was thick in the number 3 mount. I was real tired and before long I felt a tap on my shoulder. It was "Dee," my 1st class gunnersmate DEBEVIC.

He said, "Pat, if you don't stay awake, you are going out the end of that gun barrel."

I asked, "Was I really sleeping?"

He answered, "I watched you for about five minutes and you were sleeping, but you didn't miss a powder case."

Also during our stay in Korea, being in the auxiliary gang, I was told by 1st class Engineman R.N. HICKS that I was to replace a bad seal in the high pressure air compressor turbine drive. The carbon seal retained steam while driving the air compressor, which was two-stage, and pumped to 5000 pounds for clearing the guns and charging the torpedoes.

Since we were in the war zone, my name and serial number was sent by wire to the bureau of ships in Washington DC. to get permission for me to replace this seal. The compressor was still going good when I left the ship.

A couple of times in Korea I was engineer of the motor whaleboat, port side, when we would take several South Koreans ashore behind enemy lines as spies, then go pick them up a day or so later. This was always done at night for obvious reasons.

One day, the Captain and Executive Officer were taken ashore somewhere above the 38th Parallel to get information from South Korean Officers. I was the engineer that day with "Tirb" as bow hook and "Jocko" as Coxswain. The Captain told us to stay close to the boat as many buildings here were "booby trapped." It was 0 degrees or below that day so after we were there an hour or more, JOCKO started pulling siding from a building and started a small fire. This was very welcome at the time but we all got chewed out when our officers returned.

Also hanging inside one of the buildings was some bloody rope and a pool of fresh blood. We thought that they had butchered an animal there until by hand signs etc. from a South Korean soldier, we found that a North Korean soldier had been questioned there and his throat had been cut. We were anxious to leave at this time.

After the ZELLARS returned to the U.S. from Korea, we were out to sea near Cuba when the diaphragm on the fog horn went bad. The ship was underway. Again EM1 HICKS asked me to repair it.

As I sat on the forward stack working on it with the ship swaying from side to side, Hicks got permission from the Captain to test the ship's whistle which by the way was right at my side. Needless to say, had I not had a good grip on the ladder, I wouldn't be sharing this story.

242

R.N. HICKS again, "Daddy Hicks" as most of us called him: We were in the port motor whaleboat running up the engine which had to be done every so often when it was not put in the water. Hicks pushed the throttle lever too far forward and it stuck at full throttle. After a couple of minutes of trying to free it, Hicks bailed out and disappeared, leaving me to secure it.

First I shut off the starboard fuel tank valve. By then the engine, which should be run at about 1800 RPM, was running about 3000 RPM and beginning to sound like a jet engine.

About this time the Captain and several other men came out of the bridge to see what was making all the noise.

By this time the fuel ran out of the lines. The engine was screaming before it stopped in a cloud of smoke. When Hicks did show again, I asked him why he left so soon. He answered, "Did you ever see a diesel engine blow up?"

I hadn't.

RALPH C. PATTERSON EM3c

USS ZELLARS (DD777)

JOHN W. STONE

ENTERED NAVY: JULY 1951

BOOT CAMP: GREAT LAKES COMPANY

ASSIGNED TO ZELLARS: SEPT., 1951

LENGTH OF SERVICE ON ZELLARS: 2 YEARS, 8 MONTHS

RATING: SK 3C

PLACES VISITED: St. John's, New Foundland; Reykjavik, Iceland: Julianehab, Greenland; Plymouth, England: Abreystwyth, Wales; Rock of Gibralter; Cartagena; Madrid, Spain; Bremerhaven, Germany; Flushing, Holland; Cannes; Dunkirk; France; Barcellona; Sicily; Kingston, Jamaica; Cindad; Trujillo; Guantanamo Bay, Cuba; Naples, Italy; Dublin, Ireland; Hastings, England; San Jaun, Puerto Rico; Brussels, Belgium; Athens, Greece; Halifax, Nova Scotia

The ZELLARS was in drydock at Portsmouth, Virginia in the spring of 1954. We stayed on the ship part of the time, then had to move to a barracks on the beach until they finished her. While the ZELLARS was in drydock, the shipyard sandblasted her underside and repainted her.

I was a storekeeper and ran the ship's store. Of course with that position everyone was my friend. I had all the good stuff everyone wanted. I had open gangway and when we were overseas, I wore out a set of dress blues in a year.

Lt(jg) J.D. SMITH was our supply officer. We were assigned to him. We thought so much of him, we bought him a Hamilton wrist watch when he was discharged and left the ship. At our reunion in Norfolk, Virginia, he was there with his lovely wife Bobbie and guess what. He was still wearing that watch today. His wife told me he has had many watch bands but the watch is still running, which is over 40 years old.

While visiting with a Dutch fisherman he told me about the way they fished in his day versus the way they fish now. He also asked me where I was from in the USA. When I told him he wanted to know where Springfield, Illinois was located. Also he said his wooden shoes were not very comfortable, they were more of a country's tradition.

I met Winston Churchill in the lobby of the hotel in Kingston, Jamaica in 1952. I was on liberty with two of my shipmates. We went into the hotel to get something to eat and, of course, something stronger than coffee to drink. They are noted for their rum. Winston was also in the lobby checking in. He sent his aid over to ask our names. The conversation was very brief but he did mention that he was there for holiday time. He was a very impressive gentleman.

During GQ, we did most of our practice drills in Gitmo, Bay Cuba, shooting at targets pulled by aircraft and small ships. Our gun captain was GM1c PRICE at the time. He was always on our tails during rapid fire drills to get out more rounds than the other two 5" 38 mounts. Once we had a hang fire in my port gun. I was the first loader and had to dismantle the breach of my gun and throw the projectile overboard. Luckily it did not go off but my black powder man was so frightened, he jumped out of the black powder case hatch head first.

When we were in Hastings, England, we had to anchor out of port one night because the water was so rough. They cancelled liberty because they could not launch the gigs to send in for the liberty. One of my shipmates, who had met an English lass, said he was in love and had to go ashore. The water was so rough it washed him out to sea. The next day, some fishermen brought him back to the ship.

JOHN W. STONE SK3c

Penzance, England

SUNDAY, MAY 24TH
CORONATION CONCERT—NORRIS WILLIAMS, HIS
        ORCHESTRA AND SINGERS   St. John's Hall, 8 p.m.

FRIDAY, MAY 29th
ARRIVAL OF H.M.S. " BARROSA "   (Remaining until 4th June,
                                        1953).

SATURDAY, MAY 30TH
ARRIVAL OF U.S.S. " ZELLARS "   (Remaining until 6th June,
                                        1953).

TENNIS—AMERICAN TOURNAMENT   Penlee Park, 2.30 p.m.

SUNDAY, MAY 31ST
FREE CHURCHES' OPEN-AIR SERVICE   Art Gallery Playing Field,
                                        Newlyn, 11 a.m.

MAYORAL CHURCH PARADE AND OPEN-AIR SERVICE   Mennaye Field, 3 p.m.
CONCERT—MOUSEHOLE MALE VOICE CHOIR AND
          PENZANCE SILVER BAND   Morrab Gardens, 8 p.m.

MONDAY, JUNE 1ST
BAND CONCERT, PENZANCE SILVER BAND   Promenade, 8 p.m.

TUESDAY, JUNE 2ND
CORONATION DAY

FIRING OF A ROYAL SALUTE   Penlee Quarries, 12 noon
CHILDREN'S GALAS AND SPORTS   St. Clare, Ponsandane,
                                  Newlyn, Mousehole,
                                  Heamoor and Penlee Park
                                      (2.30 p.m.)

CORPUS CHRISTI FAIR   Recreation Ground, 6 p.m.
SWIMMING GALA   Bathing Pool, 7 p.m.
OPEN-AIR DANCE   Promenade, 8 p.m.
MAYORAL CORONATION BALL   St. John's Hall, 9 p.m.
FIREWORKS DISPLAYS ON THE SEA-FRONT   10.30 p.m.
SCOUTS AND GUIDES CAMP FIRE SING-SONG AND
                BONFIRE   Madron Carn, 8 p.m.

USS ZELLARS (DD777)

JAMES DOUGLAS SMITH

USNROTC: COMMISSIONED ENSIGN, USN JUNE 6, 1951. (SUPPLY CORPS)

ASSIGNED ZELLARS: DECEMBER 26,1951

LENGTH ON ZELLARS: DECEMBER 1951-NOVEMBER, 1953

RANK: LT(jg). SC. USN.

PLACES VISITED: Halifax, Nova Scotia; Guantanamo Bay, Cuba; Santiago, Cuba; U.S. Naval Academy (twice); Iceland, Plymouth, England (twice); Penzance, Southend, Hastings, Abreystwyth, Wales; Holland, Bremerhaven, Gibraltar, Cartegena, Cannes, Naples. Piraeus, and Cagliari, Sardinia.

Born and grew up in Rainelle, West Virginia. Graduated Montvale (VA) High School in 1947. Chosen for the US Navy ROTC program at University of North Carolina in the spring of 1947. A student at UNC-Chapel Hill, 1947-1951. I was commissioned as a regular (not reserve) officer in the United States Navy, June 4, 1951, Ensign, USN (Supply Corps). Attended USN Supply Corps School, Bayonne, New Jersey, September 1951.

I was then ordered to the USS SABINE (AO-25) as the assistant to the supply officer. Several of us who were destined for independent duty as destroyer supply officers were ordered for three months' temporary duty on oilers. I reported to the SABINE in New Port, RI, in early September of 1951 and left her in December of 1951, after receiving orders to the U.S.S. ZELLARS. The Sabine was short of deck officers to stand watches so I was placed in the bridge watch rotation as a Junior Officer of the Deck. Needless to say, it was unusual for a Supply Corps Officer to be given bridge deck watches.

While on the Sabine we made two trips to the Caribbean as part of task force training maneuvers. On one of these I was on the wing of the bridge, as Junior OD, checking on the distance between our ship and the ships coming alongside to refuel. I had received orders to the ZELLARS, so it was a great surprise one afternoon to see the ZELLARS approaching on our starboard side for refueling. I was very impressed with her appearance and the excellent ship handling of her skipper. However, I did not want to be seen on the deck watch because I didn't want to give anyone on the ZELLARS the idea that I might be used for deck watches once I reported on board. I asked the CO of the Sabine if I could be shifted to the port side of the bridge while the ZELLARS was alongside. When I explained why, he laughed but did shift me to the port side so I would not be seen by anyone on the ZELLARS. Supply Officers have to be versatile people, but adding deck watches to my portfolio was not something I wanted to do permanently. Actually, it was probably a violation of Navy regulations to have me standing deck watches in the first place.

I reported to the ZELLARS December 26, 1951. She was berthed at Newport News Shipbuilding, because all of the destroyer/escort piers at NOB, Norfolk were filled for the Christmas holiday season. Several destroyers were tied up at Newport News Shipbuilding and the ZELLARS was out board in a nest of three ships. Moored directly across the pier from us was the SS United States, recently completed at NNS & Drydock Company and receiving final preparations for her maiden voyage. It was a double thrill for me, therefore, to report to the ZELLARS and see the United States towering high above the pier.

My first impression of the ZELLARS was very favorable. The ship was shipshape, clean, and obviously proud to be the flag of DESDIV 162. The Commodore of DESDIV was Captain LEON S. KINTBERGER. He was a link with the past, because of his previous service on board the ZELLARS. Commodore KINTBERGER was a fine role model, Navy through and through, with a firmness that could turn brusque when warranted.

He was good company and possessed a fine sense of humor. I want to tell one story that illustrates his character. I held my first payday in early January. I felt pretty good to have completed it successfully and had returned to my (small) supply office with my DKs. I received a summons to the Commodore's quarters. I went in and Kintberger said, "Pay (master), I haven't been paid."

I said, "Commodore, I thought you were ashore."

He said, "PAY, I want you to learn an important lesson. You always come to my quarters before you hold payday to find out how much I wish to be paid. You then bring me the cash with a pay receipt, which I will sign. Pay me, and then you can hold payday for the rest of the officers and men of the crew." He was firm but had a slight twinkle in his eye as he told me what the routine was regarding his pay. Needless to say, it made a strong impression on me. I never had another problem with Commodore KINTBERGER after that.

The CO of the ZELLARS when I reported was RICHARD M. HAYES, CDR, USN. He was the CO until the summer of 1953, when he was relieved by HERBERT H. ANDERSON. More about change of command later. CDR. HAYES was a seasoned destroyer skipper. He immediately dubbed me, "Smitty," and that was what he always called me. He was all Navy and had the trust and confidence of the officers and crew. He had wide-ranging interests and conversations in the ward room at meals were generally lively. CDR. HAYES was a bachelor, and that leads me to tell a wonderful story about him. CDR HAYES was an excellent ship handler, but he was very cautious. For example, when the ZELLARS would return from being out of the Virginia Capes for a week on maneuvers, the officers and crew were anxious to return to NOB Norfolk. If there were the slightest fog, rain, or poor visibility, the Skipper would drop the hook off Lynnhaven Bay and we would spend the night and go in as soon as it was light. The officers and crew were especially annoyed by this caution when it occurred on Friday night as it often did. CDR HAYES had an unblemished record, and he simply didn't want to mess it up by taking chances with his ship on foggy, rainy nights with poor visibility. While there was much grousing about this by all hands, we knew why he was being cautious, and we sympathized with him. At least some of us did.

In the summer of 1952 the ZELLARS spent almost three months in the Portsmouth Naval Shipyard undergoing an overhaul. CDR. HAYES met a lovely nurse; they fell in love, and were married. They entertained the officers several times at their apartment off Hampton Boulevard and near NOB Norfolk. With his marriage came a change of tactics. He never again dropped the hook off Lynnhaven and spent the night. Just like the US Postal Service, neither fog, rain, mist, hail or even zero visibility would deter the ZELLARS, her dauntless skipper and crew, from reaching our birth at NOB. It sometimes took until one or two, or three AM but we always came in. As you can imagine, Skipper HAYES' reputation as a great skipper rose tremendously.

The XO was CDR THEODORE O'GORMAN, a compact, florid-faced, quiet but rock-solid Irishman. I believe that he was a reservist recalled when the Korean War broke out. In fact, many of the officers when I went aboard were reservists who had been recalled to active duty. TED O'GORMAN was relieved in late 1952 or early 1953 as XO by LCDR JOHN S. OLLER Jr. OLLER was an interesting character, a thin, nervous, type who tended to be "uptight" much of the time. One of his brothers was a Supply Officer who outranked him. It may have been jealousy of his brother, but OLLER didn't seem to think too highly of Supply Officers. We got along fairly well so long as I always had on board a stock of his favorite cigarettes, Viceroys.

I stocked the "big three" brands for the Ship's Store sales, Camels, Chesterfields and Lucky Strikes. The only other brand was the XO's "special order," Viceroy. In a strange way, while OLLER did not seem to regard Supply Officers very highly, he occasionally confided in me. These were more monologues with my listening to his words. A couple of times he would be silent, and then break the silence with, "Smitty, I can command. I know I can command." I often wondered if he was promoted to Commander or Captain and did have the opportunity to have his own ship.

Other Officers who were aboard the ZELLARS between December 1951 and November 1953 when I left the ship were RICHARD SLOCUM, a bright-eyed (mischievous-eyed) energetic graduate of Oregon State University. DICK SLOCUM had a happy-go-lucky attitude that made him fun to be around. He was a fine officer in Operations, I believe, and he took his official duties seriously. When ashore, he was the "life of the party" type. He was a recalled reservist and probably returned to his company, 3M, to become a vice-president. I don't know, but I would bet he did.

HARRY WISTRAND was a "Southern Gentleman" from Alabama and another fine officer. I believe that Harry was in engineering, but my memory has faded on that score. Again, Harry was a recalled reservist. PAUL HEUBUSCH was First Lieutenant through our summer of 1952 shipyard overhaul. As I recall, Paul was a lawyer, and recalled to active duty. He was always good company with a wry sense of humor. Paul was always thoroughly professional in everything he did. He seemed to me at the time to be the most "cerebral" of our happy band.

I cannot remember the first name of our Engineering Officer, but his last name was WEAKLEY. He was the subject of a lot of kidding as was the rule with the snipes and engineers. He was a good-natured guy and took the ribbing, giving back as good as he was given most of the time. His countenance was somewhat forlorn, and that added to the fun of sparring verbally with him.

Among other officers were PHILLIP RALPH or RALPH PHILLIP HANES. We knew him as Phil Hanes and he was a scion of the Hanes textile family of Winston-Salem, N.C. Phil was the Commodore's Aide, I believe under Commodore KINTBERGER. Phil really took his job seriously. He was a bit on the nervous side and seemed always to be worried about something. He was also a target, at times, of some joshing from his fellow officers. The Commodore's Aide who succeeded (if I have the progression straight) was FRANK NAZOR. Frank was generally more relaxed than PHIL HAYNES. Commodore KINTBERGERS successor was Captain JACOB BULLEN, and it was probably a little more relaxing for FRANK NAZOR working under Captain BULLEN than working for PHIL HAYNES. As I recall, FRANK NAZOR was a southerner and really enjoyed the Bob Crosby and Jimmy Dorsey "Dixieland" records that I contributed to the ward room record collection.

My best friends among the officers were FRED MOHN, BOB KNAUSS, and BOB GARSKE. FRED was from Northfield, MN, and a graduate of St. Olaf College. Among his many gifts was his skill as a trumpet player. If my memory serves, there was a small dance band on the ZELLARS, at one time, formed by Fred and a few of the crew who played. At any rate, I do remember an occasion or two when these guys gathered on the fantail, when we were tied up, to do a little jamming.

The highlights from an operational standpoint in the period from January and May 1952 were these. In January and February, we participated in NATO maneuvers in the North Atlantic. Everyone knows what the North Atlantic is like in mid-winter, and I won't remind you. However, the ZELLARS had an interesting assignment during the tour. Two of the support convoy, I believe both were cargo vessels, collided off New Foundland. The ZELLARS was detached with one other destroyer to accompany the two ships to Halifax, Nova Scotia. Our headway was obviously reduced to a speed of 5 to 10 knots as I recall, because the two ships were badly damaged. It took several days to make port through the heavy seas. Needless to say, we were all delighted when we finally reached Halifax. As I recall, we were in Halifax for a day and night or maybe two nights. The highlight for me as Supply Officer was the chance to replenish the fresh stores. We were able to buy delicious Canadian apples, fresh cabbage, potatoes, other vegetables and fresh milk. Our skipper, RICHARD M. HAYES, was generous with shore leave and I think just about everyone on board who wanted to, had a chance for a few hours ashore while we were in Halifax.

After our return to Norfolk from these maneuvers we readied the ship for a visit to the Naval Academy. The Skipper and the Commodore were especially interested in our appearance since we were to be "on show" at the Academy. At the time the berth for us was just east of Bancroft Hall and our bow faced directly up the walk leading to Bancroft. That berthing space has been filled in now to form athletic fields. We had a very pleasant visit to the Academy and quite a few Midshipmen came aboard to see us. The highlight of the visit was an outdoor cookout that Commodore KINTBERGER and Mrs. KINTBERGER held for the officers at their lovely home overlooking Chesapeake Bay south of Annapolis.

Before I go further, I need to add another name to the list of XO's. LCDR JOHN L. GREEN, who was XO between TED O'GORMAN and JOHN S. OLLER. I believe that John was the Gunnery Officer when I first went aboard. He was another veteran of the WWII Navy, was recalled in 1951, and left the ZELLARS in the fall of 1952. John was a colorful guy, blustery, red-faced most of the time, but an outstanding officer. He had a great sense of humor and loved to banter with his fellow officers.

One of the highlights of the summer for me and FRED MOHN was seeing and hearing the Stan Kenton Orchestra who played for a few days at the Cavalier Hotel Beach Club in Virginia Beach. It is hard to beat a great band playing on a warm summer night with gentle breezes coming off the Atlantic. The Beach Club is still there, a conference center now. But alas, where are the big bands of old?

In September-October 1952, the ZELLARS was deployed to the Caribbean on maneuvers. At this point I would like to say more about the Supply Department. In January, 1952, I relieved LTJG WILLIAM A. ARMSTRONG, USN, as Supply Officer. Bill, nicknamed "Shakey," probably from his Naval Academy days, was a first-rate officer. His records, accounts, inventories, and general condition of the Supply Department were all in excellent shape. He was very helpful to me as his relief and smoothed the way for me in succeeding him. I am pleased to see his name on the roster of members of the U.S. ZELLARS Association and am not at all surprised to see that he retired as a Rear Admiral.

My Chief in the Supply Department was CLARENCE MCGOWEN, CSC, USN. "Stew" as we all called him was a quiet, steady, conscientious, and totally honest and dependable CPO. We worked well together, and he knew how to work with our supply personnel to get their best work. I relied on "Mac" to handle the crew's mess hall, our food requisitions, our ship's cooks and stewards. He did a good job. I was blessed with some fine Storekeepers. GLEN R. ORDWAY completed a four-year hitch on the ZELLARS in 1952. ORDWAY, from New England and with a fine, regional accent, was the senior SK when I went aboard. Glenn was a no-nonsense, well respected, leader in the Supply

Department. He had a wry, New England sense of humor that quietly came forth when you least expected.

Overlapping ORDWAY'S service in the department and carrying on was JOHN W. STONE from Illinois. STONE was a little more "laid back," as we now say, than ORDWAY. JOHN STONE was always smiling, it seemed to me, and that meant he helped us all stay relaxed. When stores requisitions needed typing, inventories taken, supplies loaded, and all other Supply Department tasks undertaken, JOHN STONE was rock solid and ready to pull his weight. I was delighted to renew our ties at the U.S.S. ZELLARS Association's fifth reunion in Norfolk a few years ago. Balancing my New Englander, ORDWAY and my mid-westerner, STONE was my North Carolina man, DWAYNE MASON, who was a soft-spoken, down-home type, from the Carolina coastal plains. As I recall, he liked to work at night in the Supply office. Our cubbyhole of an office could not hold more than two or three at the most, so it was necessary for some of my men to work at night. Along with GLENN ORDWAY and JOHN STONE, DWAYNE MASON gave me a group of Storekeepers that did themselves, the Navy, and the ZELLARS proud.

I was also blessed with two fine Disbursing Clerks. WALTER LATNICK was from Rhode Island, slight of stature, a night owl, and meticulous in his record-keeping. LATNICK had a pale complexion in part because he didn't see much daylight. As noted above, DWAYNE MASON worked at night. His office sidekick was LATNICK working on the disbursing records while MASON worked on the stores records. My "daytime" DK was JOHN MCINTOSH from Massachusetts. MCINTOSH was as meticulous as LATNICK and between the two of them they were of tremendous help to me in my disbursing responsibilities. Both of them were right there beside me as we held payday, and they worked with me afterwards to be sure we balanced out exactly. No Supply Officer had better DKS than LATNICK and MCINTOSH.

Probably, no certainly, the most colorful character in my Supply Department was PATRICK PAVONE, who happily dubbed himself our "Irish Guinea." PAVONE did a little bit of everything. He helped with the Ship's store, worked in the laundry, was the ship's barber, and, in general, was ready to latch on to anything that might have some fun involved. In a word, he was irrepressible. Without a doubt, PAVONE was the biggest "character" on the ship.

In January of 1953, we were again on maneuvers in the North Atlantic. As usual, it was cold, gray, with fog or heavy mist, or rain, most of the time. Seas seemed to be running high all the time. One afternoon we were part of a circular screen formed around an aircraft carrier. The seas were running especially high and our bow would dip into a deep trough, plow into the next wave, shudder and rise to crest the following wave and then begin the descent again. (This of course, is very familiar to "Tin Can" sailors.) I was trying to do some work in the Supply Office when we sensed that the ship was changing direction to starboard. Word spread quickly that the SS UNITED STATES was approaching our formation. This meant, literally, that we were moving to make a path for her right down the middle of our task force. Everyone who could, found vantage points to watch the UNITED STATES steam through us. I remember vividly that as we dipped into a trough she was visible through the mist off our bow; when we next dipped and came up she was just about abreast midships; on the third and fourth times we plowed into the crest she moved steadily aft our stern, and then she was gone, lost in the North Atlantic mist. What a thrill it was to see that splendid vessel and to see first hand how swiftly she moved even in high seas.

We made another spring visit to the Naval Academy in 1953. Our Commodore, JACOB BULLEN, wanted the wardroom spruced-up, especially with new carpet. I remember racing to downtown Norfolk to search for just the right color green that the Commodore had requested. We put it down the day before we were to sail, and he was pleased. Commodore BULLEN was a calm, quiet, man with a face that always seemed ready to break into a smile. He and our CO, CDR HAYES, liked and respected each other.

After our Naval Academy visit, we were fully engaged in preparations for a six-months tour to Northern Europe and the Med. We had actually begun preparations for this in late 1952 by placing requisitions so that we had everything delivered on time. The Navy would not be "the Navy" however, if everything always worked according to plan. There were many anxious days wondering if all of our spare parts, supplies, ship's stores, consumables, etc., would arrive on time. When we sailed in April we were fully loaded and shared the pride of officers and crew, especially in the Supply Department, that we could say "well done."

Our first call was Reykjavik, Iceland. The things I remember best are the long boat trip into the port from our anchorage; our CO wisely restricting everyone to the ship. On May 1, the traditional big day for Communists who were strong on Iceland at the time, and who were staging a celebration; I was taking some $100 bills in US currency to the local bank president who wanted to compare the genuine bills I had, with counterfeit bills that were being circulated in Iceland. And, yes, he had a lot of counterfeit bills to worry about. Additionally, I enjoyed a tour of the thermal springs and the good seafood restaurants.

From Iceland we sailed to England. I remember so well the fog lifting off the Irish coast and the thrill it was to see the green hills of Ireland for the first time. Our first port of call was Plymouth. Later on our visit we would return to Plymouth for store replenishment before heading to the Med. I have many fond memories of Plymouth, principally because of the hospitality and kindness shown me by an English merchant, Peter Blackburn and his wife Sybil. Peter came aboard as soon as we had berthed to offer assistance. I placed a large order with him for good English ham, sausage, beef, eggs, cheese, fresh produce, and other food supplies to replenish our reefers and storerooms. Needles to say, the officers and crew welcomed this good food when it was delivered the next day. Another destroyer was berthed alongside us and Peter supplied them as well. I can not remember my fellow officer's name, but Peter took us both one afternoon to see his "old school" in Tavistock, on the bluffs of western Cornwall. It was the kind of afternoon one remembers forever. I played (badly) a round of golf with Peter at his golf club close by Dartmoor, tried my hand at cricket at his cricket club, toured a gray, windswept Dartmoor with Peter and Sybil. They entertained me at their home and I reciprocated with dinner and a movie aboard the ZELLARS. Sybil was especially impressed, because she had never been aboard a US ship. There is more I could tell, but I just want to indicate that in the course of Supply Officer's duties there is the opportunity to meet some fine people and move beyond necessary business to friendship.

Other ports of call were Aberystwyth, Penzance, Southend, and Hastings. The highlight of Aberystwyth was a grand luncheon in one of the University buildings for the officers of the ZELLARS and our sister-destroyer. Local officials and Royal Navy officers entertained us royally. Our visit to Penzance was especially memorable. FRED MOHN, BOB KNAUSS and I decided to ask the skipper if we could go to London for Queen Elizabeth's coronation. CDR HAYES heard us out, and said he thought it was a fine idea. Fortunately, we approached him first, because when others asked, he couldn't permit more than three officers to go and we were the three. I could write two or three pages about this experience. Suffice to say, it was one of those life time experiences that one savors for a life time. We took an overnight train from Penzance (having brought bread, cheese, and fruit for the next day) to Paddington Station. Our early arrival found a station newsstand with London Times headlines, "Hillary Conquers Everest." Ensconced finally under a theatre marquee on Whitehall just below Trafalgar Square, we watched the memorable tableau unfold. As their carriages went by, Queen Elizabeth II was radiant, the Royal Family happy, Sir Winston Churchill signaling his famous "V" once more, and the folks around us from all over the British Empire proud of their heritage. Back in Penzance the next day, it was hard to believe we had been there. It still is.

Our berth at Southend-on-sea afforded the crew and officers ample opportunity to visit London. Nearly everyone did so.

Before CDR ANDERSON succeeded CDR HAYES we had visited Holland and Bremerhaven. I want to tell the interesting story of my purchase of Schatz clocks. One of the most popular items that Navy men liked to purchase on tours to Europe or the Med were Schatz 300-day clocks. While we were in Bremerhaven, a German salesman came aboard to see me. He represented Schatz clocks and was approved by the Navy as the certified supplier. I took over 300 orders from the crew and officers for various models of the clocks. As I recall, we asked each man to make a small deposit with the balance on delivery. The clocks were to be delivered sometime and somewhere in the Med late in our tour before we returned home.

To jump ahead in the chronology, we were calling at our last port, Cagliari, Sardinia, in late August or early September. The clocks had not been delivered, and I was really worried about them. There was no problem with refunding the crew's deposits, but everyone was going to be disappointed to return home without his clock or clocks (some ordered more than one). Word reached me that the clocks had arrived. That was good news, but then there was the problem of transporting them in our ship's launch from the pier to our anchorage. It took several, very careful, trips to get them all on board. There was a growing problem of drugs on Sardinia at the time. The Skipper, CDR ANDERSON, ordered me to open each of the clock crates to check for smuggled drugs. My storekeepers and I spent nearly all of one day opening those crates. Fortunately, there was no evidence at all of drugs.

On our return voyage, a day or two out of Norfolk, I held a "clock delivery" session. The officers and crew presented their receipts, we double-checked the model and style, collected the balance due, and delivered each man his clock or clocks. I asked each man to check his clock for breakage of the glass dome. It was remarkable that we had only one cracked dome. Chalk that up to vaunted German precision in packing. I had ordered spare, replacement domes so we were prepared for more breakage. From a Supply Officer's viewpoint, it was a great way to end the cruise.

This narrative has run on much too long as it is, so I will refrain from recollections of Gibraltar, Cartegena (Spain), Cannes, Naples and Piraeus. I will just note that each port afforded time for trips to Malaga (from Gibraltar), for a real Spanish bullfight, along the Riveria to Monaco (from Cannes), to Rome, overnight (from Naples); to Athens, and via Corinth, to the tomb of Agamemnon (from Piraeus). Career Navy people, of course, have the opportunity for even more wonderful travel destinations. However, during my two years aboard the ZELLARS I was lucky enough to have had this memorable trip to Europe and the Med. The memory is still fresh after almost forty-five years.

It is hard to explain the bond that develops between Navy men and the ships on which they serve. Fm sure this is not always the case if one's shipboard experience has been difficult to the point of disappointment. I'm also sure that if you were to talk with the veterans of almost any Navy ship, they would fiercely defend their ship as "the best in the fleet." My own experience encompasses midshipmen cruises on the USS Astoria (CL 90) for two months; on the USS Missouri (BB63) for a month before the Missouri was ordered to Korea in June 1950; on the USS Sabine (AO 25) as noted above; and the USS ZELLARS (DD 777).

My impression after almost forty-five years is that everyone I knew, crew and officers, were proud to serve on the USS ZELLARS. There was an aura about the ship that was hard to define. I think that it must have had its bases in the deaths and terrible damage that she experienced off Okinawa. It is easy to understand why the most loyal and dedicated members of the ZELLARS Association are the plank owners and crew of that period in 1944-1945 when ship and men were tested to their limits. For those of us who came after them, while we did not share their test of courage, we could inherit some of their pride in having served on a splendid ship.

If I may offer one personal note in closing, each day since leaving the USS ZELLARS I am reminded of the ship and my shipmates. I wear on my wrist, and have for almost 45 years, a Hamilton wristwatch given to me by the men of my Supply Department when I left the ship. I am immensely proud of that watch, of having served with those young men, and above all, for the privilege of going to sea on the USS ZELLARS DD 777.

JAMES DOUGLAS SMITH, LT(jg), June 1997

USS ZELLARS (DD777)

RALPH R. HUNSTAD

ENLISTED: OCTOBER 14, 1948
BOOT CAMP: GREAT LAKES, ILL.

ASSIGNED TO ZELLARS: NOVEMBER 1, 1951

LENGTH ON ZELLARS: I YEAR

RATING: IC2c (intercommunications)

PLACES VISITED: North Atlantic Cold Weather Operations, Norfolk, VA; Guantanamo Naval Base, Cuba; Santiago, Cuba.

Shipmates: Harvey Srolovitz, Willie Randolph, (Peaches), Gregory Laprando,

"BOOT CAMP"

The beginning of the making of a sailor! My Boot training was at Great Lakes Naval Training Center, Illinois. I had brought along a small portable radio which was stolen from my personal luggage while we were being issued our uniforms. Not a very good impression of the security.

One of the first things was to get our hair cut, so we all looked like skin heads.

It was getting up early in the morning and then standing in "chow lines."

I remember that I didn't appreciate having to get up at 04:00 AM for watch duty, but then that was part of our training. While on watch duty, anytime a duty officer would come by we had to respond with name and serial number.

Another experience was when we had to get all of our vaccinations. I remember becoming feverish, (this was referred to as cat fever.)

We had many different instruction sessions. We would have inspections of both the barracks and our (clothes) uniforms.

We would have KP duty where a person was assigned a special job such as serving food, coffee runner and cleanup detail.

BOOT CAMP was also a place of learning that there are rules and regulations and it was in your best interest to follow them.

Personal experience was when we were at the Cuba Naval base for retraining out to sea, we had a "man overboard" drill and as the whaleboat was being lowered over the side of the ship, the wake of our ship (ZELLARS) caught the bow of the whaleboat (rescue boat). When the lines were being unhooked, the bow of the whaleboat went under the water. We lost a Medic man in the accident, he was the only one that had the inflatable life jacket and apparently didn't have it inflated.

My experience of coming into an area during a retraining drill to rescue a person who was supposedly injured, he was wearing a mask indicating a severe face injury, was one I will never forget, My first experience in rescue.

While on another retraining trip at sea, I was in the IC room. The observer told me I had a fire in my motor generator for the gyro compass. So I had to make a transfer to the standby motor generator, but in the process of transferring, I didn't hit the start button fast enough so I had to lock up the gyro compass frame momentarily. The person on the bridge was wondering what was going on with the gyro compass. I reported my problem. At that point they had to go back to midship to navigate by magnetic compass until I was able to stabilize my gyro. The ship happened to be in a turn so there was a lot of pressure on the gyro frame. The motor could have become unbalanced and flown out of its frame. The speed of a gyro motor is very fast. If you have ever played with a small gyrocompass, you know what force there is when you try to move the axis.

While we were in the North Atlantic on a cold weather operation, (January,. 1952) two other ships (PAs, troop transport ships) got hit in the bow area from the upper deck to the water line. I can only assume the collision happened while the two ships were changing their position in the maneuvers to omit being tracked by submarines. The ZELLARS escorted the PAs into Halifax, Canada. We actually pumped the heavy oil overboard to supposedly calm the water while escorting the PAs into Halifax. I found this hard to believe.

After returning from the North Atlantic cold weather operation, if I remember correctly, we went into dry dock for overhaul and repair, then later went to Guantanamo Bay for retraining.

RALPH R. HUNSTAD. IC2c

USS ZELLARS (DD777)

JOE HALLORAN

ENLISTED: MAY 19, 1952

BOOT CAMP: GREAT LAKES, ILL.
COMPANY, 260 CAMP DROWER

FIRST ASSIGNED TO ZELLARS: SEPTEMBER 19, 1952

RATING: BT2c

My four years in the Navy were probably some of the best years of my life. I put three months in at Boot Camp at the Great Lakes Training Center, then three months in Boiler School in Philadelphia, PA, and the rest were spent on the ZELLARS.

After going back to Great Lakes I was assigned to the ZELLARS but it was in the Caribbean Sea so I went to Norfolk, Virginia by train. I was put to work as a mess cook for two weeks, then sent to Cuba on a troop ship and landed at Guantanamo Bay air station about a week later (September 19, 1952). We, two of us, went aboard the ZELLARS for the first time. It was exciting to be shown around the ship the first day, being assigned a division, and getting to know where things were (mess deck, sleeping quarters, post office, etc).

At the Post Office the Postmaster said "I hope one of you is Joe Halloran." I told him I was, and he handed me a stack of letters about a foot high. I had given my mother and girl friend the ZELLARS address while still in the Great Lakes.

A short while after being on board ship, the Snipes (BTs) contacted me about going into the fire room. I went into the after fire room and was part of it until I left the ship in 1956.

One of the first guys I met in the fire room was ART WARD from Chicago, a nice guy who liked the Navy and planned to stay awhile. In 1955 he married a gal from Norfolk, a nice local gal that he thought the world of. A month or so later after he was married we were going out to sea again so he transferred to the U.S.S. BRONSON (DE 668). Sometime later he was lost at sea in Cape Hatteras. I really felt bad. He came from a broken home, no brothers or sisters, never heard from his mother or dad. He finally found someone that loved him and he loved. He had a lot of plans, but they ended on February 4, 1955.

Special memories I have of serving aboard the ZELLARS include:
• In 1953 we went to Northern Europe and some Mediterranean ports. We saw a lot of country and were welcomed by the people there. I spent a good while in England, met a lot of nice people there. Half of us fell in love, for awhile! When we were in the Mediterranean we saw Athens and a lot of the old city history.
• We returned to the States in the fall of 1953. Early in 1954 we went to the Caribbean for a few months then came back and went into the shipyard at Portsmouth, VA. The 40MM gun mounts were replaced by 3" guns, about a five-month deal. Then we went to Cuba on shake down. Stopped at several islands while there.

• In the spring of 1955 we went to Northern Europe and the Mediterranean again. This was another good trip. We saw a bull fight in Spain. We had to take a taxi to get to the bull fight in another town. There were 5 of us in a 1932 Chevy taxi with no doors and us in white uniforms on a dirt road. We each had our own bottle of wine and really cheered for the bulls (12 of them).

• In Athens we had a football game with a carrier crew that we crossed the Atlantic with. The ZELLARS lost bad, and the Greeks thought the game was nuts with players beating up on each other.

• Had a tour in Iceland, by U.S. Air Force people, saw a lot of ice and rocks. In the middle of the tour we stopped for lunch and had five kinds of fish and two types of eggs. They don't have much meat there.

• On tour in Brussels, Belgium, after touring the city by bus, we heard an American song playing in a bar (Mansion on the Hill). It was the only American record they had - played it and danced half the night.

• In Holland, two of us went home for supper with a fellow we had met playing billiards in a bar. His wife made a real nice meal, but the amount of meat for four people was about 2" square and 1" thick. They couldn't get meat very often and had to ration it. Sort of hard to understand for a farm kid from Minnesota.

• In Norway I and another BT went out with two gals. They took us on a cable car up the fjord to a restaurant at the top, unloaded, and went back down on the same track. We fooled around too long and had to walk down the fjord; we missed the last cable car.

• I guess my best memory was having leave in Ireland. I spent over a week with a family that was related in some way. They lived in the country by Gale way Bay. Very poor people, but a joy to be with. They lived in a home with no electricity or running water and biked or walked to most of the places they went. I was introduced to a young lady that was a school teacher and had a car. She was bound and determined to show as much of Ireland to me as she could in a few days. A very wonderful time, she was a great person and so were the people I stayed with. We were tied up in Dublin and Galeway Bay on the other side of Ireland. I had to take a train across Ireland and back. It was a beautiful trip.

• Spending a couple of days in Rome was great, too. We stayed in a hotel with no windows, just shutters over a square hole in the wall. We saw the Pope and all the history that goes with the city.

• In the PX at Cherbrough, France, we met an airman from Montana, stationed at the U.S. Air Force base. He asked us home with him for supper with his wife who also was from Montana and wasn't very happy living in a small apartment in the middle of a city in France. She wanted us to take her aboard and hide her so she could go home.

• Later in 1955, we went back across the Atlantic to Lisbon, Portugal and spent 30 days at sea, then came back to Norfolk (which took about 4 days). Early in 1956 we went to Cuba again for a few months and came back in March.

I left the ZELLARS around the 1st of May, 1956. I had Shore Patrol duty on the main base a couple weeks before going home. I was always very proud to be a part of the ZELLARS crew. It was a great crew and a great ship. The ZELLARS had the "E" twice while I was aboard. It was always nice to tell people the reason we had it on the stack, "because we were the best ship of our type." I made friends on the ZELLARS that to this day I keep in touch with. KENDALL KRAUS, from Maryland, and I talk to each other about every two weeks and have for the last 42 years. He got out in 1955.

I could go on for a long time about times on the ZELLARS. It was a wonderful 3-1/2 years. To this day I'm always proud to say I was on the ZELLARS and thankful for being able to meet and live with a crew that are probably some of the nicest guys I've known in my life time. When I go to a reunion I see the crews from the ZELLARS who were, for the most part, always a great bunch of guys.

JOE HALLORAN, BT2c

JOIN THE NAVY AND SEE THE WORLD ...

Joe did his best!

1952 – 1955

NEWFOUNDLAND

REYKJAVIK, ICELAND

PLYMOUTH, ENGLAND

BREMAHAVEN, GERMANY

PENZANCE, ENGLAND

SOUTHEND, ENGLAND

FLUSHING, HOLLAND

WHALES HASTING, ENGLAND

GIRALTAR, ATHENS, GREECE

PIEREUS, GREECE

TARANTO, ITALY

NAPLES, ROME ITALY

CANNES, FRANCE

DUNKURGUE, FRANCE

CARTGENCA, SPAIN

ORAN, ALGERIA

PALERMO, SISILY

BARCELONA, SPAIN

GIBRALTAR

PLYMOUTH, ENGLAND

VIGO, SPAIN

CHERBROUGH, FRANCE

BREMERHAVEN, GERMANY

BERGAN, NORWAY

GENTS, BELGUIM

SWANSEA, WHALES

DUBLIN, IRELAND

LONDONDARY, IRELAND

COGLAINE, SARDENIA

NORFOLK, VIRGINIA

LISBON, PORTUGAL

Joe also enjoyed several special tours: BRUSSELS, ANTWERP, BELGIUM; LONDON, ENGLAND; MARCIA, SPAIN (attended bull fights): from NAPLES, with bus ride to ROME, ITALY and back, two nights in hotel, five meals, tour of ROME, all for $32.

Joe also fooled around in the Caribbean:

GUANTANAMO BAY, CUBA:

HAITI

BRITISH, WEST INDIES

VIRGIN ISLANDS

PUERTO RICO

FRENCH, WEST INDIES

JAMAICA BERMUDA

USS ZELLARS (DD777)

BERNARD "B. J." REYNOLDS

ENTERED NAVY: AUGUST 6, 1945

BOOT CAMP: GREAT LAKES, COMPANY 1163,

ASSIGNED TO ZELLARS: NOV. 1958

LENGTH OF SERVICE ON ZELLARS: 3 YEARS, (TO NOV. 1961)

RATING: ENSIGN TO LT.(jg) (LDO)

PLACES VISITED: Naples; Barcelona; Rota; Lebanon; Bermuda; Bridgeport, Con; Norfolk, VA; Mayport; Guantanimo Bay, Cuba; Crete; Genoa; Palma, Majorca; Haiti; Tulon; Piereaus, Greece; (SP) Athens.

MPA six months; DCA 12 months; CH Eng. 18 months.

Moved from FA to BTC making E-7 in September of 1956. ZELLARS was first sea duty as an officer. I had more locker space on a Cruiser as a FN than on the ZELLARS as an officer!

During a short trip from Palma, Majorca to Naples, we encountered exceptionally heavy seas. On the 16:00 to 20:00 watch we were taking water on the bridge deck up to our knees as the ship rolled to +50 degrees. The CO, XO and I were the only officers in the ward room for the 20:00 movie as every one was already seasick. By 20:30 I had to give it up as I too was seasick.

During another Med. trip, the number 2 main engine gland sealing steam valve malfunctioned causing the number 2 main engine to be secured. We cross-connected number 1 and number 2 boilers to the number 1 main engine while repairs were performed on the number 2 main engine gland seal system. The bridge was aware of our problem but rang up flank speed anyway. We had 25 knots registering on the number-one main engine tachometer for the starboard propeller shaft; however, the actual speed through the water was more like 18 knots.

Commodore "BUD RING" (60-61) could easily be talked into giving us a few one-arm pushups on the kitchen floor about 1 AM when the ship was in port at Mayport, Florida and the officers and their wives were gathered for an impromptu party.

The CO, Cdr. JESSE HUGGINS, (59-61), became known as "BIG MOTHER" during a lower deck inspection. He opened a Jr. officer's medicine cabinet. Inside the door was an 8 X 10 photo of Cdr. HUGGINS with a hand written caption, "BIG MOTHER IS WATCHING YOU." Instead of being angry he thought that it was very funny, thus the nick name "BIG MOTHER."

The ward room always went ashore in a group with only two officers out of 12 aboard with the duty, with "BIG MOTHER" leading the way.

To add to the port calls! I could mention our ongoing contest: i.e., "The weakest kidneys in DESLANT. (Destroyers Atlantic). As mentioned before, the ward room normally went ashore as a group. The Weakest Kidneys in DESLANT was a contest to see who among us would have to visit the head first after several drinks. The honored person then would have to buy the next round. Sometimes it became painful to both kidneys and wallet.

At lunch one day, a Jr. Officer asked CO. JESS HUGGINS for his definition of leadership. The CO laid down his knife and fork, clapped his hands together and said "follow me mothers, I've got the keys to the cat house."

I took my wife, Gloria, for a tour of the engineering spaces in 1960 while we were home ported in Mayport, Florida. The snipes were very proud of our spaces. Gloria flunked the forward fire room when she spotted paint chips in the port bilges!

When brand new Ensign MIKE POPPERNICK, (59-62) reported aboard via high line at sea, he didn't have his life jacket off before he wanted to know if he was senior to anyone. We helped him get salty fast by putting his uniform brass in the urinal several nights so the continuous salt water would tarnish them. To make him think he was losing weight, we cut 1/4 inch off his web belt every week.

The XO. BILL GATTS, (61-63) and wife, Helen, both played guitar and piano. One night at the Gatts' home in Mayport, the Gatts and Reynolds made up a song, "ZELLARS ZIPPIN Z" as we had a few drinks.

Lt(jg) BOB COUSINS, (58-61) always seemed to fall asleep after a few drinks. One night in Naples we took him outside and sat him on the curb at the O club with a note pinned on his jacket that read, "My name is Bob Cousins, take me back to the USS ZELLARS." He made it OK.

Memorable port calls include Bridgeport, CN, over the 4th of July 1961 holiday. Moored outboard of the ZELLARS was a diesel submarine who's XO had previously served aboard the ZELLARS. I was the plaque custodian for the ZELLARS. The sub XO wanted a "Z" plaque. I offered to trade him a plaque for breakfast for Gloria and I on board the sub. He accepted. As we descended the vertical ladder into the sub, the XO told Gloria that on visitors day they stationed a Petty Officer at the bottom of the ladder to assist the ladies. The XO also said that it was the Petty Officer's duty to keep track of visitors on a blackboard close by that had three columns designated, "**BLACK, PINK, NONE.**"

The NAVY League of Bridgeport was our host during this port call. They kept us busy from 7 AM to midnight for six days. A wonderful time was had by all. Our crew could hardly buy a drink anywhere in town. Bridgeport was undoubtedly the best port call ever made in a USA port.

The ZELLARS completed the FRAM overhaul in Portsmouth Va. shipyard in 1960. (FRAM= fleet repair and modernization.) The shipyard removed everything above the main deck from just aft of the number 1 stack and rebuilt this area to accommodate officers' birthing, disbursing office, and personnel office on the main deck, a radio controlled helicopter hangar and flight deck on the 01 deck. Then went to GITMO for refresher training followed by then a MED cruise.

After all that steaming the ship developed a two-foot crack in the hull of the after engine room, just outboard of the starboard propeller shaft, and close to the number 2 main feed pump foundation. The ship's hull actually cracked open where you could see daylight when the ship rolled to port. (The hull is the outer skin of the ship from the main deck down to the water line.) It continued under the ship and up to the main deck on the other (port) side. About the same time, the number-five spring bearing on the starboard shaft wiped out and was replaced by MMC KENT at sea. The cause of the hull and spring bearing failure was later determined to be a very slight hull warp deflection due to sitting in dry dock so long during the FRAM conversion.

Duty aboard a destroyer provides all hands with a wide variety of experiences and responsibilities not found aboard Cruisers, Carriers and/or Battleships, or any ship with crews of 300 or more. The feeling of responsibility is awesome at times. Destroyer duty is a great stepping stone for career-minded NAVY men. Most of the senior enlisted men were brought up aboard destroyers. They have a wealth of knowledge needed to operate this type of ship. This is necessary when you consider most of the division officers are on their first cruise and the department heads aren't far behind.

BJ. REYNOLDS LT (jg)

HIGHEST AWARDS, (MEDALS)
MERITORIOUS SERVICE MEDAL
NAVY COMMENDATION MEDAL
NAVY ACHIEVEMENT AWARD.

USS ZELLARS (DD777)

INDEX